HUMAN DEVELOPMENT

National Institute Social Services Library

HUMAN DEVELOPMENT

AN INTRODUCTION TO THE PSYCHODYNAMICS
OF GROWTH, MATURITY AND AGEING

ERIC RAYNER

London
GEORGE ALLEN & UNWIN
Boston   Sydney

First published in 1971
Fourth impression 1975
Second edition 1978
Second impression 1979

GEORGE ALLEN & UNWIN LTD
40 Museum Street, London WC1A 1LU

© George Allen & Unwin (Publishers) Ltd, 1971, 1978

ISBN 0 04 155009 9 papercase
ISBN 0 04 155008 0 paperback

Printed in Great Britain in 10 on 11 point Times by
University Press, Cambridge

CONTENTS

ACKNOWLEDGEMENTS

In writing and then rewriting this book, my debt is primarily to those who have taught me. First are my teachers of psychoanalysis, foremost of whom were Mrs Eva Rosenfeld and Dr Tom Main, but there have been many other colleagues and friends. Perhaps my patients have been my primary informants; I rarely thank them, to make amends I would like to express my gratitude here.

The first edition arose out of my work at the Department of Applied Social Studies at Croydon Technical College. Here my greatest debt was to Florence Mitchell, and to Mary Barker and Nano McCaughan. But dozens of students really helped me distil much of what is written here. My colleagues Alan Wilson and Peter Lomas more intimately did the same. So also, over many months, did my wife Mary Rayner.

The second edition has been refined out of my teaching at the London School of Economics and here I have Zofia Butrym and Irmi Elkan to thank most. I would also like to thank Judy Hildebrand, Gill Bolland and Frank Orford, for their painstaking encouragement and criticism of the text. This was also done by Florence Mitchell and my wife. I owe a debt to them and to Joan Willans, who typed both manuscripts.

I have perhaps been taught most by my children Sarah, Will and Ben. I thank them.

Chapter 1

INTRODUCTION

I set about writing this book in the belief which is so obvious as to seem trite, that among other things we humans ought to strive not just to love but also to understand each other. The history of our race is a gruesome chronicle of prejudice and cruelty, lightened by glimmerings of sympathy. This human sympathy has perhaps widened and deepened just as the scale of brutality has also grown with the passing of centuries. Maybe our era is a watershed in this history, for never before has a wide moral awareness been thrown together with the dispassionate honesty of scientific inquiry. With this combination, perhaps there is hope of a firm climate of humane understanding which has not been known before. At least it is worth working for.

The argument that lies behind this book is that intuitive sensitivity and systematically tested scientific knowledge are together necessary but not by themselves sufficient to create a climate of sympathetic awareness of other people. Each one of us needs to use the knowledge gained by others through scientific inquiry. But we also have to discover everything anew for ourselves and practise it. Only through practice can we really believe what we feel and know. What is more, we are so prone to self-deception that we need to be critically aware of our tricks of thoughts as well as our effects on others if this climate of understanding is to be cultivated. This awareness of the feelings and thoughts of oneself and others can be called 'dispassionate empathy'.

Such sensitivity can of course be applied either over a wide abstract vista in comprehending other cultures, or in much narrower focus when making sense of another family's life. Most intimately it is applied when understanding the predicaments of one other person. This last is the concern of the present book.

There are very many ways of exercising sympathetic understanding of others; informally it has been done for centuries in listening and talking and also in prayer and meditation. But the past decades have seen the growth of a multitude of innovations: psychotherapy, counselling, group therapy, sensitivity groups, encounter groups, role play and many others.

This book does not consider such direct encounters, it is complementary to them but stands at a slightly greater distance, and is concerned with some of the predominant experiences of people as they grow up, age and die. Its focus will be upon the intimate, personal or inner thoughts, feelings and actions of individuals or 'single-selves' and how they may structure their private worlds as they go through life. It is primarily addressed to those beginning their careers in the helping professions, but anyone interested in attending to himself or others going through life might enjoy it.

You may wonder why the helping professions should be expected to appreciate a single individual's experiences. There are so many immediate problems of vital importance such as health, poverty, housing or class intolerance which require a wider vision than understanding individual experiences, that surely these must come first? But we are now in a culture which is in revolution or at least in rapid flux. Nearly every traditional way is being questioned as to whether it is inadequate or even destructive of happy living. As ordinary citizens we cannot help participating, if only by default, in the creation of changed systems of culture. And the recipients or victims of these cultures will be individual human beings. If we do not deeply study the needs of individuals and attune our cultural practices to them they are likely to become expendable items in new social dreams. Only individual people experience suffering and joy, never social systems.

More specifically, a member of the helping professions is always intimately relating to people of all ages whether they be colleagues, clients or patients, either directly or indirectly. If we do not attune our minds to their experiences and predicaments we will probably be experienced as heartless, classifying machines and be hated or at least found useless.

It is, of course, essential to learn about each person as one goes along, but it is as well to have a pool of ideas to draw upon and sensitise oneself to issues which might be useful in each new case. It is in order to build up these useful ideas in the back of one's mind that the scientific method of testing hypotheses and refining them into theories is essential.

This understanding of individual experiences may be clearer if the stage is set by a brief consideration of biological evolution. Looking at the world we see that a characteristic of all living things is that they are self-perpetuating organisations. Digesting from its environment and excreting into it, each organism is continuously changing its constituents but keeps its own form. It has a characteristic spirit of its own until it dies. With evolution the breadth and variety of some organisms' exchanges with the environment have developed enormously. The vertebrate, for instance, can hunt and escape in ways that are impossible for the protoplasm. This is particularly so with mammals; a combination of large brains and prolonged infancy has enabled them to develop a range of activity by the use of *learning* which far exceeds lower animals. They have developed a *central control system* which, through the ability to learn, has made them relatively free of innate reflex patterns.

The primates function at a higher level than any other mammal with these characteristics of central control; they can also, unlike most other animals, be sexually aroused almost continuously. A million or so years ago the human seems to have been a meat-eating, group-living, erect, large-brained primate. Thus he must have been a hunter, intelligent about the environment, guileful with prey and wary of threats.

As he lived in a group, the human must have developed sensitivity to and co-operativeness with his fellows. The fittest who survived must have been those who could *submit* to group decisions and also control their sexuality as much as those who lorded over them.

The articulation of all these features becomes possible with an enormous brain which allows for central control by the use of *thought*; it is not visible nor can it be heard or touched but it is omnipresent. If central control breaks down a human goes mad or demented. This all-important feature is often referred to in technical literature nowadays as *ego functioning*, it used to be phrased more poetically as 'the human spirit' or simply the mind.

Man's large brain means not only that he can learn at an incredible pace, especially when young, but also that he can imagine what is not actually present, he can *symbolise*. This means he can create mental representations of events and make *choices* between alternatives before taking action. What is more he can discriminate between that which is his own body and that which is not. He can discriminate his *private world* of imagination and feeling from other worlds of things and space. Being able to imagine means also that he can delay and conceive of time, the beginning middle and ends of things. He can imagine his own future death.

Being imaginative with a sense of inner and outer reality, of space and of time, he can be reflective and aware of his *self* in a world of other selves. He is capable of wonderment. But there is a price to pay, there is a tragedy in it, he *must conform* to survive. He is thus at the mercy of others and their madness and limitations as well as finding comfort and enjoyment with them. In conforming a human probably must lose some of his potentialities, often to a crippling degree, and as conformity starts at a very early age the experiences of limitation can be very profoundly felt. Yet without conformity a human can have no order or security.

In being imaginative and needing to be dependent and conform to others, the human experiences *threats* as well as delights from self and others. He can be aware of *helplessness* especially when young. At the same time he can imagine his effects on others. He can thus be aware of or imagine his *value* and *guilt*.

To summarise, the human is a large-brained, group-living primate capable of being sexually aroused at almost any time. He is capable of creating mental representations of his world and of choice in using these representations. He can experience helplessness, wonderment, value and guilt. It could be said that the human is a religious primate.

Some readers may have noticed that this survey has moved from a biological to an existential point of view (Becker, 1971; Tillich, 1952). But it has only outlined what humans in general are capable of. It is quite different to recognise what a particular person from a specific background at a point in his life actually does experience and do. Scientific research has made it plain that any one person's vitality of thought, feeling and action is delimited by a vast web of influences: by the coding of his genes, by his uterine environment, by the bias of the society of his early family which itself is delimited by its culture. Then, a person is delimited by the pattern of relationships between his family and those around, his friends and school. Later he will be influenced by work, friends and the new families he encounters as he marries, has children and ages. But this is not all: each person's actions affect those around him and they in turn affect him. A person grows and lives in a living web of circular or *feedback* relationships.

Every person has his own delimited capacities for feeling and action. The meaningfulness of the world and our usefulness to it is different for each one of us. Every person is idiosyncratic. And when the question of enhancing the individual, idiosyncratic person arises, teachers, social workers and therapists must come forward and those skilled in abstract generalisation – evolutionary biologists, philosophers and academic scientists – must step into the background.

This is the viewpoint of this book. I am a specialised worker with individuals, a psychologist and psychoanalyst by profession, and my underlying argument will be a psychoanalytic one though the observations of many other disciplines will be drawn upon. That is, historically the book is largely based upon the intimate, detailed work with individual people originated by Freud over half a century ago (Freud, 1915b). Since then psychoanalytic ideas have been modified and enlarged throughout the world, but especially in America and particularly in Britain by such thinkers as Melanie Klein, Fairbairn and Winnicott (see Guntrip, 1961). In his theorising Freud tended to view the individual as centrally struggling throughout life to relieve instinctual biological tensions which were basically antipathetic to social mores. Later psychoanalysts, particularly in Britain, have felt this model to be essential but limited and have emphasised the individual's fundamental love and yearning, at every level of development, *to relate to objects and objectives*. These objectives may be physical things, intimacy with other people, mastery of actions or attainment of ideas. In other words this view stresses the importance of recognising the individual's urge, usually against odds, to make his experiences more meaningful. It is rather less pessimistic than Freud's position, and is not so much a testable theory as a way of attending to people.

Here is a hypothetical example of such a way of attending:

We eavesdrop on a young housewife's mind for a few minutes. She is thinking about making dinner, puts a pan on the stove. As she does so she listens for the baby waking up, looks out of the window to check the older ones are all right. Her mind shifts to her husband coming home and looks forward to his being in a good mood. She flicks on the radio and its rhythmic beat sets her hips moving. With it comes the fleeting thought of a past lover and the fantasy of future ones. She feels hot and flushed, puts it out of her mind but is slightly uneasy and irritable. Then the baby cries, she curses, thinks of the freedom of going out to work again as she picks him up. He smiles and she cuddles him with gratitude that he is alive. A memory of her own mother comes to her mind and she feels a strange mixture of haunted sadness, fondness and annoyance. It stays with her and somehow adds savour to her laughing with the baby.

You will note that this description moved between observation of the young woman's behaviour and identification with her thoughts and feelings. Dispassionate empathy is being used. The description also notes her not only relating behaviourally to objects (pans, baby, children, radio) but also relating to memories and imagined objects and objectives (husband, mother, lover, fantasy lovers, freedom of future work). Each thought of the woman is webbed with other thoughts which well up and add meaning to her experiences.

Many of her thoughts and actions would be consciously reportable by the woman, others are so automatic as to be unnoticed. Other thoughts have a dimness, yet are deeply felt (her uneasiness after putting the idea of lovers out of her mind, being haunted by her mother's image). These qualities of dim yet deep feeling would make us intuitively feel that highly charged unconscious ideas were perhaps active. This hunch is, of course, untested in our account. With this woman the unconscious ideas seem to contribute to the private richness of her experiences and further inquiry would be an intrusion. But if she were chronically irritable, anxious or haunted it might serve her if we inquired further into the thoughts and feelings that moved her chronic moods. Illuminating them might make them less mysterious. This was the view first systematically introduced by Freud and will be in the background throughout this book, not so much in order to investigate mental disturbance in detail, but as a means of approaching disturbing emotional events which seem to be the fate of all ordinary people.

Freud was, I think, the first person in Western culture to both empathise and think systematically with individual people over long periods of time. Because of this he was able to formulate ideas about the intimate emotional lives of some people in ways that had not been coherently recognised before. It is to him that we owe the beginning of a consistent empathetic point of view. His revolutionary contributions came from his clinical studies, which incidently seem to be largely ignored by most general writers on the subject. At 'the same time it must be remembered that Freud was brought up in the nineteenth century and trained in the science and medicine of that time. Thus his underlying theoretical framework was couched in terms of nineteenth-century physics and biology. The culture of scientific thought has changed since then; the idea of gaining absolute knowledge, as in Newtonian physics, for instance, has given way to Einstein's relativity. This revolution is not confined to the specialty of physics, it has permeated our general ways of understanding things. As the term suggests, the object-relations point of view has moved psychoanalytic thought some way in the direction of thinking relativistically. Instead of thinking simply in terms of a human being driven by 'absolute' forces of instincts, as Freud tended to do, there is now more recognition that there can be no absolute knowledge by one person of another. One person can only know another by the way they relate together. What is more, a person can only know himself by the way he relates to others, in *external relationships*; and also by the ways aspects of himself relate to each other *in internal relationships*. Even with this advance, I think background theory lags behind the vast, informal knowledge of people that has been amassed. Our concepts often still have a nineteenth-century flavour to them. I feel that the formulations of this book are limited in this way. If I am fortunate enough to rewrite it again in a few years time, I hope I shall be clearer about these issues. Background theory is not as unimportant as many practical people think. For instance, the question whether a person has knowledge of absolute truths independent of his own position as an observer sounds a theoretical quibble. But when a person is convinced of the absolute rightness of his beliefs he is prone to a ruthless dogmatism which can have serious practical consequences, especially if he holds power over others. A sensitivity to the relativity of knowledge can be conducive not only to self-doubt but also to tolerance and open-mindedness.

From this it will be clear that frames of reference, other than the psychoanalytic one, can be equally valid in their own way. For instance, the viewpoint taken so far is very close to an *existential one* (May, 1967) in that both are interested in experiences and what things mean to a person. However there are also differences. The existential point of view, having grown out of introspection, is less interested in observation of a person's behaviour and his effects on others than is that of the psychoanalyst, which grew out of medical diagnosis and work with cases. Furthermore, the existentialist tends to be most at home with abstractions about 'man' in general. Whereas the psychoanalyst, with a long tradition of case study behind him, tends to be more skilled in thinking about the individual's's idiosyncratic complexities of thought, especially those which are *repetitions* from his past.

The background of this book also has kinship with physiology and anatomy. It was evident from my description of the young woman, and will be stressed throughout the book, that feelings always seem to be rooted in bodily events. But whereas the physiologist's focus of concern is the patterning of events of body chemistry, mine is upon a person's experiential events and actions.

The book is also close to social psychology, sociology and anthropology because all are concerned with a person growing in relation to societies of other things and people. However, social psychology is primarily concerned with comparing and contrasting events between people, and sociology and anthropology are concerned with comparison of events between groups of people. Whereas this book's primary concern is events *within* individuals. This does not imply that these social disciplines have nothing to offer in our understanding of individual experience. I will be stressing how each person's ideas seem to be strictly delimited by his culture, so that without sociological sensitivity this book will be meaningless. Because of this I personally feel that those of us who deal with individuals can perhaps learn more about our own trade from the social sciences and medicine than from any other discipline. One of the disappointments of this book may be that there is little detailed reference to and discussion of sociological work. I have omitted to do this because here I am merely an enthusiastic amateur; moreover the book would be unwieldy. The reader must therefore be served by other books and tutors who have been steeped in social thinking.

Even closer, and hence more confusing, is the relationship between this book and the standpoint of research psychologists. They, like the book, are concerned with individual behavioural or mental events, but their primary interest is in enhancing the body of generally valid science. As such they are devoted to testing hypotheses which can be verified by other independent observers. As only behaviour can, in principle, be recorded by independent observers it is upon this that the research psychologist has focused his work life. In consequence he has not traditionally been very interested in the nature of personal experiences, nor in individual fantasy and emotion-laden imagination, nor in the vagaries of the sense of self and individual meaningfulness. The analytic worker on the other hand, being centrally concerned with helping individuals in the enhancement of their lives, has been interested in these matters. He is thus more adept than the research psychologist at thinking about how individuals structure their personal worlds in both useful and self-destructive ways as crises arise through the course of their lives. He usually has a rich pool of ideas available on these questions for use in his work. His authority is that he has, unlike academics and researchers, a case-loaded or *person-loaded mind*. The price paid, of course, is that many of the analytic worker's ideas are only tested informally through his experience, reading and conversation with others. They do not meet the criterion of formal testability in an experimental design which is espoused by the research psychologist.

This book will use the findings of research psychologists, particularly in the regions of infancy and childhood. But it must be recognised that it is written by someone with an essentially person-loaded mind and stands (or falls) between many disciplines. It is focally concerned with the growth, and disturbance in growth, of the individual's mental events of ideas, action and feeling.

This position has grave weaknesses. As mentioned already, its theories are often woolly, certainly more loosely verified than exact science. Psychoanalysts are prone to make sweeping generalisations from limited evidence. Such arrogance can be irritating to any thoughtful person, and is particularly so to those whose central love is science. In writing the book, I have probably been prone to this arrogance. I will, however, attempt to differeniate those conclusions which have experimental evidence to support them from those which have less-formal case support.

It must also be stressed that the book is culturally biased; its baseline undoubtedly originates in the British nuclear family. The justification for this is that one must start somewhere and as this is my background and that of many readers, it is a reasonable starting point. The length of the book will not permit any detailed cultural comparison, but I will attempt to distinguish those observations which seem to apply to all humans from those which are culturally limited. The fact that this book is British-based does not imply that this culture is considered the best. The reader himself can go on to make his own evaluations, guided by sociological and anthropological literature.

The book may prove a disappointment to some on broad moral issues. I will reach certain conclusions about what I think is conducive to growth and what is deleterious. These are thus personal value judgements but I will try and specify whether these are widely accepted or not. They can at best be only temporary as new evidence will change them. I hope their expression will help each reader to argue for himself.

No doubt everyone will be annoyed by at least some aspects of the text. This may be due to my real misunderstanding of vital issues. It may also be due to the fact that the book points towards truths which we would prefer not to know about. When something loved is threatened one automatically feels fear or anger, even if the loved thing is a fallacious idea. As we cannot talk together it will be impossible to work out in the book where my own, as opposed to a reader's fallacies, lie. This can only be achieved in thought and conversation with friends and teachers.

At this juncture it is worth recognising that just as my viewpoints are limited, so also will be the opinions of others. Experts and professionals, in particular, tend to espouse narrow-minded, moralistic stances from which they criticise others for not conforming to their own codes. For instance, a caseworker is easily made indignant by the scientist's apparent lack of concern for human or animal suffering. The scientifically minded expert is no less a moralist and has often indignantly castigated both casework thinking in general and psychoanalytic ideas in particular for not conforming to scientific codes of testability (e.g. Eysenck, 1953). It is my opinion that the scientific researcher can valuably question the woolliness of the therapist or social worker; but when he assumes, and this is common, that the *only* valid means of gaining understanding of human predicaments is by his own limited methods then he becomes arrogantly silly.

There is a further point to be considered before finally starting on the main text. It is concerned with the logic of thought and I can do no more than allude to it here, partly because there is not space to consider it fully, but also because it involves questions which I do not think have yet been fully clarified. Nevertheless, it is necessary to be at least sensitive to the existence of such questions.

In order to think and then act efficiently with regard to the *world outside us*, it is necessary for our thought to operate in strictly disciplined ways. Even in ordinary everyday matters disciplined thinking is obviously necessary. In preparing a meal, for instance, it is necessary to propose to onself the rule that if nobbly brown things called potatoes are to be edible then they must first be cooked. Whereas if round orange things are to be edible they need not be cooked but must be peeled. It is one of the businesses of childhood to formulate slowly, at least subconsciously, the natural laws which things around us seem to obey.

The job of systematic science is to extend this realm of common sense by reformulating and refining our ideas about the natural laws of the behaviour of things around us. The study of logic proceeds from this and is concerned with formulating the rules which must be obeyed by thought if it is to be valid in making inferences about these things around us. The first great investigators who tried to make these rules of inference explicit and clear were of course the Greeks, Aristotle in particular. Probably the greatest strength of Western thought has been its deep facility to use rules of inference. Science and technology rest upon them (Persig, 1974).

But we become very lame if our thought is limited to the logical rules applicable to dealing with *external things* when in fact we are concerned with inner experiences. Here is a notable example. One basic rule of reasonable thought about external things is the Aristotelian law which says that you cannot validly make a proposition that a thing is true and at the same time say that it is not true. In other words, it would be logically crazy to propose that a thing is both a potato and not a potato or that a thing is both an orange and not an orange.

However, when concerned with *inner* experiences it is sane to propose just such contradictions. In this region it is important to think *paradoxically* (Fromm, 1927). In order to be sensitive it is necessary to be able to make such propositions as: 'He loves her and yet he doesn't' or, 'In order to be sane you need to be able to go mad' or, 'He feels both male and female'. All these seem to run in the face of Aristotelian rules. Also apparently contradicting these rules is the very act of dispassionate empathy itself. In this we need to identify ourselves with a person in front of us. In other words the subject becomes identified with the object; a very odd piece of logic by the standards of objective science. Without the use of such paradoxes we can only be crass about other people's feelings. Yet at the same time we must be able to think of people as external to us and apply Aristotelian logic when appropriate. A fundamental clarification of the apparent contradictions between these two modes of thought has recently been attempted by a combination of mathematical logic and psychoanalytic thinking (Matte Blanco, 1975). I think this may herald a breakthrough in our understanding of psychodynamics. But it requires specialised knowledge and, for the time being at least, must lie outside the scope of this book, which will move continuously between these modes of thought.

Lastly a few words about the sequence of the book. It is laid out in age phases from birth to death. This is partly to give an acquaintance of some of the common experiences of each phase. These will note the emergence of new patterns of mental activity which continue on in modified form into later life. Thus the discussion of earlier phases of life will naturally introduce concepts about mental activity which it is useful to be aware of no matter what age is being considered. This is the developmental point of view. It proposes that however mature thought may be, there is nevertheless primitive thought and feeling still active within it.

This form of sequence is intended to introduce a way of thinking about people. It attempts to make use not only of scientific knowledge but also of intuition, paradox and self-knowledge. I hope that it is a contribution towards a climate of sympathetic understanding between people.

FURTHER READING

1 Becker, E. (1971), *The Birth and Death of Meaning*. An approach to psychodynamics from the point of view of evolution.
2 Freud, S. (1915), *Introductory Lectures on Psychoanalysis*. The classic, and still the best, introduction to the psychoanalytic way of thinking.
3 Fromm, E. (1957), *The Art of Loving*. Contains a simple discussion of paradoxical logic.
4 Hunt, S. and Hilton, J. (1975), *Individual Development and Social Experience*. Useful to read in parallel with the chapters of this book as it emphasises the experimental rather than the psychodynamic approach.
5 Lowe, G. (1972), *The Growth of Personality*. Can also be read in parallel with this book. Its approach is psychodynamic.
6 Persig, R. M. (1974), *Zen and the Art of Motorcycle Maintenance*. A personal exploration into the nature of intellectual understanding giving a clear exposition on the nature of scientific and technological logic. A beautifully written and unusual book.
7 Rycroft, C. (1968), *A Critical Dictionary of Psychoanalysis*. Useful as a source of definition of psychodynamic and psychoanalytic terms.

Chapter 2

BEING PREGNANT

The Early Organisers of a Child's Environment
Let us first consider the infant in his physical and social environment. He must from the beginning exchange substances with his environment. But his central control system, his capacity to discriminate and react selectively to the world of objects around him, his ego, is only rudimentary. He is incapable of surviving alone. He must attune to organisers, his parents in particular, and they must attune to him to provide the substances and patterns of stimulation necessary for his survival. Only slowly is the necessity for them outgrown. Even then the memory of these early organisers is probably indelible. It is one of the main contentions of this book that, just as it has been seen that genetic constitution delimits the pattern of a life, so it must also be recognised that early organisers can delimit too.

In our culture and in many others the infant usually has one central organiser. This is most frequently his (I will use the traditional 'his' to apply to both sexes) biological mother. Naturally this central organiser may be a foster, adoptive or grandmother, a nanny, wet nurse or father. Or there may be no one central organiser but several. Here we will be concerned with the preparations of a biological mother before birth.

The Nature of Preparation
Let us consider the nature of preparation generally for a moment, not just in pregnancy. To be conscious of preparing we must be aware, even in dim or distorted form, of having a self with a body in a world of other selves and bodies. We must also anticipate the future in our imagination. The nature of this anticipation may in part depend on memories of similar eventualities in the past but, since the future cannot be certain, much anticipation must rest on inexact imagination or *personal fantasy*. In so far as we anticipate fulfilment in imagination, we usually feel confidence. And in so far as we imagine or fantasise failure, we experience *anxiety*. It is common to avoid or flee in imagination from the conscious experience of anxious anticipation. Such pretence of not being worried is an

everyday 'cowardly' mental trick and defines *defensive* mental activity. When we openly imagine both possible fulfilment and failure and yet set about a task we are being *courageous*. And in so far as we discipline this imagination to fit what we know of the real world about us we set about *problem-solving*. It is possible to recognise any person at any time as a rich mixture of defensive cowardice and of courage as he strives in problem-solving. This is the *psychodynamic* point of view, which for practical purposes can be considered here as synonymous with the object-relations viewpoint mentioned in the last chapter.

Now let us consider the pregnant woman's preparations.

Conception

Naturally intercourse is the first step in an individual's biological contribution to continuing our species. But, equally obviously, humans have found that biological reproduction is not the only fulfilment to be found in love making. Of all the hundreds and thousands of times a man or woman enjoys making love during their lifetime only very rarely do they both want to conceive. And even more rarely do they want to conceive *and* rear their conception. What is often unrecognised is that many women deeply wish and will go to great lengths to be impregnated, while at the same time recoiling from the idea of mothering a child. Likewise many men will go to similar lengths to impregnate without wanting to father their child. The difference between the fantasy of procreation, stirred no doubt by physiological drives together with anxious competitiveness about fertility or potency, and the years of devotion entailed in rearing viable members of the next generation, is very great indeed. Let us look at the first months of these years of devotion.

Early Pregnancy: the Mother's Experience

In utero the human life proceeds from one cell to an infant of 2 million million cells in the course of nine months. This entails enormous chemical, particularly hormonal, changes in the mother's body (Chamberlain, 1969; Smith, 1970). The manifest symptoms of these changes will be a woman's first indications of pregnancy. Briefly these are as follows. She will miss her periods; will probably feel unusually tired; notice tingling in her breasts; probably suffer bouts of nausea; her vulva, nipples and cheeks will appear darker; she will need to urinate more frequently; and she will put on weight.

With a first pregnancy a woman will usually need confirmation from a doctor. When it is confirmed she very often finds herself swept by such feelings as, 'This is what life is all about'; these are often openly felt even with unwanted pregnancies. The destruction of a new life is very frequently deeply mourned after abortions. This depression can happen to men as well as to women. When a young woman intends to keep the baby, one of her first impulses is usually to share the news with others. She particularly wants affirmative enjoyment from her husband, family and friends, probably because they are going to be needed to take on responsibilities. Being pregnant without this gladness on the part of husband and relatives is nearly always a very lonely experience. I know of no definitive research which correlates this loneliness with specific physical disorders for either mother or infant. There is only some evidence that stress generally can affect the foetus (Hunt and Hilton, 1975). But health visitors and welfare agencies who have worked with isolated, pregnant women will usually affirm how much they need friendly help. Being pregnant is a social event from the beginning.

The Emergence of Fantasy in Pregnancy

With widespread hormonal changes and her excited yet anxious anticipation of an uncertain future, the old ways of a woman's personal adaptations tend slowly to be broken down. This change is subtle and does not become obvious until late in pregnancy, but it usually starts early. There is a proneness to lability of mood, to swings between elation and tearful depression, with unexpected, vivid thoughts suddenly coming to consciousness. She often has quick and idiosyncratic likes and revulsions about drinks, foods, smells or sights. Usually, if they are not too anxious, women need to be left alone to keep these ideas private with perhaps no more than the good-humoured recognition that *fantasies* are occurring.

It is appropriate at this point to digress briefly to introduce the *concept of fantasy* which will be used a great deal in this book. Here it will be used in a wider sense than the common one of pleasant daydreaming, that is in the way psychoanalysts use the term. (They often spell it 'phantasy' to indicate this special usage – Segal, 1973.) They agree that imaginative activity underlies all thought and feeling. This imaginative activity is, except in sleep (when it continues in dreaming), usually being continuously checked, refined and tested in response to the input of the external sense organs and to meet the demands of the individual's tasks. This testing and refinement is presumably one function of the system of central control or ego activity. The outcome of such refinement is referred to as *adaptive* thought and behaviour. But this adaptive activity is accompanied, enlivened and affected by vaguer, often unconscious, happenings which are laden with feeling. This is fantasy. Being laden with feeling (which we know involves somatic activity – Dunbar, 1946) suggests that fantasy is often a close mental representation of *bodily functions*. Thus, for instance, we have just noted that pregnant women have impulsive thoughts about drink, food and smells. These are oral fantasies breaking through the control of the ego. The actual conscious images or intellectual elements in much fantasising is often minimal or non-existent. When they do emerge they are normally confined to the unexpected happening of visual dream-like symbols that are usually thinly disguised portrayals of physiological events. Here are some examples:

I suddenly had the idea of a concrete mixer being fed with ice cream.
I had the thought of a waterfall in a wooded cleft in the rocks.
A woman took her parents out for the evening. She felt she was very insensitive to their needs and reported that she felt 'like a lump-headed idiot'. The following night she dreamt she 'had a tumour on the brain'.

In this last example the woman did not have an explicit, conscious image of a body representation breaking through in her waking life, she used a metaphor about the head instead. However, the body imagery broke through quite clearly in her dream.

Although this notion of fantasy is really a simple one, it is often particularly difficult to grasp because we are so used to thinking about tasks rather than moods and bodily rooted feelings. Perhaps a better term than fantasy would be 'feelothoughts', for we have no appropriate term in the language. This concept of fantasy is not on the whole subscribed to by academic and research psychologists. Behaviourist psychologists in particular tend to reject it because its occurrence is not verifiable by observable behaviour. My own opinion is that they are the poorer for this because fantasy seems to be an omnipresent aspect of experience. Others, like the educational psychologist Piaget, are interested in fantasy but tend to ignore the personal feelings involved. Psychoanalysts and therapists consider these to be of prime importance.

Returning to the pregnant woman, the direction of her fantasies and hence the adaptive thought arising from them will depend to an extent upon the nature of the world and society around her. Let us take some of the more predominant facets of these in turn:

A Woman and Her Culture
The pregnant woman's feelings and anxious fantasy will naturally depend upon the general expectations of her culture. One instance of this is that in many cultures, especially in the past, it was generally felt it was good to be fruitful, hence easy to be joyful about pregnancy. But many societies valued male children far above female ones. In such climates it is to be expected that women would be more prone to worry about the sex of the infant than they do in Britain today. In this country, where birth control is felt to be a necessity, a woman is more likely to be worried about whether she ought to be having a child at all.

A Woman and Her Own Mother
One common trend which runs through many women's doubts about themselves is an implicit comparison and rivalry with their own mothers.

Such feelings are not often consciously expressed, but when they are they have a poignancy which rings true. For instance:

My mother believed that childhood was the golden age and a mother must surrender everything to the children. I don't want to do that, but I am terrified not to.

Mother never lost her temper with us. I am sure I shall. I am awful, aren't I?

Mother always made us go to the lavatory every few hours; I am determined that my children shall not suffer such agony and indignity.

It seems that pregnancy involves a complex of feelings of conflict, rivalry and conformity between the generations (Deutsch, 1944; Bibring, 1961). It is usually very important to a woman that her own mother should be pleased and appreciative of the pregnancy. For instance:

A young woman who was a very active and convinced rebel against the absurdities of the older generation said some months after her baby was born, 'My mother is a crazy idiot, but I forgive her everything and love her dearly because she dotes on Ann, the baby. I could murder my mother-in-law because she has just blatantly ignored us since I got pregnant.'

It is possible to detect a thread of anticipatory thinking in most of these comments about mothers. The women seem to be forming resolves about how they will behave as mothers and comparing these with their own, perhaps distorted memories of childhood. This, incidentally, can be a most enjoyable activity. It also seems likely that such anticipatory thinking serves very definite preparatory functions. It helps a woman to form a preliminary attitude towards handling a baby. This in itself is valuable because it helps her to be certain of what she feels to begin with. Then, depending on how things turn out later, she can alter her ideas to match her experience without to much floundering. If she does not have any preliminary attitude she is much more likely to feel lost and helpless. Here is a sort of hypothesis testing or informal scientific method.

A Woman and the Professional Helper

Most women want to get on with being pregnant with the minimum of interference from professionals. At the same time they anxiously rely on their examinations and advice, and often feel very sensitive to being in their power. Some women find it easy to be in such a state of helplessness, others are terrified and enraged that they are treated like cattle. This is not so often experienced with a home confinement, but long waits and peremptory treatment by busy staff in hospitals has broken the calm peacefulness of many pregnant women. On a more personal level, a few district midwives have been felt as the terror of the neighbourhood, leaving young mothers weeping helplessly in fright, hating them yet not daring to say anything because they will be in their hands at the birth.

We have no way of estimating the lasting effects of these bad experiences. They are probably not very great, but the more time a woman spends feeling angry and anxious, the less time she has to relax and 'just be' with her baby inside her. If she has other personal anxieties also impeding her relaxation, this may be the straw which breaks the camel's back (Caplan, 1964).

A Woman and her Husband

The person who is usually most important for a woman's ease in pregnancy is her husband. With him there is the obvious yet fundamental need for assurance of financial and physical security and for intimate valuing of each other. Lost intimacy can act like a malignant thing.

A woman will often say how sensitive she is to her husband's moods. It matters very much that he should want the child, for without this a woman is alone and often feels guilty both towards her husband and the baby. Even though he wants a child, it is not uncommon for a husband to be physically disgusted by his pregnant wife, and when this happens she is likely to become listless and depressed. When the baby is born, the husband's disgust may wear off and the wife's depression lift. Probably nearly all women worry that they will be sexually unattractive to their husbands during and after pregnancy. Love making will inevitably be interrupted at the end of the pregnancy and immediately after birth. It may even be many months before easy intercourse is re-established. Husbands often find this abstinence difficult to bear and become impatient and bad-tempered, perhaps because they have not anticipated these difficulties. Quite a few men seem tempted at least to be unfaithful in this situation.

The importance of the feeling of togetherness is reported so often by women that it is clearly one factor which can shatter the ease of a woman's maternal preoccupation. It is often quite sufficient for a woman to feel that her husband is with her in spirit. She can be quite happy if her husband is thousands of miles away if assured of his regard. Nevertheless pregnant women do repeatedly stress the value of day-to-day contact with their husbands. This has probably become more important in recent years as husbands and wives often have to support each other rather than being able to turn to other members of an extended family.

One responsibility of a husband in day-to-day contact is to act as a receptor and container for his wife's anxiety-ridden fantasies. How one person helps ease the anxiety of another in this way is not yet well understood. One instance of it would be when a wife worries that the baby will be deformed and her husband sympathises with her, but points out that it is unlikely. Naturally enough, husbands can also increase anxiety both by panicking themselves or perhaps by being disdainful. In whatever way a husband responds, his wife is likely to be sensitive and easily stirred by him.

Later Pregnancy: Changing Image of the Self

At about four or five months a woman will first notice the quickening, this is the flutter of a baby's movements *in utero*. This is usually very exciting for the mother, a living thing which is not herself is inside her. She frequently starts up imaginary conversations with her baby, often giving it provisional names. The actual anticipation of birth and mothering is likely to become more omnipresent in her mind. At the same time she is getting heavier and thus less able to move with her old vivacity. If she is going to relax and enjoy the pregnancy and early mothering a woman must give up many of her old ways of organising herself and her life. The process of allowing this to happen has been termed *Primary maternal preoccupation* (Winnicott, 1958). This summarises many of the changes of pregnancy mentioned already: becoming slower in movement, a pleasant withdrawal into ideas of self and infant, opening up of fantasies, loosening of old habits, and a *regression* into allowing the self to be dependent in more childlike ways than previously. The easy functioning of this process is epitomised by quietness.

The fact that many adoptive mothers both enjoy being and make themselves enjoyable mothers makes it plain that this primary maternal preoccupation in pregnancy is not necessary for good mothering. But I would argue that if a woman is to enjoy the stresses of later pregnancy, childbirth, lactation and early mothering in a relaxed way then it is necessary to allow old habits of vigilance and defence to break and preoccupation to take its course.

Since the preoccupation involves the breaking of old modes of adaptation, then the loosening of fantasy allowing new modes of activity to be tried and tested, later pregnancy is a *life crisis* (Caplan, 1964). This concept of crisis will be discussed on several occasions later, particularly in Chapter 9 on 'Adolescence'. Pregnancy is not usually a noisy crisis and is most frequently benign but, as it is a time of fundamental life change, it is worth regarding it as crisis. And as with any crisis anxiety is more or less inevitable. Furthermore, in later pregnancy, as a woman cannot both relax into preoccupation and remain fully vigilant, she does need to depend upon others to be vigilant for her. If her husband cannot do this then she needs other helpers.

Let us now consider a few quite commonly expressed anxious ideas in this time of preoccupation.

A pregnant woman often feels that she will not be able to cope with her new life. There also comes rage at having to change her old ways.

A common occurrence today is that a woman may have invested a great deal in a career, identified with it, and gained a unique sense of self-esteem from it. The coming of a child threatens this, and it is often possible to see how a woman cannot let herself relax into maternal preoccupation because she needs to cling to her career and old sense of herself. This affects some women so deeply that they seem to deny their pregnancy for as long as they can. Then, when they can deny it no longer, they become angry, tense and depressed.

Less tied to external circumstances, and hence more difficult for outsiders to comprehend, is the problem of lack of self-esteem which all mothers experience to some degree and some feel chronically. Some women seem, as an underlying characteristic, to doubt themselves as having any value, so that when they become pregnant they have not got the self-confidence to say to themselves, 'Now I can relax, I am good enough to be a mother and I shall know intuitively what is right'. For instance:

A woman was convinced her own conception had been a mistake. Her parents had spent all their time running a shop, so she lodged with her grandparents or aunts throughout most of her childhood. She was swept by anxieties during all her pregnancies, obsessed by the thought that it was all a mistake, that she didn't want the baby and couldn't cope. However she repeatedly got herself pregnant, perhaps to prove that that next one would be wanted after all.

Such an illustration cannot be a convincing general proof of the importance of early childhood experiences, but it alerts one to their possible importance. That they are important is given added support by the observation that most women who felt predominantly at ease with their parents as children seem to feel more or less serene about their own maternality as long as they are happy with their husbands. It must be added that I know of no formal survey that confirms or denies this, but it is a common-enough experience of those working with pregnant women.

At the same time as a young woman will probably be anticipating the birth and after, she may be frightened of the pain and shame of losing control. Dealing with this is, of course, one of the main functions of childbirth classes (Chertok, 1969).

Of more long-lasting importance is anticipation of later mothering. Thinking about coping with children must be a private preoccupation of most young women. Such anticipation no doubt carries a great deal of anxious fantasy but, as I have already mentioned, it may also be useful as a realistic, problem-solving activity.

Perhaps the most commonly felt anxiety about mothering is concerned with aggressiveness in one form or another. The mother often expresses this as a fear of losing her temper, or of not being able to stand up to her child's demands. Many women feel they should show no aggressiveness towards their children and suffer agonies when, out of frustration, they quite naturally find it rising up in themselves. This fear of aggressiveness seems to vary from person to person, from family to family, and from one culture to another. Probably in Britain, where social norms are more fluid than in traditional societies, a woman is more or less allowed the freedom to find her own way with her children. But this freedom of choice means that a great burden of responsibility and hence guilt rests upon her shoulders. If anything, the burden has increased with greater understanding of the needs of children. To many mothers the professional adviser has something of the aura of the priest of old who purveys gloomy knowledge of what is right and wrong. No responsible parents can ignore technical understanding of the needs of children. But if they blindly obey the conflicting pronouncements of every expert on the subject they are likely to be driven crazy with doubt.

The Father's Experience

So far we have been identifying with a pregnant woman and her husband has only been mentioned as an important adjunct. We have not discussed how he might feel about the matter. It does not take much exploration to discover that his wife's pregnancy usually brings to a husband a sense of fulfilment and passionate pride which is very close to the emotions of his wife, so that they can intimately share in each other's feelings.

Just as for his wife, with her pregnancy he is called upon to change his old ways of life and thought, though to a less obvious degree. Here are a couple of examples.

After that first feeling of 'Ah, we've done it', so I began to feel scared. Would my wife be all right? What would I be like as a father? And then all sorts of worries about whether our housing would be all right, would I earn enough money to keep the family, came upon me.
Money seemed my main worry. My wife had worked before and now it was up to me – quite exciting in its way but scaring all the same.

A very common anxiety for a man is that his wife will withdraw from him and not dote on him as before. Probably every man wants to be mothered, and looks to his wife to meet this need. With a real baby as rival this satisfaction is threatened. Here is an extreme example:

I know I feel an outsider. My wife says I make myself one. But I know something disappeared for me when the first child was born which has never returned. And the second child seemed to finish things. I am very fond of both children but something went dead between me and my wife.

For most men such alienation is probably hardly felt at all. They shift happily enough to sharing. But it seems rare for a man never to feel afraid of being left out, if not in the first pregnancy then in later ones. In some ways it is inevitable, because a woman turns into herself and it would be an insensitive man who did not feel it. Thus in pregnancy the wife needs her husband's concern perhaps more than on any other occasion, yet this is the time when he is very likely to feel alienated.

As with their wives, pregnancy stirs many men to fantasies. These often have their roots in childhood just as those of their wives do.

My parents counted up our misdeeds until the end of the week, when we were beaten for them. I am determined never to lay hands on my children.

I find it easy to look after children. I suppose I got it from my mother, who was always a nice, warm person.

My father enjoyed playing with us and I am looking forward to doing the same.

And, just as with the wife, such ideas must usually remain private to himself and are not often discussed, except perhaps with her.

Second and Further Pregnancies

Much of what has been said about the first pregnancy applies equally to later ones. There may not be the extremes of pleasure and fear which can be experienced with any event for the first time. Both parents will probably be surer of themselves, at least if all has gone well with the first child. In a sense the first child, simply by being alive and well, contributes to the parents' confidence. This will not be by any conscious intention of unselfishness or kindness on the child's part. But it is communicated in a very real sense none the less. Winnicott (1964) has called this a child's *contribution*.

Just as the parents have to change when they have a first baby, also the first child will have to accept a change when the second one is on the way. Most children are very aware of the changes that take place in their mothers in pregnancy. This will be perceived in her body shape and also in her tiredness and withdrawal. It is usually possible to see signs of anxiety about this if one listens and watches. It is not something a child can easily talk about, and being unable to communicate makes it all the worse for him. The child tends to be in the same position as the husband whom we described above, alienated from his mother, who because of her pregnancy is not able to respond to him as sensitively as before. It is noticeable that many kind and devoted parents ignore this pregnancy anxiety of the child. It is often thought that the child will be jealous of the baby after the birth. This may be so, but anxiety before birth, related to the mother's withdrawal, seems also to be common. It is often thought that because a child is too young to understand the facts of life then he will not be frightened about the changes in his mother. However the younger a child is, the less he understands, and hence the more puzzled and frightened he can be by the mysterious differences in his mother.

Summary
This brief discussion of a woman's and her husband's feelings and fantasies gives us few definitive conclusions except that of the importance of 'vigilant helpers' who will allow a mother to be preoccupied in a relaxed way at her own speed. It also demonstrates how pregnancy, like the rest of childhood, is a private matter of each individual's fantasy and problem solving. But it is also a public process where these private activities affect all other individuals involved in the business of bringing up a child. This web of related private worlds makes the psychological environment for a new born child.

FURTHER READING

1 Chamberlain, G. (1969), *The Safety of the Unborn Child*. A useful summary of the physiology of uterine development.
2 Green, J. H. (1968), *Basic Clinical Physiology*. It is essential to have an acquaintance with physiology before reading *Human Development*. This is a good text.
3 Segal, H. (1973), *An Introduction to the Work of Melanie Klein*. This book is not about pregnancy but it includes a wider discussion of the concept of fantasy than I give. Also useful for later chapters.
4 Smith, A. (1968), *The Body*.

Chapter 3

THE FIRST MONTHS

For a baby, birth means a fundamental change in his whole psychological organisation. *In utero* ventilation, nutrition and excretion took place through the placenta and umbilical cord. Now ventilation starts suddenly with the first breath through the lungs, feeding by sucking commences within a couple of days and so also does bowel and bladder excretion. None of the reflex patterns organising these functions can have been fully exercised before.

Early Abilities
A cursory glance at a newborn baby indicates that he is asleep nearly all the time, most relaxed when fairly tightly wrapped in his cot with a minimum of stimulation, rather like *in utero*. In the brief periods of about six minutes at a time when he is awake, it becomes plain that each child has his own particular style of movement, sensitivity and reflex reactivity. No two babies are the same in style and it is likely to be a mother's first post-birth task, after resting, slowly to attune herself to her baby's rhythm of sleeping, waking movement and feeding. This is a major task and we will discuss it later.

It was assumed until recently that the newborn baby of up to about a month was capable of very little except sleep, a few rudimentary reflexes, and a slow development of feeding ability. But experimental observations on babies using sophisticated recording techniques such as slow-motion videotapes show that only a few days after birth they are capable of a great deal during their periods of wakefulness (Lewin, 1975). A baby can focus his eyes clearly within a few days. The rudiments of even spacial discrimination are discernible within a month. Thus hand-grasping movements towards objects can be detected. And a 'defensive' gesture is made with the head when an object approaches to within about 30 cm, whereas objects presenting a larger retinal image at a greater distance will not evoke this reaction. Odour discrimination is, as might be expected, particularly acute. A baby is also soon capable of a rough localisation of sounds and responds differently to variations in sounds. His startle reflex to loud noises has been known for a long time. Only recently discovered, however, is that the whole body, and mouth in particular, responds in minute but quite specific ways to different patterns of sound. There is evidence that he mimics his mother's spoken mouth movements with similar 'linguistic' mouth movements of his own by the time he is a month old. This is matched by a mimicry of other body movement by a similar age. For instance, he is able to respond to his mother's smile with the beginnings of a smile of his own. These observations make it clear that the rudiments of echoing another person's pattern of muscular activity, by movements of similar muscles, is present very early and probably has an innate basis. The clarity of this mimicry seems to get confused later in infancy, presumably through a baby's proneness to adapt to external stimuli. What is more the mimicry is only brought out in the first place by an adult who fits into his arousal pattern.

The person most likely to do this of course is a baby's mother; it is clear that mothers and babies develop a *synchrony* with each other in the earliest weeks. What is more, within a similar period the baby can discriminate his mother's from other faces. By this synchrony, *conversations* between mother and child establish themselves within a very few weeks. These conversations often involve sound, not meaningful words, of course, but rather visual-muscular and auditory *gestures*. Even though they become confused in later months, such gestures must, together with feeding experiences, form the *roots of human communication* and hence of language.

Sleep, Arousal and Distress

As already mentioned a baby moves in a cycle between sleep and arousal; if disturbed in this he becomes distressed and usually cries. These three states involve definable differences in the activity of the nervous system of adults as well as infants which are important to recognise when considering stress, anxiety, anger, defence and aggression, as we shall be throughout the book. Early recognition of this pattern was made by the physiologist Cannon (1929) and has been followed by much research since.

A summary of each state in turn is as follows.

(1) *Sleep.* There is: synchronous activity in the central nervous system (CNS); inhibition of the sympathetic nervous system; and activity of the parasympathetic. Of subjective emotion there is none (except when sleep is disturbed).

(2) *Arousal.* There is: partial desynchrony of the CNS; a patterned mixture of inhibition and activity of the sympathetic and parasympathetic systems. And subjectively we experience interest ranging from pleasure to anxiety.

(3) *Distress.* There is: desynchronous activity of the CNS; sympathetic nervous activity and parasympathetic inhibition. Subjectively the experience is extreme rage, fear or excitement with hyperactive behaviour and hypersensitivity.

Distress is thus characterised by nervous disorganisation and hence mental disturbance. Also present are elements, often in confused form, of animal *flight* and *fight* reactions. Those in turn affect breathing, temperature control, digestion and excretion. Distress is a *psychosomatic reaction* (Parks, 1972).

What evokes distress in young infants? Well known for many years have been the following: sudden loud noises, loss of body support, choking, hunger, pain and cold. Less well known and recently added are: *overstimulation* (e.g. erratic jigging which disturbs the sleep–waking rhythm), *confusion* (e.g. after the baby is a month or so old a strange voice interposed with his mother's face will distress him), and *rejective gestures* by a familiar person like his mother (again this occurs only after there has been enough time for a person to become familiar). Distress is relieved, of course, by stopping the disturbing stimulation and also by nursing, holding, caressing and cuddling. These all involve *gentle* movement and skin sense stimulation. They are *gently erotic*, rather than excitingly so, and have more than superficial similarities with a lover's embrace. That young babies actively seek this comfortable pleasure not only when distressed is obvious enough to any interested mother. The necessity for this has been systematically studied in primates (Harlow, 1961). But until recently the importance of erotic holding and play has been largely ignored by academic research, which has concentrated on more intellectual development. Psychoanalysts, on the other hand, while backward in investigating intellectual discriminations, have long stressed the importance of erotic comfort (Bowlby, 1969; Winnicott, 1965; Escalona, 1969).

Baby and Mother
The idiosyncratic style of each baby and mother has already been stressed. Some babies are born very active, others placid; likewise mothers differ in their characteristic movements, not only from one mother to another but also from culture to culture. If a mother cannot attune to her baby's rhythm then distress is likely to result. This in turn stresses his mother, probably upsetting him more so that a vicious circle is likely. Although babies are usually more robust than inexperienced mothers fear and 'forgiveness' comes quickly when a contented rhythm is re-established, nevertheless a mother needs all her vitality, ingenuity and patience to melt such vicious circles. It is naturally most enjoyable for both if they hardly occur. I have already argued that for this to happen a mother needs to

B

become loose and flexibly attuned in a relaxed sort of way to her baby's rhythm and pattern.

This is why relaxing and regressing into maternal preoccupation seems to be important. A mother with only half her mind on a baby, or over quick and incisive in her movements, is unlikely to provide that smooth pattern of moderate stimulation when awake and minimal stimulation when asleep which seems necessary for the relaxed synchrony of an infant's growth. However it must not be forgotten that the mother–child relationship is a two-way process. From birth some babies seem to be impossible to please even with the most devoted mothering. And even if this is not the case a mother can only rarely be blamed for conscious wilfulness. When things go wrong a mother is, as often as not, as baffled and distressed as the baby.

Nevertheless, I would suggest that it is under these loose conditions that mother–child conversations of feeding and gesture come most easily. In them a mother seems to experience her baby paradoxically as separate from her and yet at one with her. 'Separate and yet at one' is naturally beautiful to watch. It is most obvious in mothering but also in fathering and in later life between lovers and very good friends; its beauty is also evident in anyone playing or working with consummate skill. This vital state of being together and yet separate is, I think, what is essentially being referred to by the word *loving*. It is wonderful to experience and I have been arguing that it is also vital to growth. However, it can also be fragile for, with experiences of togetherness, separateness can be lost into engulfment; and with separateness, togetherness can be lost into alienation. This theme of loving is central to the book and will be referred to time and again in different guises and forms.

Returning to the baby, it must be becoming clear that, as he is awake so little, only very few people, one or two at most, can have the time really to attune harmoniously with him. What is more, if a mother herself is to relax with him, it is naturally necessary for her helpers to continue to be vigilant for her. This is where the baby–mother–father triad can be a most enjoyable and economical unit. A husband who is lovingly attuned to both his wife and baby can move easily between looking after her and helping her out with attending to their child. A husband is the most likely person to fulfil the needs of a vigilant helper, because not only are husband and wife usually close but so also are father and baby.

There seems to be no other reason why the nuclear family should be sacred at this time of life. Children thrive, in infancy at least, throughout the world with indifferent or absent fathers so long as other trusted helpers are available. Nevertheless, I would argue that the reasons given so far are sufficient to value and preserve the nuclear family, at this phase of a child's life at least.

The necessity for an infant to have only one 'mother', feeding her child herself with attendant father, has often been questioned. Successful adoption makes it plain that breast feeding is not essential. And the participation of nannies, or other members of an extended family, is common throughout the world without apparently catastrophic effects (Mead, 1950). Let us summarise the observations so far and come to provisional conclusions. They apply to babies in any culture.

Breast feeding in early infancy is optimal (but not necessary) in that it is a most mobile food factory, provides a balanced diet, and gives immunity to many infantile infections. It also provides the possibility of enjoyable erotic, visual and vocal conversations which do seem to be necessary for optimal development. These conversations may also be deeply enjoyable to mothers. But it is also plain that the infant can enjoy relating to more than one person so long as they are familiar and also attune themselves to him in a quiet relaxed way (Rutter, 1972). A chaotic whirl of unfamiliar helpers is known to be extremely distressing (Spitz, 1965; Bowlby, 1953). The grave long-term effects of this will be discussed in the next chapter.

In conclusion I would suggest that a very small number of affectionate and familiar parents (biological or otherwise) are necessary for an infant's vital development. A biological mother breast feeding with close affectionate helpers is optimal. This is usually most easily attained, in British society at least, in a nuclear family.

Intellectual Development in the Early Months

We have considered so far a baby's competence in sensory discrimination and motor activity, together with the conditions of his general well-being. The development of new sensori-motor patterns has been the subject of study for many years. The appearance of a new integration of activity is popularly called a *milestone*. A summary of common milestones is termed a developmental schedule (Sheridan, 1968). Such schedules are commonly used by health visitors, medical officers and paediatricians as useful preliminary checks upon an infant's development. But they can only be rough guides since babies develop particular skills differently, both individually and from one culture to another.

The means by which new integrations come about is presumed to be by an interplay between the maturing of innately delimited patterns (alternatively called innate reflexes) and *learning from experience*. Recently it has become evident that infants must learn at an amazing speed. How they do learn has long been the subject of psychological research and debate.

Passive or associative learning is known to be possible *in utero*. For instance, the following classical *conditioning* sequence has been observed in the eighth month of pregnancy. A buzzer sounded close to a mother's stomach evokes no response from the foetus, but a vibrator resting on the skin evokes kicking movements. If the buzzer and vibrator are applied together several times then naturally kicking also occurs. If the buzzer now sounds without the vibrator the foetus will still kick in response. Similar conditioning or passive learning of associations takes place after birth. For example, a mother's face is soon conditioned to or associated with feeding as is evident from a baby's preparatory sucking movements (Jehu, 1967). Hundreds of concomitant impressions associated together must link to form new meanings for a young infant.

But if all learning were passive, meanings would be overwhelmingly confusing for the infant. With regard to this it has been noted, particularly by Piaget and his associates (Piaget, 1953), that a baby is from very early days *active* in being interested in certain things and in ignoring others. What is more, he spontaneously *explores* stimuli and hence begins to integrate meaningful intellectual structures or *schemata* for himself. For instance, he may by chance lick his lips, seem to get pleasure from this and try to repeat it. On subsequent days he will repeat the licking with greater sureness, apparently just enjoying the active mastery for its own sake. This repetition of a sensori-motor pattern is called a *circular-reaction* by Piaget. He suggests that by this active exploration and repetition the infant builds up for himself integrated structures or hierarchies of meaningful activity as days and months go by. They are termed hierarchical because new patterns of activity are clearly dependent upon simpler ones mastered previously. For instance, in early weeks a baby is relatively passive in feeding except for the sucking of his mouth and tongue. This in itself becomes more assured through repetition. Then he fairly quickly associates his mother's face with feeding and actively orients his whole body and manipulates her breast to start efficient sucking. Thus the original sucking is subsumed in a hierarchical way under a wider pattern of activity.

Piaget and his associates have developed a comprehensive theory of intellectual growth delineating how these early sensori-motor *schemata* are slowly transformed, through the stages of childhood, to fully logical, abstract rational thought which is only to be achieved later in adolescence. Each new stage arises out of integrations of earlier modes of mental activity and cannot develop without the mastery of earlier stages. Other psychologists (like the behaviourist Skinner, 1953) affirm the importance of a process akin to the circular-reaction of Piaget, in stressing *operant conditioning* in early learning. They fiercely criticise him, however, not only for the small samples upon which he made his observations, but also because they doubt whether his theory is justified even by his own observations, let alone by the findings of other workers. Nevertheless, no other worker has approached the breadth of Piaget's ideas which have had a great impact on psychological thought.

As already mentioned, psychoanalysts have made little direct contribution to the understanding of intellectual development, concentrating as they have on fantasy and feeling. But they are very close to Piaget in stressing how later developments are always dependent upon the patterning of earlier relationships. Likewise both Piaget and psychoanalysts agree upon the importance of mouth, hand and eye co-ordinations in the early months of life.

Because of the importance of the mouth this has been called the *oral phase*, and psychoanalysts stress how oral feeling and fantasy is still active in adult life, albeit much of it unconscious. This can be seen in our ordinary language by the frequent use of such phrases as 'I am afraid I've bitten off more than I can chew', 'I can't swallow that one', 'She's a sweet girl', 'The team were hungry for goals'. Here, I am arguing that these phrases are not chance metaphors, but that oral fantasy is active to give meaning to both speaker and listener. (As we know now that sight, smell and hearing are also important in the early months, perhaps this period should be referred to as the 'snout phase' rather than the oral phase.)

The Infant's Experience of Self and the Outside World
As he cannot speak we can only know about a baby's experience by empathy and inference. From the observations about himself and other objects, particularly his mother, already discussed in the earlier parts of this chapter, we can say that his behaviour is object-related or objective-related from the start. We also know that he is very active in learning and in trying to develop meaningful patterns of ideas. He certainly soon manifests contentment, excitement, rage and confusion. Perhaps after a few months it can be said that he is joyful or elated and also depressed. But there is no evidence for such complex feelings as sadness, hope, pity, concern or revenge. These emotions involve complex structures of intellectual discrimination and feeling akin to: 'I have lost', 'I expect to get but haven't got', 'He, not I has been hurt' and 'I, not he has been hurt'.

Thus, from comparing gestures indicative of emotion in infants with those in older children we have one line of evidence to suggest that infants of up to a few months old have not yet discriminated, in any stable way at least, that which belongs to themselves from that which belongs to their bodies and to the outside world. In other words, much intellectual learning must take place before a baby can sort out what belongs to his self and what is not-self. This leads me to conclude, along with most other psychoanalysts, that *self–object discrimination* is, at most, unstable and rudimentary in the early months of life. If this is so, then, in the experience of a baby, a mother's smile is not meaningfully conceived as being less or more his possession than is a hunger pang. And the sensations of a bowel motion are no more or less outside him than the joggling of his pram. They may be discriminated but this is not the same as being conceived in terms of belonging to the self. The signs of early self–object discrimination will be considered in the next chapter. Here I would like to stress only how important this state of non-differentiation seems to be. Its presence has already been stressed when describing the child's early relationship with his mother and its mutual mimicry. The early state of non-differentiation is not only very enjoyable to both mother and child, but learning also takes place at a very great pace at this stage.

Even as adults, we experience partial losses of self-object differentiation when, for instance, we are in excited conversation and cannot remember when who has said what. We also experience it, partially, when in sympathy with others or when intuitively understanding them, this is particularly so when making love. It is also felt with the physical world in mystic and deeply religious feelings.

When such non-differentiation chronically persists for a person, then he is able neither to think rationally, nor relate to others realistically, nor to adapt to the external world. Such a chronic state of self–object non-differentiation is *psychotic* and is naturally very disturbing for the sufferer and those around him. But it seems to me that transient or partial states of this kind are both normal, in that they are frequent and also probably essential for deep communication and health. Non-differentiation is primitive but not necessarily pathological, just as drinking milk is primitive but not necessarily pathological.

Thinkers in the Western world, and psychiatrists in particular, probably undervalue transient non-differentiation. Freud himself was very sceptical about the 'oceanic feeling', tentatively relegating it to a disease symptom. Perhaps this scepticism is a by-product of our deeply ingrained assumption of the unique superiority of Aristotelian logic which assumes subject–object differentiation as Persig (1974) suggests. Certainly in the East the prejudice has for centuries been, if anything, in the other direction. The Buddha, for instance, propounded that unnecessary human suffering originates essentially from *spurious* self–object differentiation (Ling, 1973). Zen and other Buddhist masters have cogently argued and refined this point of view ever since (Susuki, 1949). A clarification of this question, however, does seem to be appearing in Western thought. Matte Blanco (1975), for instance, has very recently tackled the question by combining the specialised techniques of mathematical logic and psychoanalytic thinking. He makes it plain that the undifferentiated thought described here is very close to that employed in dreaming and is also an undertone in everyday thinking. It is close to what Freud called *primary process* thinking or the language of unconscious thought. He stresses how important this undifferentiated thought is in everyday life, but that it needs to be 'contained' by logical thought which differentiates both relations between objects and between the self and objects in the external world. It is likely that the whole question of human psychological development can be viewed as centering upon how an individual comes to articulate higher, logical or scientific thinking out of undifferentiated ideas. Certainly the main theme of this book can be seen in this light.

FURTHER READING

1 Jehu, D. (1967), *Learning Theory and Social Work*. Clear descriptions of conditioning theory.
2 Landreth, C. (1967), *Early Childhood*. A summary of experimental evidence concerning both infancy and early childhood.
3 Lewin, R., (ed.) (1975), *Child Alive*. A summary of the most recent research on infant behaviour in earliest infancy. Very readable.
4 Parkes, M. (1972), *Bereavement*. Contains a summary of the physiological and psychological characteristics of stress. Also recommended for its main content, bereavement.
5 Richmond, P. G. (1970), *An Introduction to Piaget*. A good introduction to the theories of Piaget. Also recommended for reading later, in parallel with *Human Development*.
6 Sheridan, M. (1968), *The Developmental Progress of Infants and Young Children*. A much-used summary of 'milestones' of development.
7 Winnicott, D. W. (1964), *The Child, the Family and the Outside World*. A very readable and sensitive account of parent–child relationships, from a psychoanalytic point of view.

Chapter 4

THE SECOND SIX MONTHS

Observable Behaviour

The second six months are usually remembered by parents with special delight. The early days of worry and drudgery have passed and routines have been established. The time has yet to come when the child is really mobile, 'into everything', provoking clashes of will and fears for his safety. During these intermediate months, parents often have time to be relatively idle. There is plenty to enjoy. The baby will usually be eagerly interested in most things that come into his orbit be they human, animal or simply shapes, colours or movements. This is a time of enormous, easily observable, thrusts in sensori-motor development and these in turn lead to crucial emotional developments.

During the first six months the baby will have been progressively awake for longer periods during the day. He will probably have dropped his night feeds, much to his parents' relief. By the middle of the first year a British baby will usually still be feeding from breast or bottle but will also be using spoon and cup. He will be kicking and wriggling, and probably sitting up for long periods, at least when supported. Sitting up means that he has a much wider scope of vision and use of his hands. He will continually be examining things, not only by looking but also by manipulating them with his hands, and often with his feet. He will take things to his mouth, suck and chew them, twist them round and look at them. This chewing also gives him relief from teething pains. He will be clearly attentive to sounds, turning towards them and singing and babbling to himself. He will also probably be beginning to play intentionally with his parents, both with things and in cuddling, tickling and babbling, usually to the delight of all concerned.

In the latter months of the first year he will be sitting up unsupported, and later start moving on his own initiative. This is usually by crawling, but babies find their own modes of progression. Some never crawl but move on one arm or by sitting up and propelling themselves with their hands. By one year a child will probably be able to stand and may be walking. In this again, babies are very variable. Some quite normal children do not walk until they are getting on for 2 years old. Having found another means of progression, they do not seem to bother to learn to walk.

When a baby has learnt to sit up, and then to move, a new range of experience is open to him. He can actively explore new places. He throws things away and looks to see where they have gone. He bangs things together to make noises and manipulates toys in relation to each other, not just towards himself and his mouth. Towards the end of the first year he will use *instruments* in his play.

Most gratifying of all for many parents, perhaps, he will be more and more actively interested in other human beings. He tends to be puzzled and tentative with strangers, reacting quite differently to them compared with his parents. But given time he will readily turn away from his parents, at least for short periods, and enjoy playing with others. Towards the end of the year he will probably show definite signs of self-conscious *coyness* and a wish to *show off*. He will also not simply mimic others in the minute ways described in the last chapter, but will, again with apparent self-consciousness, intentionally imitate and play at imitating them. Playing with sounds is enjoyed by babbling and repeating intonations to himself which are seemingly meaningless. These sounds will later be refined to become recognizable imitations. Probably by about 1 year, or a little older, the first recognisable words for objects will be developed.

Mother, Father and Baby
This brief description emphasises the value of *variety* of stimulation for the child acquainting himself with new meanings. The previous chapter stressed the importance of gentle stimulation for the very young baby. This still applies, but older babies usually enjoy more and more vigorous handling and play. With regard to this, cultures vary greatly in the patterning of infant stimulation; for instance, many African mothers and babies enjoy gymnastic performances which quite frighten unwary, unathletic Britishers. Perhaps this early physical enjoyment accounts in part for the natural grace of African dancing and athletic movement, compared to their hesitantly formalised European counterparts.

We have also stressed the danger of confusion in overstimulating a child. However now, for short periods at least, a child very obviously seeks out new experiences. Piaget epitomises this by referring to the demand for *moderate-newness*. A father with his different body movements, often harder than a mother's, clearly provides moderate-newness in body-gesture conversations with his baby. In the earliest months he usually has to inhibit muscular aggressiveness in order to attune gently, now it is possible to be freer. Thus at this stage a father can become not only the mother's vigilant helper and assistant mother, but can also use a facility which tends to be special to his sex – his passion for muscular vigour.

Forms of Pleasure

In considering sensori-motor conversations between parents and child it is worth distinguishing three different general forms of pleasure. Taking these in turn:

(1) There is *homeostatic pleasure*. This is experienced when a chemical balance is restored in the body. Thus a thirsty baby is active, even distressed until he has filled his stomach with liquid. Then he flops back with a satiated sigh. A similar satisfied sigh is also noticeable after urinating or defecating. There seems to be something *orgasmic* about this satisfaction, in that pleasure seems to shiver through the whole body (Winnicott, 1958; Rycroft, 1971).

(2) *Erotic pleasure* is also distinguishable. Rhythmic stimulation of the skin and movement senses, such as being rocked, hugged, tickled, stroked and bounced, evoke paroxysms of laughing delight which have something of the quality of little orgasms. This pleasure is close to, yet quite different from, the pleasure of being held which involves contact but little or no movement. In parallel with these, an infant also enjoys such self-stimulation as thumb-sucking. This is *auto-erotic* activity of which more will be said later.

(3) *Mastery and meaning–finding pleasure* is also detectable. Here there is delight when a new skill has been achieved, or some meaningful, new mental realisation has been made. Most adults are familiar with the culmination experience, such as when a goal is scored or the shout of 'Eureka' when making a new discovery. Such pleasures, often accompanied by a laugh of triumph, again with a slightly orgasmic note of a mental kind, are easily noticeable in older babies.

Psychoanalysts have stressed (Guntrip, 1961) the first two pleasures, together with that of being held (Winnicott, 1965), when developing theories about the fundamental yearnings of human beings. They have tended to ignore the third. Research psychologists, on the other hand, have tended to stress the first – homeostatic pleasure – or the last – meaning pleasure – , but have ignored the second. Piaget, for instance, rightly I think, stresses meaning pleasure but, wrongly I think, tends to ignore homeostatic and erotic pleasures.

A parent, especially a mother, is frequently a necessary participator in all three forms of pleasure, especially when feeding. But certain pleasures are probably essentially found in *solitude*, excretion for instance. And much meaning and mastery pleasure can only be found by a baby when to all intents and purposes he is alone. Here Winnicott (1965) has stressed the importance in development for a mother and older baby to be alone together in the same room. In this situation a baby seems to feel 'held' by his mother's vigilant presence, but both are able to go their separate ways.

Displeasure and Distress

A parent, the mother particularly, is, I think inevitably, also experienced essentially as a *source of distress*. As already mentioned, this arises in young babies with pain, frustration (having to wait), overstimulation, understimulation, rebuffs and confusion. By the time the baby is several months old a new trigger for distress becomes apparent. He will have begun to settle meaningful *schemata* about events in his mind, and hence to shape his activity with an underlying expectation that 'the mother thing' will respond when called. If there is no reply he is distressed. So we must now add *loss* to the list of distress arousers. Distress is most often relieved by gentle *holding* which often leads to sleep. *Sleep and dreaming rhythm* is essential as a long-term salve to distress.

We have already noted that distress involves desynchrony of the central nervous system, hypersensitivity and hyperactivity, and also confused flight and fight reactions. From the point of view of an adult we know that this desynchrony readily makes us experience things in *bits*. Things, ourselves included, are experienced as a strange chaos of impressions and quiet meaningfulness is lost. People say, 'I just went to bits'. I will be suggesting throughout the book that anxious anticipation of 'going to bits', is present in us all throughout our lives. It is a fear of going mad. Fortunately it is usually not in the forefront of our mind and is relegated to unconsciousness. When a person is in acute, confused distress we say he is in a *panic*. When he keeps some organisation going in his ideas by means of fighting reactions we say he is *madly angry*. When he keeps some organisation going predominantly by flight we say he is *phobic* or as a characteristic, 'cowardly'.

When a person chronically remains in bits, distinction between what belongs to self, the body and the outside world continues to be confused in a malignant way. When such a person attempts to create some order in this personal chaos by believing in certainties in which other people cannot believe, we say the person is *deluded* or *psychotic*. This psychotic loss of distinction between self and the outside world has some apparent similarity to the non-differentiation of an infant. But it is fundamentally very different in that the former is a chronic distress reaction whereas the latter is a natural state of immaturity.

I will be arguing that these states of madness and the fear of their occurrence, *psychotic anxiety* (Segal, 1973), are not normal in the sense that they are happy. But they can be normal in that they occur, albeit transiently, in everyone. People probably minimise such states from childhood onwards by moulding their lives to avoid their occurrence. In other words, they develop mental *schemata* or structures of ideas about the self and the world in fantasy and action which keep the risk at a minimum. Such *defensive schemata* may be inadequate, absurd or cowardly, but are necessary for equanimity. I will also argue that transient or benign experiences of madness are probably necessary in passing through essential crises of life. These are probably difficult notions to digest and further explanations will be given in later chapters.

Very little of what has just been said applies to a young baby, except that we do know he suffers, sometimes chronically, from distress. It is also plain that mothers, by overstimulating, confusing, rebuffing or leaving their babies, very frequently provoke chronic distress. (How parents can drive their children mad has been much investigated and discussed in psychiatric writing in recent years – Laing and Esterson, 1964; Lidz, 1963; Haley, 1968; de Mause, 1974.) I will not give illustrative examples here; they abound in the literature, some of which is essential reading.

Good and Bad Experiences

When considering a baby's pleasure and distress in relation to his mother, I think it is very useful to follow a distinction, first introduced by Melanie Klein (1948), between the experience of a mother as a good object and bad object. When a mother is experienced as *enhancing* a child's pleasure (homeostatic erotic or meaningful) she is obviously welcomed with joy, in which case it is said she is 'good'. When, on the other hand, she is experienced as arousing distress it is said she is being 'bad'. What is more, babies tend to react in *all-or-nothing* ways, so experiences are either totally good or totally bad. These notions of good and bad only refer to the *immediate* experience of the child. They do not refer to what is good for him in the long run. Quite clearly, not only is it impossible for even the most devoted mother to be good in this sense all the time, but also, as we will argue later, what is felt as bad for a baby in the immediate experience may well be good for him in the long run.

Spitz (1965) has stressed a similar distinction between good and bad in the mother–child relation, but in the opposite direction to that of Klein. Klein pointed out the importance of a *baby* feeling his mother to be either all-good or all-bad. Spitz, on the other hand, has pointed out the importance of the *mother* feeling her baby to be good or bad. These states, he suggests, are signalled by 'yes' and 'no' gestures from a mother to her baby. 'Yes' gestures, sometimes consciously intended but often quite automatic, are made by the mother when she is enjoying what her baby is doing. They help to affirm to the baby that he is good for his mother, and hence, since mother is most of his world, that he is a good person worth being alive. 'No' gestures, on the other hand, negate what a child is doing and probably tend to instil in a child a sense of being a bad person who is not worth having around. We can detect here the possible roots of *guilt* which will be discussed in the next chapter. What is more, when a mother makes 'no' gestures she rebuffs the child who is then likely to become, if only transiently, distressed. Hence, mother and child naturally feel mentally bad for each other.

In summary, when a mother evokes distress, and all that that entails, she is experienced as bad. As a mother must inevitably be at best both bad and good at times, then she is the child's first enemy as well as his first lover. Furthermore, the patterning of these good and bad experiences seems often to set the style of child–parent communication and hence, perhaps, for the climate of much of his later life.

Loss, Separation Anxiety and Deprivation

It is now well known that a child of over a few months old who has got used to enjoying his mother becomes distressed when she is absent for even short periods. In particular, if he is separated from her in a strange environment he is at first distraught and screaming. He is in a state of *extreme distress*. After some days he seems to quieten down and behave 'better'. If the separation continues for a long period he becomes apathetic and unresponsive, manifesting most of the symptoms of *depression* (Bowlby, 1973).

Although sensitive parents have been intuitively aware of this reaction to loss for a very long time, it is remarkable how many cultural practices have ignored this, not only in this country but throughout the world. In Britain, Bowlby and his colleague Robertson were the first to bring this question towards formal recognition, by pointing out this syndrome when children were sent to hospital or to children's homes.

Since then there has been a great deal of research and argument about how much a young child can be separated from his familiar mother without serious damage (Clarke, 1975). This has been summarised by Rutter (1972). In general, his conclusions can be briefly stated as follows. If a young child is separated from a familiar mother and placed in an unfamiliar and, to him, chaotic environment then the picture of distress passing to depression, as described by Bowlby, does take place. If, however, a child is separated from his mother but placed in a familiar environment with a foster person with whom he is also familiar then there is little sign of distress and probably few, if any, serious long-term effects on development. This contention is movingly argued and demonstrated in the well-known films by the Robertsons (quoted by Rutter).

A similar, but not identical, problem with regard to infant development was raised some time before Bowlby by Spitz (1965). This is the question not of the loss of a good mother but of *deprivation* in mothering. Spitz observed that children in large institutions, where they were well nourished and clean but left chronically devoid of consistent stimulation, became extremely retarded. Furthermore, they were excessively prone to infections so that mortality rates were far higher than less sanitary but more friendly environments. Thus deprivation of affectionate stimulation was seen to have not only psychological consequences but also serious somatic ones.

More recently, health visitors and social workers have informally noted how frequently these deprivations of consistent stimulation and conversation can occur even for a baby at home with his mother. Deprivation is not confined to infants in hospitals or large institutions. This concept has been extended to that of the *cycle of deprivation*, which points out that parents who were deprived in their childhood probably tend to repeat the pattern with their own children (Kelmer-Pringle, 1974).

It is worth recognising at this point that the overall concept of deprivation can be a crude categorisation. We ought, perhaps, not to rest content with it but rather specify in what specific functions a child seems to be deprived. Some children are deprived of nutrition, others of affection, others have plenty of affection but little quiet consistency of stimulation, and yet others may be deprived of variety while experiencing plenty of affection and consistency. Proneness to crude categorisation by workers can be most unjust to mothers who are doing their best but failing, probably unconsciously, only in certain aspects of their responsibilities. There is a certain brutality in negating all a mother's sense of worth instead of affirming some aspects while critically drawing attention to others where failure is really occurring.

Fantasy in Infancy

Returning now to the differentiation of the idea of self from the external world, I want to recall the concept of fantasy. In the chapter on pregnancy it was defined as that personal, imaginative activity which underlies thought and feeling. In waking life it seems to be continuously checked, refined and tested by a system of central evaluation and control – the ego. But, at least when life is experienced richly, adaptive activity is always accompanied and enlivened by fantasy laden with feeling. I also suggested that such fantasising seemed to involve close mental representations of physiological or body functions.

We have, of course, little direct evidence of fantasy occurring in infancy because babies do not talk and report their inner feelings. But we do know that little children who are not much older are full of fantasies, often of a very rich and lurid kind (M. Klein, 1932). We also know that fantasies continue when asleep and that they are particularly open during the regular periods in which we dream each night. These periods can be detected experimentally by noting changes in electroencephalogram rhythms which are concurrent with other physiological changes – rapid eye movements, sucking motions, and erection of the penis in males (presumably there is some similar clitoral arousal). When woken during these periods adults report vivid dream material (Kline, 1972; Mee and Mayes, 1973; Witkin and Lewis, 1967). With slight differences from adults, this dreaming cycle is present in babies, even *in utero*. This is not direct evidence for infants fantasising when awake. But it does argue for a continuity from earliest infancy of mental processes in which fantasy seems to take place. We also have no reason at all to believe that fantasies begin at some time after infancy and yet just before children can speak.

If an infant does have fantasies then his mental life is likely to be rich and vivid because, as we have stressed before, so much of what he experiences must be vivid, 'all or nothing' and yet baffling. As Piaget has stated, a baby is extremely active in trying to form meaningful representations, but this meaningfulness is rudimentary, fluctuant and unstable. Furthermore, since a baby's mental life is at the start centred around the mouth, nose, eyes, ears and hands we would expect his most insistent fantasies to focus on these zones of the body. Thus infantile fantasy is frequently of tasting, swallowing, gulping, biting, chewing, grinding, puncturing and spitting. And, as he does not discriminate himself from the outside world, he probably just as readily fantasises passively of being swallowed, bitten and spat out.

We can assume that, when contended, a baby's fantasy is experienced as mild and pleasant. But in distress it is likely to be violent, explosive, in bits and discordant. Grinding, slashing, engulfing, ejecting, tearing, exploding would be some likely fantasies. It is known that these are prevalent in the waking life of older children and adults when disturbed. So that there is good reason to believe that they are also present in distressed infants. At this age every experience must tend to have an urgent overwhelming immediacy, for there is hardly any idea of future or past for a baby.

However, after he is about 6 months old, there are signs that a baby is beginning to grow beyond awareness of only immediate urgencies and to stabilise ideas of past and future, inside and outside. Let us now turn to this.

Self and Not-Self
During the second half of the first year various subtle changes in a baby's behaviour can be detected by any ordinary observer. An infant's interest in inanimate objects changes in that he will now look actively for things that have gone out of his field of vision. At about this time also, or a little later, he will *play at* throwing things away in order to have them retrieved. After he has begun to sit up unaided he will use his whole body to search for hidden objects. Similar changes occur in relation to people. In crying, a new note comes into his voice which can only be described as *calling*; it is not the simple 'whow whow' of earlier days but more of a 'Come here I want you'. Separation anxiety also becomes evident, in

such ways as whimpering when his mother puts on her coat to go out.

All these activities suggest a growing awareness that things and people can disappear and arouse anxiety, but they can also return. A structuring of ideas is growing into an awareness that physical things can come and go, and yet maintain a *constancy* of their own independent of the baby's wishes. The same occurs with regard to people; they are beginning to be recognised as having an independent but constant life of their own. The delightful side of this realisation of separate existence can be seen in a baby's fun at playing such games as peep-bo, or tickling a parent to get them to giggle and then wanting to be tickled back. *External Reality* is beginning to be appreciated. Self and not-self is being discriminated. It is the psychological birth of an infant.

What is the self? It has, of course, been an abiding concern of civilised mankind in both East and West for thousands of years. The religious and philosophical literature on the subject is vast and quite beyond my capacity to summarise. In past decades, perhaps the most rigorous analysers of experiences of self have been existential thinkers (Laing, 1959; May, 1967; Tillich, 1952). Academic psychologists have on the whole bypassed the question because it has not seemed in principle to be a concept that is open to scientific verification. A notable exception is G. A. Kelly (1963) whose theory of personal constructs has given birth to a vigorous school of research and testing both in Britain and America. Again, until very recently, psychiatrists have likewise had little to say on the subject, except when concerned with disorders of the body image. With the exception of Jung, psychoanalysts and therapists have also only recently directly addressed themselves to the question when, it has become of very active interest (Jacobson, 1964; Winnicott, 1965; Kohut, 1971; Khan, 1975). Mahler (1975) and her associates have perhaps been the most systematic psychoanalytic investigators of the development of self-differentiation in infancy and early childhood. It is to them we owe the felicitous phrase of 'psychological birth' which they see as occurring crucially from about 6 months to $2\frac{1}{2}$ years old. Led probably by the original thinking of G. H. Meade (1932), sociologists have recently produced a very great deal of searching work on the social contexts of self-feeling (e.g. Goffman, 1959). A visitor from another planet would probably be struck by the present intellectual ferment on this question in the West. There will be no answers to the question of self in this book, but I will briefly argue about one or two facets which I hope may provoke further questions.

The necessary substrate of each person's self-feeling must, of course, be simply that he is able to be aware or to have experiences. We can only have indirect access, through word or gesture, to other people's experience. And we do not know when an infant's awareness begins: it seems to be wakefully present at least from the earliest days after birth. In the past it has been usual to equate awareness with wakeful consciousness, but our understanding of *dreaming* (Freud, 1900) indicates that a form of awareness of experiences continues in sleep. The recent physiological studies, already mentioned, indicate that this dreaming occurs in infancy, even *in utero*, as well as in adult life. Experimental studies of subliminal-perception likewise stress the presence of subconscious awareness (Kline, 1972).

But awareness is not the same as self-awareness which is our present concern. It is a practice of old Zen masters when questioned on this subject to reiterate the pronouncement of Joshu, a Chinese master of a thousand years ago, which was simply 'no-thing'. It seems useful to follow this advice and divest ourselves to begin with to thinking of the self as a concrete entity. Rather let us recognise it as one side of an *act of discrimination* or differentiation. This is what I was referring to a few paragraphs back when describing the infant's behaviour towards things and people: he seemed to be discriminating self and not-self. If the sense of self is essentially part of a process of discrimination, then we cannot meaningfully talk about 'the self' as if it were an entity in isolation but only in relation to not-self experiences.

One essential facet of not-self feeling is the experience of *external reality*. This seems clearly to be forming in the second six months of life. For instance, a baby playing at throwing things away and getting them back or looking for lost objects seems to be discriminating that 'things are real out there'. Let us consider this for a moment. Obviously ideas of external reality are dependent upon patterned information from the exteroceptors: sight, hearing, touch and movement. But ideas of *constancy* are also involved, that is that things can disappear from sensory contact and be conceived as still present somewhere in order to return later. Stable memory and imagination are obviously important in this.

Emotionally, constancy can be seen to entail two sorts of experience: first, awareness of *loss* and, secondly, expectation or hope of *return*. For these to occur, and hence for a baby, or grown up, to feel something as real, he must recognise it to be out of the control of his *whim*. For instance, you feel the chair you are sitting on is real and constant not only because you can touch and see it, but also because you intuitively know it is not subject to every whim which might arise in you. If you wished, perhaps you could smash it up but you know you could not eat it or magically turn it into a butterfly.

This inability to control must entail *frustration*, especially for a baby. And we know that frustration evokes distress and rage. This being so, the development of a sense of external reality inevitably involves feelings of destructive aggression as well as the experience of loss. Furthermore, if the sense of self is the counterpart of external reality then the feeling of oneself as a separate individual is also born out of experiences of frustration, distress and rage. This rather solemn conclusion is not, I think, widely discussed in the literature: it is however explicitly stated by Freud (1915a), Winnicott (1958), and Rochlin (1973). It is also implied by such existential writers as Tillich and May.

But the experience of reality cannot simply be one of frustration and distress. Enjoyment and satisfaction also really happen for both infants and ourselves. What is more, it is plain from the work of Spitz, Bowlby, Mahler and many others that the most frustrated babies are certainly not likely to become the most realistic children. On the other hand, it is common knowledge that a child who is exclusively cosseted and pampered to satisfy his every whim becomes a distressing tyrant to himself as well as others. Clearly a baby must develop his differentiation of self from external reality by a rhythm of satisfaction interspersed with frustration. In a mixture of Spitz's and Mahler's phrases the pattern of a mother's 'Yeses' and 'Noes' provides the background for his psychological birth. Without steady satisfactions and enjoyment from his parents, a baby cannot develop those hopeful ideas of future pleasure that make painful frustrations bearable. When distress becomes chronic, then it seems that a child's mind resorts to a variety of pathological, defensive activities where self and reality discrimination is distorted if not disabled. This will be the subject of later discussion.

What I am alluding to in these paragraphs is the first dim, vague, but deep beginning of an underlying sense of external reality. I am not trying to describe clearly structured and precise thinking which we call realistic or rational thought, only its origins. The evidence, particularly Piaget (1929, 1954), suggests that realistic thinking only slowly develops throughout childhood and after; it is the product of imagination or fantasy being tested and refined by immovable experiences. A child, if healthy, continuously creates hypotheses about the world from his imagination. These are modified, and also distorted, by what he is told; they are also tested by what he experiences for himself.

Sociologists have further pointed out how the sharing of a model of reality with others of the same culture gives its individuals a conviction of the truth of this model, even though members of other cultures can see its fallacies. This being so, we must recognise that no representation of external reality, even a formally tested scientific theory, is a final truth. Reasoning doubt must be a hallmark of sane intelligence. Provisional conviction about a view of the world is necessary for decisive action, but it seems that a person holding a conviction of the final truth of his ideas is under a delusion.

If our conception of external reality is created and slowly tested throughout life then so also must its counterpart, the sense of self, slowly develop and solidify.

If my argument that the senses of self and external reality are counterparts in the same process of discrimination, then various conclusions about the origins of the sense of self can be made. Like external reality the self-feeling must be born of the combined experiences of enjoyments and frustration. As I mentioned earlier, the part played by frustration and distress may at first seem strange, and it must be admitted that the evidence from infancy can only be indirect and, except for Mahler, is little researched. But evidence from introspection supports the contention that something of a sense of *loss*, *aloneness*, and the ability to bear *loneliness* is intrinsic to sure self-feeling and integrity.

I would also tentatively suggest that just as with his developing representations of external reality, so too does a child, perhaps more vaguely, create and test representations of himself. These are necessarily incomplete and fluctuant but become progressively more stable over the years. This stability is probably always only partial. It develops and changes until death unless stultified by encrusted defensive postures.

Sources of Information in Creating a Self-Image
I suggest that it is worth while distinguishing two sources of information in the building up of self-representation. The first source comes from what *other* people communicate to the individual about himself. Secondly, this is integrated with what the individual *privately* remembers, perceives and imagines of his effects on others, and they on him. For example, the communication 'You are a brainless fool' from another person may be integrated by an individual with his private perceptions and memory so that he thinks, 'It does seem that I have been foolish on this occasion but on many other occasions I have acted intelligently and I see no reason why I should not be intelligent again. I have been foolish but as a character I am not a fool.' On the other hand, a person's integrative capacity, and hence his self-knowledge, may be weak and shattered by the scornful pronouncement, so that he can do nothing but believe he is a fool in an overwhelmed way. This can occur very easily with a young child whose memory is short and integrative capacity vulnerable.

It has been suggested that knowledge of self in infancy is derived primarily from the first of the two sources just mentioned: from communication by others. G. H. Meade (1932) cogently argued this point of view some years ago. As well as using other evidence, he pointed out how in primitive speech a child first uses his name (given to him by others) to refer to himself, e.g.' Sarah want drink'. This is later replaced by the passive pronoun 'Me want drink'. Lastly comes the active 'I want a drink'.

This line of approach has underlying similarities to the psychoanalytic one of Spitz (1965), where he stresses the fundamental importance of maternal communications, in both gesture and speech (Yeses and Noes), for the development of a child's feeling about himself. Thus a child who is enjoyed by his mother clearly feels he is worthy. Whereas a child who is repeatedly rebuffed is prone to feel depressedly useless.

But hand in hand with these social sources of self-feeling must go a child's private discriminations of what is possessed by his aware self. The constant presence of parts of his body is signalled by the interoceptive senses and its surface is indicated by touch sensations. These constant patterns must contribute towards the integration of the sense of self as possessing a body. Less constant, but nevertheless cyclic, within this *body image* are experienced urges to suck, swallow, bite, spit, urinate, defacate, reach, grab and lick. And we have suggested that these seem to be the sorces of many imaginings or fantasies. Thus the body image is filled with fantasy and is probably very unstable in early life. What is more, disturbed states later in life show how prone we are to unstable possession of body image. Feelings of strange body shape, of not possessing parts of the body and unwarranted, hypochondriacal ideas of body malfunction are very common indeed. Like the representation of external reality a coherent body image develops only slowly, can be unstable and changes throughout life.

Memory, both long and short term, is perhaps the most central pool from which we derive coherent self-feelings. By remembering his past, a person can check the validity of his own present imaginings as well as the communications of others. 'I am what I remember I did' is largely true.

The sum of the representations of our body image, its urges and fantasy together with our memories is referred to often as our *inner world* or inner reality as distinct from the *external world* or external reality. Let us not forget that they are both incomplete, vague and subject to distortion and, as will be discussed later, the two can often be confused in experience. This is particularly true of the young child who, having a short memory and unstable intellectual structures, has a very unsure sense of himself which is easily swayed both by distress and the communications of others. Only after years does a determined self-conscious sense of identity cohere, and even then it is likely to change until death.

Lastly, let us draw some threads together and consider the general notion of central control, the *ego* as I called it in the first chapter, and the self as now discussed.

The concept of the ego was first systematically introduced by Freud (1923). At this time Freud was taking the position of observing *other* people's behaviour. He noted that they seemed, on the one hand, to be impulse ridden and yearning to satisfy themselves. He gave a name to the source of these impulses and called it the *id* (as if it were an entity). On the other hand, he saw that people learned and were adaptive, in some measure developing controls over impulses in order to adapt. He was impressed by the central organisation in this and gave it a name (again as if it were an entity) which is called, in translation, *the ego.*

Many writers, being unhappy about this formulation, have often used the terms according to their own whims so that something of a Tower of Babel exists at present in the literature. Some have largely given up the term 'the ego' and refer to ego-functioning more loosely to refer to adaptive activities generally. At all events, the notion of ego seems to have an *objective* frame of reference. The self, on the other hand, is a concept that is derived subjectively from introspection. In so far as a person is aware of his being adaptive as others would observe him, then his sense of self is likely to be close to his ego-functioning. But, if he is riven with fantasy, then his consciousness of self is likely to be a long way from an objective assessment of his ego-functioning.

Infantile and Psychotic Mental Events

The considerations just mentioned give some idea of how tenuous the sense of self can be. It can be riven with fantasies of many things. For instance, the fantasy of one's effect on others, of *power* can grow to delusional proportions. Delusions are fantasies held with utter conviction. If we are sane our experience of reality is toned both by a sense of the effectiveness of our ego but also by an underlying sense of being partly helpless. We adults have a tenuous enough sense of our effect on others, a baby must be far more doubtful. If the deep feelings of older people are anything to go by, the infant must experience fantasies akin to grandeur when he chortles with self-satisfied delight and is worshipped by his doting parents. Likewise when rejected, unwanted and swept by distress he shows all the signs of experiences of helplessness and despair. Something akin to the fantasy, 'They are dead to me and I am dead to them' is likely to be active. This is depression.

Our discussion has already touched on many characteristics of *psychotic processes* observable in disturbed adults. In the psychotic depression or melancholia of adults, for instance, we can recognise: chronic listless apathy, agitation, a feeling of loss of good experiences, a deep sense of unworthiness, of people being dead to oneself and oneself being dead to them. This sense of worthless helplessness may in melancholia be interspersed with feelings of grand effectiveness: 'I have done it, it is all my fault, I am utterly bad.'

Likewise we have alluded to processes characteristics of *schizoid* conditions. These are: being in bits, feelings of catastrophic explosions, of the self disintegrating, of not being in one's own body, and of self-not-self confusion. We have also alluded to the characteristic schizoid defensive withdrawal into autoerotism, this can proceed into *autistic* preference for fantasy.

None of this is arguing that an infant is really psychotic nor that a psychotically ill adult has simply regressed to infancy. Rather it argues that the benign operation of these psychotic-like fantasies can be strongly inferred in infancy. Just as I have argued already, these can be, even ought to be, part of normal, mature adult life. As mentioned earlier, psychotic processes are only malign in adulthood (and probably in infancy also) when the central control system or ego is no longer basically integrative. This seems to occur in chronic distress, and can be brought about by environmental agencies or disorders of body chemistry or both, but these are psychiatric questions which are outside our scope.

Defence Mechanisms

If it is problematic for an adult to keep sane and content how does the more vulnerable infant manage it? First, it is obvious from our earlier discussion that this is not within the baby's power alone. He remains contented largely by other agencies, that is by having loving, empathetic and consistent adults around him who provide the conditions of moderatenewness of stimulation.

But we can also detect the rudiments of *defence mechanisms* or mental tricks which reduce immediate distress. Thumb-sucking, autoerotism and then withdrawal into autistic fantasy are some that have been mentioned.

Another one concerns good and bad feelings and their 'all-or-nothing' quality. It is easy to observe how a baby or young child has a short time span of attention for one activity. He gets deeply absorbed in a thing, then suddenly switches off it to become deeply engrossed in another. So engrossed is he that it is as if the previous thing is of no importance at all. This switching is very frequently used to recover from distress. One moment a baby will be in a paroxysm of rage, kicking and screaming at his mother, then he is picked up and kissed and he switches, the rage has gone, he is all smiles. 'Bad' mother has suddenly turned into 'good' mother again. The bad experience seems to be forgotten.

This underlying proneness to dichotomise is, it seems to me, omnipresent in adult emotional reactions as well as in infancy. Sociologists and anthropologists (such as Lévi-Strauss, 1966) emphasise the dichotomisation underlying many cultural practices. For instance, exogamous clan systems are dichotomous, so are many supernatural beliefs. It has been pointed out that even monotheism is really a duotheism between God and the Devil.

At the individual level psychoanalysts refer to this dichotomisation as *splitting* (Segal, 1973). This refers in the first instance to experiencing something as absolutely good or absolutely bad. In the process of splitting, when a thing is felt as good, the distressing memories or experiences are *denied*. This is just like the baby who seemed to deny his unpleasant experience of his mother immediately after she had picked him up, kissed him and he was all smiles.

Splitting seems to act not only as a defence, in that it quickly blots out distress or bad experiences, but also saves an immature child from helpless confusion. If he remains aware of distress and pleasure coming from the same source he is utterly mixed up. Structuring his awareness by splitting allows him to remain coherent to himself, if in an inadequate way. It seems to take much experience and assimilation for a child to develop a coherent sense at any one time, of his mother, say, as potentially 'both good and bad, distressing and enjoyable'.

What I have just described is defensive splitting, which, like all defences, is necessary for equanimity. It cannot by itself be categorised as pathological. Only when it is used chronically and in some way prevents further development can it be so regarded. This would be the case, for example, when a child splits so that he keeps the image of his mother as totally good, whereas all school teachers are evil and he refuses to go to school.

I have alluded also to another distinct form of splitting which occurs in the actual experience of extreme distress, this is the shattering of the feeling of self and objects into 'bits'. This can hardly be said to be a defensive manoeuvre to ward off distress, it is part of distress itself. However in psychosis individuals do seem to identify themselves with these bits of experience in bizarre ways in frantic efforts to feel some certainty about themselves. For instance, after writing the first edition of this book, one night I felt myself to be the pages of a book. It was most unpleasant, but fortunately my common sense or ego was also still working and I felt first horrified and then slightly amused at its happening. If, on the other hand, I had become chronically convinced that I was a book, then I would really be in trouble.

This is our first introduction to defensive tricks. I will be saying much more about them later.

FURTHER READING

1 Bowlby, J. (1953), *Child Care and the Growth of Love*. An abridged version of Bowlby's original work on separation.
2 Goffman, I. (1959), *The Presentation of Self in Everyday Life*. Probably a classic on the sociological approach to the self.
3 Kelmer-Pringle, M. (1974), *The Needs of Children*. Particularly worth reading for its sections on the cycle of deprivation, but also for its more general considerations of parents and children.
4 Kline, P. (1972), *Fact and Fantasy in Freudian Theory*. A long and highly technical book, but contains a very good summary of studies on dreaming.
5 Laing, R. D. (1959), *The Divided Self*. A very well-known book on the self and schizoid experiences, primarily from an existential point of view.
6 Rutter, M. (1972), *Maternal Deprivation Reassessed*. This is just what its title describes.
7 Spitz, R. (1965), *The First Year of Life*. An exhaustive and technical work on the early months of life, from the psychoanalytic point of view.
8 Winnicott, D. W. (1965), *The Maturational Processes and the Facilitating Environment*. A collection of technical papers, but the early ones on 'Development' are particularly relevant to this chapter.

Chapter 5

ONE TO TWO YEARS OLD

Observable Behaviour

At the beginning of his second year a child will probably be just about taking his first floundering steps: by the end of that year he will usually be moving with assurance. At the beginning there is a slightly anxious pleasure in discovering his movements: at the end of the year, and on into the third, he usually shows a sheer joy in progression, and the discoveries that come with it. A young child's life is all movement. He absorbs himself in exploration, finding new things and then manipulating them, thus discovering what can be done with them, what they will fit into, what noise they make, and so on. *Play is sensory and manipulative.* For instance, sand is ladled from one cup to another and run through the hands, water is splashed about, not only to see what happens to it, but also for its feel. Primitive tools are used to prod things, draw them closer and, of course, to make noises. He will be feeding himself with a spoon, and incidentally using this to ladle food into other places as well as his mouth, partly through clumsiness but also, it seems, to discover the relation of food to other things as well as to himself. The first primitive scribbles will be attempted, not apparently to represent things, but for the pleasure of movement and to see the marks. Although he cannot draw representational pictures, he will recognise photographs or pictures of familiar objects. Probably by the end of his second year he will be trying at least to be clean and dry during the day (for milestones, see Sheridan, 1968).

The child will be understanding words and increasing his spoken vocabulary almost daily. At the beginning of the year he may be using a few approximations. By the end of it he will probably have refined a vocabulary of many words, all clearly recognisable and articulated into simple sentences.

Trust in Self

As a child explores and goes through ecstasies of pleasure at his new-found powers of progression, investigation and manipulation, he seems to be concerned with growing a *trust in himself* and his ego-functioning (Erikson, 1963). This is never entirely smooth. He may try too much for instance, and fall over and burst into tears, not only because he has hurt himself but because confidence in himself is dashed. Tears of frustration and anger at his own inability are very common at this age.

Consider this trust from the point of view of the child for a moment. By his explorations he must be developing a representation of his self as someone who can do some things and not others in relation to reality. We can make such inferences when we observe his anticipatory activities. He may, for instance, be quite happy about clambering upstairs but, with trepidation on his face, will refuse to go down after having tumbled on one or two occasions.

Erikson has stressed the importance of developing *trust in the environment*, particularly parents, during the first year of life as a prerequisite of trust in self. Now we can consider the relation of one to the other. Where a child feels at ease and trusts his environment, he is free to explore spontaneously and develop his own skills, hence trust himself. He will also find it easy to learn from such an environment, to imitate his parents, for instance, and hence be helped to develop the skills that lie behind trust in himself.

If his parents have been prone to distress him, then *mistrust* is likely to be a predominant mood. He may be able to discover a lot about the environment but not *identify* himself with other people in a relaxed, coherent way. Identification seems to involve first the mimicry and then imitation (already mentioned) which is repeatedly played over and tested to become part of a child's self-possession. With mistrust, mimicry and ill-coordinated imitations are likely to occur but, lacking relaxation with other people, structure of self-possessed identifications will tend to be broken up and discordant. For instance, a mother may confuse him by saying, 'Get out from under my feet. Go and play in the garden where there's lots to do.' The child then goes out into the mud and gets dirty, at which his mother says, 'Look at you, those nice, clean clothes all ruined. Come out of that filthy garden.' Here the child is put into a *double-bind* (Hayley, 1968) where doing something to please brings a parent's displeasure. This pattern has frequently been stressed by investigators of mental disturbance, it epitomises how parents can confuse their children. Under these circumstances, relaxed identification is impossible and trust in self impeded.

Communication and Language
We have already noted the infant–mother mimicry of body movements in the first weeks of life, extending to the vital communication by gesture

in later months. The growth of understanding and use of *words* and the formation of these into *grammar* is much more complex and the subject of very active research at present (Lewin, 1975; Britton, 1970).

Let us first generally recognise that words are *signs*. They are sounds which stand for things and actions, and then later for abstract ideas. Signs are distinguishable from *symbols* in that they need bear no similarity to the form of the thing referred to, whereas symbols are representations having some similarity of form to the thing. The word 'rifle' is a sign, whereas a stick being played with may be a symbol for a rifle. Or the word 'fire' is a sign whereas 'bang' is nearer to a symbol.

Cursory observation of older babies makes it plain that learning to passively *understand* words as signs develops before learning actively to use them in *talking* recognisably. Late in his first year a baby will readily turn to things which have often been mentioned. This shows that the repeated concomitant use of a word in proximity to a thing has led the child to associate the sound with the thing. The sound has gained meaning; passive understanding is taking place.

Active talking is by itself not necessarily linked with understanding the meaning of the sounds; parrots can talk and children can parrot. It is generally agreed that talking, whether parroting or meaningful language, develops out of babbling. Babbling is sound-playing; it is a sort of fantasising in that it is a mental activity in which there is neither a clear representation of anything nor does it obey formal rules. However, listening to a child suggests that there is much active and intelligent trial and error of mimicry and imitation in it. More exact research bears this out (Lewin, 1975).

With this playful trial and error, the child seems to approximate closer and closer to voicing recognisable words. When parents think they recognise a word they are usually delighted, hugging and kissing their child for his brilliance. The child for his part is then usually delighted with himself too, crowing with pleasure and repeating the word to get more of his parents' pleasure. My feeling is that such parents are not absurd to be so delighted, finding words is an incredible feat of perseverance and discrimination. After this a child usually races ahead trying out and finding many new words. Early speech always involves comical mistakes or approximations, for instance: bissica for biscuit, blabbi for blanket, wowies for trousers, toon for spoon, pisgetti for spaghetti, even coddispeeper for compost heap. These approximations indicate the *creative* invention that goes into learning to talk. Invention comes first, testing their conformity to rules comes second. Perhaps adults find such delight in children's early language because it is so freshly creative with a freedom that they cannot hope to match, engrossed as they must be in the routines and rules of adult life.

By the end of the second year the toddler will probably have progressed to linking words into simple grammatical sentences. The development of grammar is another fascinating puzzle. In recent years the linguist Chomsky has initiated a revolution in our understanding of grammar by first of all distinguishing the surface structure of sentences from what he calls their deep structure. Secondly, he has pointed out how different languages throughout the world all have the same *deep structure*, although very variable *surface structures*. As an example, the sentences 'John is easy to please' and 'John is eager to please' have the same surface structure but different deep structures in that in the first sentence John is the main actor, whereas in the second someone else is (Cromer, 1975). In understanding sentences, we are somehow unconsciously able to distinguish these deep structures behind the surface ordering of the words.

At first children do not recognise these deep structures but soon set about investigating them. For instance, at first a child will imitate adults and use 'went' as the past tense of 'go'. But then, after discovering the general rule of past tenses, will use 'goed' instead. Only later will he revert to 'went'. This points to how children very actively and intelligently search for meaningful rules. They seem to do this largely independently of their parents' habits. For instance, adults will consistently say, 'I don't think it will rain today', not of course meaning that they are not thinking. Although children hear only this idiomatic form from their parents, they will use the more simple, logical structure which is 'I think it will not rain today'. Only later will they take over the adult usage.

Chomsky has suggested that because of the universal similarity of deep structures of grammar there must be an innate readiness to acquire these forms of grammar. How this might be, remains uncertain and there has been much argument about the question. Probably there are common bases to the structuring of thought generally, which rest on the innate propensities for mimicry as suggested in the last chapter. This thought structuring is then reflected in grammar.

With speech and grammar, the 'flattish' world of infantile impressions is broadened and deepened immeasurably. By using words he begins to be able to communicate precisely what his inner wishes and feelings are. To say 'drink' when he is thirsty is much more economical and peaceful than the crying and shouting he had to resort to before speech. By the time he is 3 years old he will speak coherently of his inner states. For instance, 'I feel sad, Jenny wouldn't play with me', or, 'We had a super picnic in the park'. Also, with language the child is brought into a clearer apprehension of other people's wishes and feelings. He will recognise his parents' wishes – 'Don't do that, it is very annoying', or, 'Mum feels tired now', or, 'Well done, that is a lovely sand pie'. Later still, the vast, moving and intricate web of other people's inner feelings will be opened up to him through everyday speech, novels, biographies, poetry and drama.

It is not only in the communication of feelings and wishes that language has such value. The realm of physical facts is widened immeasurably. By attaching known words to a new object, that object immediately gains meaning. For instance, walking down a strange road a mother points to one building and says, 'That is where they bake bread', and points to another, 'That is where the milk van has its garage'. With this, unknown buildings are brought into contact with familiar things and, in a flash, gain meaning for the child.

Language can, of course, in certain circumstances, be condensed into signs and symbols to such a degree that they seem to be unrelated to ordinary words. This occurs in mathematics, where symbols condense what might take pages to write in ordinary language. It is perhaps a good exercise to try and imagine what our world was like before we learnt the meaning of words. With a little imagination we can get the impression of an inner and outer world where sound is only noise, where there are no sure signs to indicate hidden connections, and which is thus full of mysteries and terrors.

Child, Parent and Socialisation

With the ability to walk and the mastery of language to express himself, a toddler must achieve a vastly enhanced experience of his separate self and his effectiveness. He seems to be working on and playing with trusting himself. These powers also give him a much wider appreciation of the world, its dangers and mysteries. It is a world of precipitous stairs, high balconies, hot irons, boiling pans, fires, curbs, grinding lorries, inexorable cars, mysterious ponds, weird neighbours with secret houses and of bosomy, booming people towering over you so that all you see clearly are their skirts, stocking tops, trousers and flies.

Thus, just as a child develops a sense of power, so paradoxically he must become even more aware, however dimly, of his helplessness. This sense of helplessness is an unavoidable consequence of growing intelligence. It cannot be said to be neurotic but rather an existential or *normal anxiety*.

What is naturally puzzling can be explained or further confused by parents. For instance:

One mother might explain to a rather worried child faced by an eager dog, 'Yes he is rather big but I think he just wants to be friendly, just stroke him gently and see'.
Whereas another mother might say about the same dog, 'Come away from that vicious creature'.

A child is not only faced with the mysteries of the physical world but also the contradictory vagaries of other's fantasies. For instance:

A child crying and bleeding from being bitten by a dog was smilingly told
by its owner, 'He was just trying to be friendly'.
Some little children playing in a small park which was an old graveyard
were terrified by an old man shouting, 'You little sinners the dead will
rise and punish you'.

If a child was unable to split off, deny or ignore a vast amount of the
fantastic verbiage of many adult communications he would probably be
much more prone to confused distress than most children apparently
are. But if crazy contradictions are insistently repeated by his parents he
cannot escape their double-binds. Here are a couple more examples:

In a restaurant a mother says, 'Don't use a spoon for the peas, behave
properly, sit up and use your fork'. The child sits up straight, picks up
his fork, and with quivering hand lets the peas fall as he tries to get
them up to his mouth. His mother then shouts, 'Oh you hopeless boy'.
The child breaks into tears which evoke the words, 'Stop that immediately, you are disgracing me and ruining everyone's dinner'.
A father, very proud of his pretty little daughter, takes her around with
him in his car when visiting for his work. He is delighted by the attention both of them receive, but becomes irritable and scornful when she
herself shows signs of being a flirtatious show-off.

It seems that not only does each child have his own idiosyncratic
forms of activity, but also each family presents for him its own mixture
of enjoyable impressions and useful information interwoven with confusing or stultifying, contradictory fantasies. Furthermore, not only do
families differ in their competences and crazy fantasies, so also do cultures.
Since each child is exposed to and has to adapt to a different environment
from other children, he must structure his mental life differently from the
child next door or in the next continent. He is being socialised in ways
particular for him (Danziger, 1970).

Vigilance, Rules, Conflict and Compliance
With mobility a child is into everything in order to discover and understand. A mother's presence is usually demanded but interference is not
(Bowlby, 1969). However, such exploration not only presents dangers
for the child (fires, cookers, electric plugs, stairs, roads, ponds, balconies),
it also threatens a mother's precious possessions and habits. The looseness
of primary maternal preoccupation has to give way to a more *vigilant
preoccupation*. Fromm (1957) has distinguished unconditional love, which
he associates with mothering, from conditional love associated with
fathering. This is, I think, an interesting but slightly Victorian view;
rather it would seem that a mother alone (quite apart from a father) is

needed to be fundamentally unconditional in her loving during much of the first year of life but more conditional in the second.

The second year of life is epitomised by commands, entreaties and threats: 'Don't pull the tablecloth', 'Come away from the fire', 'Please don't bring that mess in here', 'Where have you put that spoon?', 'Don't do that you'll hurt yourself'. This is a far cry from the Madonna and Child picture of the first year, yet it is just as central a part of mothering. It is very exhausting and essentially involves battles of wills. A toddler yearns to satisfy a multitude of striving for meaning and erotic and homeostatic enjoyments. And, when thwarted by his mother's words, gestures or stronger arms he is likely to be furious.

This fury is of a different quality from his paroxysms of distress in early months. Then, with very little sense of time and a rudimentary sense of self, frustration was likely to be felt as cataclysmic. Now, if it has been a steady and enjoyable first year, his more coherent and stable *schemata* of himself and his parents can be held in experience when feeling angry. Psychotic anxiety is thus not likely to overwhelm him but be modified into a milder trepidation.

Even so, the switching of all-or-nothing reactions is still in the forefront, so that when frustrated he is likely to feel dimly something of, 'It has gone dead on me', and fantasise his mother as an all-bad killer. Such moods may be fleeting but frequent, and probably leave their impressions on his puzzled mind.

There is no evidence that a child innately wishes to be naughty. On the contrary there is plenty of evidence from the earliest days of mimicry that a child has strong urges to comply. But at 1 or 2 years old, frustration of yearned-for activity can be felt as an absolute end, fantasised as akin to a death. And, with memories of these experiences inevitably building up in the child's mind, so then *schemata* of resented parents naturally develop. The results can be seen easily enough in the sulky frowns or bitter snarls on the faces of toddlers.

Social conflict seems to be inevitable. If a mother inflexibly and harshly repeats forbidding gestures then her child may slip into a characteristic, bitter, self-assertive resentment. Alternatively, a façade compliance may develop where vital spontaneity has died or is severely inhibited. Here, something akin to a *false self* may have developed (Winnicott, 1958). On the other hand, if a mother surrenders to a child's every whim he is likely to be left with a fantasy of himself as magically powerful or *omnipotent*. This is extremely frightening because within such a fantasy everything is in danger of crumbling before him. It is a common clinical observation that children left quite unrestricted do not become freer but lapse into anxious doubt and depression.

The solution to all these conflicting claims seems to lie in a mother exercising her dispassionate empathy. With this she recognises, with pleasure, her child's inner vitality and at the same time notices, expresses, and enforces if needs be, her own wishes and the needs of others.

Toilet Training

There is no need to say that this is a much-discussed aspect of socialisation both by parents and experts. Everyone has opinions about it, but there seems to have been very little systematic study and observation of the subject (see Newson, 1963; J. Klein, 1965).

We know that at birth the nervous system is neither structurally developed nor functionally organised to cope with the complex organisation that has come into play to achieve sphincter control. Let us look at the sequence of thought that must take place in the child for control to take place.

He must first be aware that he *has* wetted or soiled himself. He must then become aware of the sensations *just before* he wets or soils himself. He must understand that other people want him to *communicate* this inner state of affairs to them. He must also *inhibit* the relaxation of his sphincters long enough for him to be brought to a pot. Lastly he must learn to relax his sphincters when over the pot.

Clearly a child does not necessarily learn this sequence in the order presented here. Many children, for instance, quickly learn the last part – opening the sphincters over the pot – long before they master the first part of the sequence.

One suspects that there are as many methods of achieving the sequence as there are mothers in the world. And more: because there are also experts on child-rearing who are willing to pronounce upon the subject without ever having gone through the business of training. Perhaps we could distinguish two main schools of thought. First, the 'start it early and repeat it often' school who advocate potting from the earliest months to get the child used to the situation. Some mothers of this persuasion emphasise routine, and will put their children on the pot for half an hour or more after meals to establish a routine and a habit. The other philosophy could be called the 'wait till he wants to' school of thought. This emphasises that a child will learn quickly and easily when the situation of potting means something to him so that he himself wants, for his own as well as other people's sakes, to control his bladder and bowels. Those who wait for this usually have to put up with nappies for eighteen months at least. But they may then find that learning to control himself has an element of fun and pleasure for the child as well as the parent.

It is an open question as to which school of thought is best. I know of no statistics on the subject. My own recollections suggest that there is not much in it as far as the final age of being clean and dry both day and night is concerned.

Potty training is not usually an openly difficult affair whichever method is used. Yet anal and urethral fantasy is omnipresently active not only in psychotherapists' consulting rooms but in everyday life as well. For instance, pleasure in dirty jokes is fairly universal in spontaneous children who naturally get very excited about lavatorial humour. Later, when they have learnt to talk about sex, these are transformed into sexual joking, but the underlying lavatorialness seems to remain.

Less fun than joking is the continuation of anal fantasy into the habitual *character structure* of many adults. For instance, there is strong evidence that meticulous cleanliness, meanness about money and possessions, self-righteousness and preoccupation with obedience to rules do all tend to form constellations together as characteristics of some individuals (Lowe, 1972; Kline, 1972). There seems little in common to bring these together except for an underlying, unconscious concern about excretory control.

If toilet training itself is not usually a desperate struggle, why then should fantasies about it continue so troublesomely to cloud many people's adult lives? The answer to this seems to lie somewhere in the following direction. First of all, because the anal and urethral zones of the body are highly sensitive, they easily arouse erotic sensations and these in turn stimulate exaggerated fantasies. In addition, these zones mediate the expulsion of contents from inside the body. We know, too, that the body and its contents, in fantasy, are some of the self's most necessary and private possessions. And in toilet training these precious possessions have to be controlled and then surrendered to another person. This being so, toilet training would epitomise, and generate exaggerated fantasy about, the surrender of self to others. This problem of the surrender of self to others is not a trivial business for anyone, and for some is catastrophic. It seems that *conflicts, originating in many other areas easily become focused onto excretory functions* because these above others are readily represented in fantasy.

Furthermore, it is not simply the child's fantasy systems that are involved but his parents' as well. He grows up throughout childhood fighting with and submitting to his parents' fantasies. Toilet training is only one event in a long sometimes benign, often chronic, history of struggle.

Here is an illustration, evidence but not proof, of this contention.

A boy was brought up by parents belonging to a religious sect which was strict, rule-ridden and unquestioning. His mother was kind but a convinced believer and also meticulous, very busy and matter of fact, did not play games and was rather joyless, certainly not erotic. She toilet trained her boy successfully by routine from an early age. He remembers being fond of his family and passionately wishing to conform. But an underlying element of dreariness in life was eptomised for him by hours in chapel which were appallingly painful because he had to keep still all the time. However, the rebel was still alive in him. He secretly discovered how to explore erotically with pet dogs, and also how to play more open, ordinary games in fun with other children. When he went to school the relaxation of other families disturbed him and he became overtly rebellious. He seemed to express this at times by frequently peeing on the carpet outside his mother's prized and very clean kitchen at night.

As he came to adolescence the revolt became more open by refusing to accept his parents' ideas and challenging their beliefs and habits. Neither side could budge and at home he lapsed into a generalised sulking mood. Rebellious and intelligently free thinking in his general philosophy as he was, his parents' ways had nevertheless entered into him. He found himself in obsessive dilemmas about petty things that wasted hours of time, prissily meticulous about other people's faults and hairsplitting in arguments. He tended to find himself mean and over-careful about money. As an outlet he took to obsessive orgies of gambling, priding himself, however, on the meticulous, carefully worked out systems which he used before staking his money at the tables.

This illustrates not only a child's long-term struggle with parental habits but also suggests the association, which has been generally recognised for a long time by psychoanalysts, between early childhood control, rebellious aggressiveness, and *obsessional* thinking (Kline, 1972).

Shame and Scorn
A child of this age, beginning to be self-conscious, is easily upset by his failures. In the presence of others he is often obviously bashful or coy. And when he fails to do things in front of adults or older children, it is evident that he feels *shame* which he shows by hiding his face, running away or getting cross. When laughed at over his failure, *scorned* or shown *contempt* he shows every sign of being bitterly *hurt*.

It is odd that we should use the word hurt where no physical damage is caused, but when scorned we do feel almost physically hurt. I think something of the following happens in these events. We are hurt most by those we love most. In love there is perhaps always a fantasy at least of finding a near-physical unity with the loved one. When that loved person is contemptuous the sense of a loving bond, with all its tender physical feelings, is savagely cut; we are dismissed or disowned and our self-esteem broken. It is as painful, often more so, than a physical wound.

But the experience of shame can be dodged by using two mechanisms associated with the splitting I have already mentioned. These are *projection and denial*. After these are used, the end result can be that a person feeling shame can convert it to contempt.

Here are a couple of examples of projection and denial.

C

I myself feel rather ashamed of being very incompetent at foreign languages. However, I am very competent in my knowledge of the London underground. When a lost foreigner hesitatingly asks me the way, I find myself sometimes welling up with a superior, scornful feeling of 'You fool, don't you know your way around', and 'You can't even speak English properly'. I think I hide this well enough and perhaps am often over-solicitous, for I particularly dislike scorn.

Georgie Porgie pudding and pie, kissed the girls and made them cry, when the boys came out to play, Georgie Porgie ran away.

In both these instances a person feels inferior about himself. Myself at languages; Georgie Porgie was and must have felt a coward. But this shame can be denied in perceiving weakness in others for it relieves one of feeling weak or incompetent in oneself. I myself feel superior in seeing a foreigner flounder; Georgie Porgie must presumably have got a similar pleasure in making the girls cry. When an attribute *originally experienced about oneself is emphasised about someone else projection is said to occur.* Violent projective processes probably underlie all bullying, shrewishness, scorn and contempt. As will be obvious these malign activities abound throughout the world, not only individually but also seeming to be particularly rampant when shared in groups, by cultures, nations and races.

A process in the opposite direction from projection is also common; this is termed *introjection.* Here an attribute is first experienced as belonging outside oneself, but is 'swallowed' so that it becomes a possession of one's own self. Its most common occurrence is perhaps when a person first feels distressed by a loved one. Blaming a loved one is often frightening, so a person will readily leap to the idea that it was really his own fault. In a less painful way, it is probably used by children a very great deal when they themselves feel posh if their parents do or have something grand. Introjection is a very common activity; it is often less malign than projection and goes on daily when learning skills from a teacher or parent. It is a fantasy associated with imitation and hence with identification. But it should be distinguished from full identification. This involves not only imitating another person and introjectively feeling like him, but also playing over and testing out to steady mastery the actual skills involved.

Lastly, in the context of shame, scorn and contempt, the experience of *envy* should be mentioned. This occurs when an individual is *unable* to introject and then identify with something he wants to do badly, but still perceives it as the possession of another. It happens when imitation, introjection and identification fail. It can, of course, be corrosive but is also a spur to learning. It is hard to say how often it is acutely present in little children. In older ones it is very prevalent indeed, and, as the younger children are actually surrounded by people with much more than they have, it is probably very active in them too.

Primitive Guilt

Very close to shame is the experience of guilt. Both involve actual or fantasised awareness of being observed by others. They differ, however, in that shame is a reaction to failure to meet up to an *aspiration* of one's own. Guilt, on the other hand, may involve this but essentially involves the experience in fantasy or fact (conscious or unconscious) of one's *effect* of causing *distress* to another person (damage, hurt, disappointment or confusion). The essential point is that it is concerned with the individual's experience of his effect on others. Psychoanalysts have stressed for many years that *fantasies of effects* on others are often much more powerful in experience than are actual effects.

I will argue, as do many other psychoanalysts (M. Klein, 1932; Winnicott, 1965), that primitive manifestations of guilt can be detected in the behaviour of children under 2 years old. One can see gestures of fending off expected retaliation, running away, and also attempts to kiss mother better or to offer her titbits of food to placate her after a misdeed.

The credit for first investigating the natural personal development of guilt, rather than assuming it as a given of human nature, must go to Freud (1917). Since then academic psychologists have largely shied off the subject with a few but growing number of notable exceptions. Piaget (1935), for instance, has investigated the development of moral concepts in young children. Also, particularly, Kohlberg (1969) has developed and refined Piaget's experimental methods, indicating subtleties in the later development of moral conscience which Freud and other psychoanalysts have not articulated.

Psychoanalysts themselves have not been very interested in statistical, experimental studies of guilt and conscience. Rather they have been concerned with their presence, genesis and habitual structuring in individual minds. Melanie Klein, for instance, was the first to point out the omnipresence of intense, guilt-ridden, primitive fantasies in very young children which were paralleled by adult patients. The following discussion is drawn largely from her work; though in modified form, for she tended to envisage primitive guilt almost solely as a process internal to a child. This differs slightly from my presentation which envisages it as a consequence of both social and internal processes.

The toddler's primitive guilt is, as Piaget pointed out years ago, *premoral*. That is he has not developed a stable, coherent sense, or mental structure, of conscience which he identifies or possesses as his own.

It seems that in the first instance, as would be expected, commands, pleas and threats about a child's actions are experienced as coming *predominantly* from *outside* the self. This is natural, for it is from outside a child that they do in fact come. We observed the precursors of commands in the first year of life in a mother's 'Yes' and 'No' non-verbal gestures. It is in these, I think, that we must look for the origins of guilt. We have noted also how a mother's 'No' gestures and rebuffs evoke depressed distress in an infant. This depressed distress seems to have fantasies akin to a sense of *death* in them, so we would expect ideas of death to be closely associated with profound guilt and remorse. This is certainly heard in the remorseful utterances of suicidally melancholic people. It is also seen more widely in culturally shared fantasies like 'The judgement of sin is death', and 'Hell is for the wicked after death'.

As time goes by we would expect the young child to develop *expectations of punishment*, often fantastic in quality, based upon his experiences of a mother's rebuffs. This can be observed in little children cowering or hiding in expectation when no punishment has in fact been meted out. Here it is plain that, although punishments are felt as coming from outside the self, the child is beginning to develop representative *schemata* or mental structures about punishment or revenge that have a lasting quality.

This observation is confirmed when we note a slightly older child talking to himself, saying such things as 'Don't do that John it's dirty', using his mother's voice. From our point of view, the child is clearly internalising his mother. But, from the child's point of view, expected punishment still seems to him to come from the outside, not from within his own conscience.

In general, up to this age a child predominantly (but not exclusively) experiences his self consciously as a *passive recipient* of influences and effects from the outside rather than as one affecting others. This is natural enough because he is really small and powerless, very much at the mercy of huge, mysterious adults. His anxiety is largely concerned with what others will do to him rather than what he does to others. In psychoanalytic jargon it is said that his anxieties tend to be *persecutory*. That is, he feels his self as small, weak, passive and innocent in the face of powerful, unpleasant outside forces or persecutors. It is also said that, because he tends to experience himself as *passive* in the face of powerful, possibly cataclysmic, forces, he is primarily in a *schizoid position* with regard to his image of himself and the outside world. This is perhaps not a very happy term for it suggests serious pathology which is not intended. It is used to indicate a normal developmental stage and to draw attention to the nature of the anxiety involved in it. This assertion that a child settles first into a passive position may seem puzzling. For it has already also been suggested that he probably has fantasies of his omnipotent effects on others, and this seems to contradict my present assertions. But I am saying that while a child can quickly deny his omnipotence, being really small and weak he cannot deny his passivity, so he settles into that idea of himself first.

But, also as has been noted already, a toddler grows up, walks and very evidently gains confidence in his own powers and cannot help noticing his *active effect* in pleasing and distressing others. With this he seems to begin to experience *concern* about the, often fantasised, damage he has done. For instance, he kisses or hugs his mother better, or makes other reparative gestures. These are only rudimentary at this stage, but the work of internalisation is beginning to take effect so that a new form of schema is developing. Around 2 years old or so, it is possible to hear little children say, 'Mummy, John will be a good boy today'. Then later, perhaps at about 3 years old, more internalised, 'I'll try to be good today'. Because this process is primarily concerned with the *effect of self on others*, and consequently with self-accusations and remorse, it is referred to as a *depressive position*. Again it is not entirely a happy term because it is not intended to be equated with pathological depression but to a normal mental activity.

It is of note that, although G. H. Meade (1932) was no psychoanalyst, nor particularly interested in the development of guilt both he and Klein had a similar point of view about the sequence from passive 'me' to active 'I' in the development of a child's awareness of himself and his world. It seems that, rudimentary though it may be, the achievement of stable 'depressive' feelings is of the most fundamental importance. Genuine sympathetic kindliness and then the formation of a moral conscience seem to originate in them. But more than this, the very sense of self in a setting of a real external world seems, in part to be dependent upon them. This is because depressive feelings are concerned with the self's effects on the outside world. And without an awareness of the effect of self on others, one is being only half realistic. Thus *concern about effects on others is an essential component in being realistic* both morally and intellectually. However, this concern can be enormously exaggerated especially in children. We have already noted this in our earlier discussion of fantasies of omnipotence. So this concern or guilt can be very painful and frightening. All sorts of tricks or defences may be used to avoid full conscious awareness of them. Thus guilt is perennially defended against, but without its experience we cannot be fully realistic. This seems to be a problem not only for children, but probably for older people too. As any person comes to a new situation he is faced with the question of his effects on others. Painful fantasies of inordinate shame and guilt may make him avoid awareness of this. But if he does not face these experiences and *test out*, at least subconsciously, his effects on others then he cannot be realistic in the new situation. This depressive experience has to be 'reworked' at every phase of life. Without this happening, a person is weakened and probably prone to breakdown.

Defences against Primitive Guilt

It has just been restressed that little children often seem, albeit quietly, to experience guilt in fantastically exaggerated, all-or-nothing ways. For instance:

A 2-year-old boy seeing a bombed house said, 'Michael [himself] didn't do it.'

The play of disturbed children often shows obsessive preoccupation with fantastic guilt. Many less disturbed people can look back into their childhoods and remember dim, omnipresent, helpless feelings of responsibility and unworthiness, especially if their parents were unhappy in themselves. Here is a personal memory of fantastic guilt.

I remember myself, as a rather older child challenging my old grandfather, of whom I was very fond, to a running race which to my dismay he won. A few months later he died and I privately worried a great deal that the effort of the race might have killed him.

With guilt being such a painful, all-or-nothing experience it is no wonder that it is vigorously defended against in the mind. One of the most frequent mechanisms or tricks (and the most malignant socially and personally) is the use of *splitting, projection and denial*. In the instance of the bombed house just mentioned we can see denial operative. First of all Michael must have thought 'Did Michael do it?', then denial, 'Michael didn't do it'. In this case, the denial matched reality and his nurse confirmed it, but this does not always happen. Another instance shows projection operative:

A 4-year-old boy was severely spanked by his mother for some misdeed and she shouted the words 'you disgusting little brute'. He spent the rest of the morning interrupting his little brother in his play, hitting him and screaming, 'You disgusting little brute, look at all the mud on you, look at your vest, look at your filthy hands.'

Here, apparently after experiencing guilt himself, he spent the rest of the morning actively projecting it into his brother while he presumably felt clean and pure by comparison. Here, badness originally belonging to the self has been split from it and projected into his brother, so that the boy can feel his self to be pure and good.

The splitting projection and denial, the syndrome of 'It's not me, it's him', 'It's not our fault, it's theirs', is, I think, pervasive throughout the world. It is present in 'goodies' and 'baddies' games, and thus in all goody–baddy hero–villain films which appeal to millions. It can also be seen in wicked, witch–fairy godmother, beauty–beast, God–devil fairy stories. It is, more seriously I think, prevalent in the group behaviour of chronically acrimonious party politics, in racism, class wars, belligerent nationalism and religious intolerance. It is very prevalent in private but often equally painful ways in marital conflicts. At an individual and marital level it has been much studied and is well documented (Dicks, 1967). It seems a great pity that, although we are beginning to understand so much of what happens in people's minds, the leaders and participants in horror-ridden social conflicts seem often to utterly ignore what they are doing. Perhaps violent splitting and projection are essential ingredients of 'evil' activity anywhere.

FURTHER READING

1 Britton, J. (1970), *Language and Learning*. Particularly for its chapters on early language development.
2 Erikson, E. H. (1963), *Childhood and Society*. A classic study of development from the psychosocial point of view. Recommended for its discussion of trust, but also more generally for its description of development phases throughout life.
3 Freud, A. (1937), *The Ego and the Mechanisms of Defense*. A technical book, but a classic description of Defences.
4 Hayley, J. (1968), in Handel, G. (ed.), *The Psychosocial Interior of the Family*.
5 Klein, J. (1965), *Samples of English Culture*, vol. II. A summary of surveys on attitudes to child-rearing and discipline.
6 Lewin, R., ed. (1975), *Child Alive*. Appropriate to read here the chapters on language development.
7 Newson, J. and E. (1963), *Patterns of Infant Care*. A survey of different parental attitudes to child care and discipline.
8 Segal, H. (1973), *An Introduction to the Work of Melanie Klein*. Recommended for its discussion of primitive guilt and defences.
9 Winnicott, D. W. (1965), *The Maturational Processes and the Facilitating Environment*. A collection of technical papers recommended here for the papers of primitive guilt in development.
10 Wright, D. (1971), *The Psychology of Moral Behaviour*. For its wide discussion of the psychology of conscience.

Chapter 6

_____

TWO TO THREE YEARS OLD

Introduction
The period of toddlerhood is epitomised by the discovery of a rudimentary sense of self-trust in physical movement. With this established, a child moves into the pre-school years. Vitality, full-blooded feeling and fantasy are the hallmarks of this period. In discussing this time of life it would be wrong to separate out each year apart from the others. Many things that apply to a 2-year-old can equally be said of a 4-year-old, and vice versa. Developments are taking place at a rapid speed, but one child will develop in one direction but not in another until later, whereas with another child it will be the other way round. However, I shall stick to age differentiation and highlight some functions which are particularly important at each phase, while remembering that they apply to the whole pre-school period and have consequences in later life.

This chapter will be particularly concerned with make-believe or symbolic play. The next will focus upon the group play of children and also upon feelings about adults; I will then draw my considerations together.

Motor and Intellectual Development of the 2-Year-Old
With the firm knowledge that automatic movement is possible, the 2-year-old will be seeking out new and more refined movements to achieve. From toddling, the child goes on to walking steadily but, not content to rest at that, will want to run everywhere, practise climbing, jumping and skipping. Perhaps the most immediate impression one gets of a group of pre-school children is one of continuous flowing movement, eager, excited running, bouncing up and down from dawn till dusk.

This sense of physical autonomy is perhaps reflected in the child's conception of himself. As a toddler he referred to himself by his first name, which had been given to him by others. Now, less passively, he uses the word 'I'.

The young child's vitality is seen also in his talk, play and ideas. His chatter is predominantly a stream of observations, 'There's a bus', 'Ooh, a train', 'Look, a pram', 'I saw a cow today'. Later, at 3 and 4, these simple observations give way to complex stories of events, and to questions, 'Why?', 'How?' and 'What?'.

In both movement and ideas, the young child throws himself into one activity and then switches, often without warning, to something quite different. This flow of imagination, shifting from one activity to another, is exhausting to an adult as well as a delight. It is tiring not only because of the physical movement involved, but also because the adult, to keep up with the child, must allow his own imagination to range freely at the same speed as that of the child. He must give up his well-tried modes of thought and action and allow free play to his own 'childish' fantasies. To do this, and at the same time remain a realistic, responsible adult, is not easy. However, to many parents the pre-school years of their children are unforgettable. There is enough drama of joy, pain, anguish and violence from one family to fill a hundred theatres.

The 2-year-old's capacity to speak gives us the opportunity to understand his point of view with a precision that was not possible in the earlier years. We see that, while most 2-year-olds are zestfully interested in the world, it is a puzzling place which often frightens him. He still rushes back to his mother when it gets too much.

As he goes about the place he often seems to be talking all the time. His speech may be about what he feels – 'I want a biscuit', 'Don't want to go to bed', 'You are horrid'. But most often it communicates an observation: 'We did go to the swings today', 'We did see an elephant', 'There's the moon', and so on. Although stated as observations, these require an answer and a child will become very angry if there is no reply. He is not only making an observation, but he is also asking for confirmation that his conceptualisation is correct. He is trying, as we have mentioned before, to build up coherent and meaningful representations of the host of impressions that impinge upon him (Piaget, 1955). A lot of his observations sound silly, but are perfectly sensible from his rudimentary point of view. For instance, many children search behind a television set or look under a telephone to 'find the people'. Or when told, 'We are going to post a letter to Granny', he may burst into tears at the pillar-box because 'Granny locked in there'. Again, on seeing a chimney smoking, he puzzles and says, 'Bonfire on the roof', Such observations indicate the feats of learning which every child must accomplish (Fraiberg, 1959; Isaacs, 1930).

The Child Learning from Others
The child is usually quite content to have his observation simply confirmed by his adult companion. But he also relies on the adult to explain and fill out his direct perceptions. Obviously it would be a very careless person who just said 'Yes' to the observation about bonfires on the roof. A child's parents and siblings are continuously required to correct, fill in and expand the child's knowledge of the world. Thus a child when

drinking says 'milk', and his mother may reply 'Yes' and no more – in which case his concept of milk is confirmed but not expanded. On the other hand, she may say, 'Yes – do you remember the cows we saw yesterday? Well, milk comes from cows'. The child usually readily picks this up, and may speculate with quite vivid approximations or fantasies as to how milk comes from a cow. He says: 'Cut cow open and milk comes out' or 'Milk in cow's tummy'. This would be refined, perhaps, when the mother and child again see a cow, and she points to the udder and says it is where the cow makes the milk, and that it is sucked out through the teats by a machine and then put in bottles.

Naturally, the social chemistry of this information exchange varies from one family to another. Equally, my illustrations are all British and children from other cultures will often be exposed to quite different information and develop different forms of competence.

Concept Formation

I have just begun reiterating what has been described earlier, that is, that the child has to make sense of his body himself, and the external world. Fundamentally, he must feel baffled and helpless, and he is *continuously building up representations out of his spontaneous fantasy*, and then testing them to give ordered meaning to what he feels, sees and hears. The very development of language is a sign of forming *concepts*. In the formation of a concept the child's mind seems to range widely over a host of perceptions and memories and then *abstracts* certain common features which seem significant. Lastly, a distillate of these features is formed with a word attached to the common characteristic. He then uses his mental representations of the abstracted characteristic to understand new perceptions as they arise. For instance, he may begin by thinking that all four-legged animals are dogs. But soon he will notice that some heavy four-legged creatures eating grass are called cows. After this he may see a similar creature in a yard and know it also as a cow. Thus he has begun to recognise and to build up coherent and meaningful representations of the host of impressions that impinge upon him (Piaget, 1954).

Mother, Father, Others in the Family and the Outside World

The physical movement of a child at this age indicates his eagerness to get to know the world outside his family. There is much evidence of his fears if separated from those he knows very well for more than short periods (Bowlby, 1969). But this does not mean he is uninterested in and cannot learn from other people. Many people will testify that other members of the family – grandparents, aunts, uncles, siblings and nannies – can become objects of as much affection as a father or mother.

At this point it is important to stress the question of a child's *ambivalence*. We have noted already how a child switches quickly from doting affection to active dislike, from all good to all bad experiences. We have also noted how this splitting is useful in saving the immature child from confusion. But it seems that, if equable enjoyment and tolerance of other people is to develop, then a child must develop a structuring of ideas in his mind whereby he can experience good and bad feelings about one person *at the same time*. Anyone will recall how disturbing the company of other adults can be if they are all with you one moment but against you the next. I would suggest, like most other psychoanalysts, that the development of tolerance of this ambivalence is central to growth into useful and sociable maturity. I think this is a universal question tied to no one culture.

It seems that close family members, mothers in particular, play a vital part in helping or hindering this tolerance of ambivalence. If a mother is present to receive and respond to all forms of her child's mood, good and bad, then he can slowly create an image of a person, his mother, who is good, bad and in between. She is then experienced not so much as either wonderful or terrible but as lovably interesting. Forming this representation of a person as a whole, with a continuity between the multiplicity of feelings of good and bad, sadness and joy, rebuff and gladness, takes a long time of exploration and experience. In times of extreme distress it may shatter and for some children it clearly is never remotely achieved. Psychoanalysts refer to this achievement as *whole object* formation. This process is only beginning at this age; it will be years before it is well integrated.

The importance of this development argues strongly for a child having one person (most frequently his own mother) to love and hate, with continuity, at this age. If intimate loving and hating is chronically split between two or more people the child's tolerance is not so likely to develop. This argument, however, does not imply that a child ought to have only one person to love and hate. On the contrary, if there is only one person he has no one else to turn to for comfort in moments of intense hatred. This is often intolerably distressing, quite apart from the other impoverishments entailed.

The easy presence of another person, a father perhaps, allows a child to run to him crying, for instance, 'She's horrible, horrible. I'm going to smash her into little bits.' The other person can hold the child in a way a hated mother could not at that moment.

Quite clearly the role played by the other person in helping to resolve a child's ambivalence depends on the position taken. If a father, for example, replies by gesture or word, 'Yes she's horrid, I'm much nicer than she is' then the splitting is exacerbated. On the other hand, if he replies, 'You are to say no such thing about your dear mother' then the child is left all alone with his hatred. But if he says something to the effect of, 'Yes, she's horrid sometimes but lovely too' then a child is probably helped in resolving his splitting.

I have given this instance in terms of a father as the 'other person'. It could equally apply to anyone else. However, a father can be particularly well placed for this function because he above others is likely to know, love and be annoyed by his wife as deeply as the child, yet also can be dispassionate. He can share feelings with his child with both conviction and fairness.

This argument is laid out in the language of a British nuclear family. In more general terms, the necessities for maturing out of primitive ambivalence into more 'whole' experiences of people simply seem to be: at least two, mutually intimate and tolerant grown-ups. These can be found in family patterns other than the stereotyped nuclear one. I would add, however, from my own experience of people who have grown up in large, extended family networks and in other countries, that the nuclear triangle of mother–father–child within the wider network very frequently remains of vital and long-lasting importance to the growing person wherever he may have grown up.

Girls and Boys

Along with other discoveries at this time, a child is likely to notice and become interested in the different body contours and colours of people of all ages; and also in the differences between female and male. Girls will notice and question about their similarity with their mothers and differences from their fathers; boys likewise. There will be the first open glimmerings of *feelings of affinity* with those of the same sex and difference from those of the opposite sex. In a child's play one will begin to notice girls often beginning to actively model themselves on their mothers, and boys on their fathers.

At this point it is appropriate to summarise findings on the psychological differences between the sexes. There is a great deal of research material on the subject collected in recent years (Maccoby and Jacklin, 1975; Hutt, 1975). Very briefly we can say the following. Until about the seventh week of pregnancy, human foetuses are identical in form, except of course for chromosome pattern. This form is essentially *female*. At the seventh week the male hormone begins to be manufactured and its action generates the development of male characteristics. Female development is not the same active process, it simply occurs in the absence of male hormone. The development of male characteristics entails the following sex differences after birth. Boys tend to be stronger muscled, have a higher vital capacity and metabolic rate than girls. They thus tend to be more physically aggressive (in the sense simply of using their muscles thrustfully). Girls, on the other hand, have more body fat; this together with the lower metabolic rate tends to make them less muscularly aggressive. Perhaps partly because of their imbalance of X and Y chromosomes, males statistically tend to *extremes* more than females. More male foetuses abort.

There are more male stillbirths, more males born defective. In intellectual achievements there tends to be an overweighting of males at both the dull and brilliant ends of the scale (though this is undoubtedly coloured by cultural factors). In childhood, girls tend to develop intellectually earlier than boys, but this evens out in the teens. Girls tend particularly to be higher in verbal abilities, whereas boys excel more at spacial-motor abilities (this again may be culturally coloured).

Apart from these, there seems to be little evidence of differences. Ideas of superiorities and inferiorites are encrusted, fantasised, often shared between people into prejudices.

However, the fact that boys and girls physically metabolise differently must mean that they tend to *generate fantasies* rather differently in their own spontaneous ways. Those who argue, for instance, that children's play preferences, which are often markedly different between boys and girls, are solely a function of cultural indoctrination ignore this. In so doing they probably do an injustice to children's vital spontaneity. Let us now move on to a consideration of play generally.

Symbolic Play and Make-Believe
Brief reflexion about any sort of play will suggest that it rests on an active but relaxed manipulation of materials (in adults these materials may be purely mental). During play, distress must be at a minimum. The pleasures of play can be erotic but are more frequently those of meaning acquisition. From the earliest days of life, the infant plays in sensori-motor ways; so do other animals.

In the latter half of the first year a new form of playing develops out of this sensori-motor activity. This is when something is made to *stand for*, be a sign or symbol of, something else. We noted particularly how this occurred in the acquisition of speech signs. Later in the second year intentional symbolisation begins to appear in play.

It is plain that this *make-believe* play is not confined to humans. It has been noted, for instance, that monkeys make characteristic 'let's play' gestures before gambolling together. In the absence of these serious fighting can ensue. Bruner (1976) argues that some measure of discrimination of a separate-self is necessary for true make-believe, even in animals. In other words, in order to play someone else a person must be able to experience, 'I'm me and it's it and now I'll *pretend* that it's something else'. Or if two individuals play together they must both be able to agree, 'I'm me and you're you, now let's pretend we are doing something else'.

Bruner and many others before him (Millar, 1968) have stressed the importance of play as essential in acquiring serious skills. Although oddly ignored by multitudes of parents and educators in the past, this is so well recognised today that further argument by me is unnecessary. Let us return to the young child.

Towards the end of the second year the toddler will begin to state explicitly that such-and-such is something else, and then play with it *as if* it were the real thing. For instance, he will pick up a stick and gleefully say 'saw', and start a sawing movement with it. Then in the third year (when he is 2, that is), he will probably multiply his instances of make-believe. Here are just a few. A stick can be a saw, a screwdriver, fishing-rod, sword, gun, crane, hosepipe, wireless aerial, telescope, kerb to a road, aeroplane wing, or knife. A grocer's box can be a cot, a bath, a seat, car, train, aeroplane, boat, pig-sty, oven, table, cage, or house.

Make-believe takes place in two directions. First, the stick or box is made to stand for something imagined. The visually recognisable similarity between a toy and the thing for which it stands makes this possible. It is here that the child is using his capacity for abstraction. But also the child pretends that *he* is somebody other than himself. Thus when he uses a stick to saw he is perhaps 'being Dad', or at least himself as a person who can use a saw. Again, in using the box as an oven, he is being 'Mum cooking'.

In make-believe there is an 'as if' suspension of reality. This is naturally only partial. Children usually know very well that they are playing. We have already mentioned how both children and adults may on occasions doubt whether their fantasy is real or not. When this occurs, play ceases and distress takes its place.

There is something oddly paradoxical about play; it is an essential means of acquiring skills, in mastering reality, but in doing so a person stops bothering about reality to enjoy fantasy. The reality gains are a spin-off of the manufacture of fantasies.

Make-believe play is at least partly moved by fantasy, and this in turn is aroused by ever-present body feelings. One particular feeling about the body that underlies so much of a small child's life is his helplessness or incompetence. We noted this in the last chapter as a vague, not necessarily unpleasant, feeling of general or *existential anxiety*. With this, little children *play at being bigger or stronger*. Nearly always they play at being adults, big, strong, clever or precious things. Their play is of lions, horses, cooks, nurses, mummies, soldiers, cowboys, doctors, tractors, aeroplanes and cars. Sometimes they play at being little things like mice, but then they are usually clever enough to escape, or good enough to be preciously quiet. There is *wish-fulfilment* in play.

We see fantasy, probably arising from different parts of the body, in play. From the skeletal muscles there is play of diggers, cars and tractors. From the mouth there is lions, tigers and doll feeding. From the bowels and bladder there is messing and splashing, cleaning and tidying. From the penis, there is probably boys' enjoyment of sticks, guns or spears. Fantasy from the penis is seen more evidently when a boy puts a broom between his legs saying, 'Look at my willy'. And from a girl's clitoris and vagina probably come fantasies moving her to play at the insides of things, dolls, houses and flowers.

But it is not simply body functions that are played over, it is the child himself in *relation to things*. When a child plays at being a digger or at being a mother with a doll, he can forget his smallness in relation to the world and for a time he is its master or mistress.

As with the world generally, so too in relation to people. What has been passively experienced can be played actively. For instance, having been nursed and fed by his mother a child can play at actively nursing a doll. In like manner, we can infer that active games of killing have been preceded by passive experiences of things going dead for the child. Herein, perhaps, lies an argument against preventing battle games by little children, for in doing so adults deprive them of the opportunity to play over experiences of being made 'dead' or depressed.

Perhaps the morality of allowing some forms of play and not others should centre not on the content of the play but on the material of the playthings. We have, for instance, no reason to believe that dolls or little soldiers object to being knocked about. But when the plaything is a child it is another matter. When a spanked child goes and spanks a doll it is one thing. But when, as described in the last chapter, a spanked child goes off and sets about spanking another child without any 'let's play' agreement beforehand it is quite different. Different rules have to be set for monologue as opposed to social play.

Let us now turn briefly to a general consideration. Play obviously does not cease with childhood; in the adult world creative play takes place with the minimum of physical objects, for instance a chess set, a writing pad, a drawing block or a musical instrument. Playing is embedded in all satisfying work, particularly in the design stages of a task. But the childhood need for physical objects in play often goes on into adult life without recognition. A child, being small, needs only a patch of mud to play in. Adults can readily enlarge this patch of mud to vast tracts of the earth in the urge to play their games – albeit unconscious and no doubt with other rational or rationalised motives as well.

Adults and Children's Play

The arguments given above stress how children need time and space to play. The need to give physical *room to play* is now well recognised. More subtle are the limits set on play by adult attitudes. A child is prevented from playing over an activity not just by materials being unavailable but also by forbidding and rebuffing gestures spoken and unspoken. An 'Ugh' or 'Don't do that' prevents relaxed play as much as any wall. It seems only fair to a child that his adults should, except in emergencies, reflect 'Why?' before they forbid a game. Otherwise a child is surrounded by incomprehensible, fantasy-driven rules which are not rules but whims.

But children need adults in play not only as rule setters. Under about 3 years old, a child usually can only play solitarily or at most in parallel. But even at this age he does usually seek to play with an adult. Parents on the floor, and songs and stories at bedtime are usually remembered as times of bliss long afterwards. And adults who do it are remembered with deep gratitude. This is not surprising because at such times a child can feel that an otherwise huge adult is a human with experiences like himself. The wholeness of the parent is enhanced. It is a time of sharing democracy. In particular, many of the frightening fantasies and puzzles which assail him in solitude can be transformed into fun when experienced with an adult who has similar fantasies but who is humourously unafraid of them. In this, I think, lie the principals of play-therapy and most other psychotherapies for adults as well as children. It seems more economical as well as deeply satisfying if parents can pre-empt such measures by having some fun themselves.

FURTHER READING

1 Bowlby, J. (1969), *Attachment*. Highly technical discussion from the points of view of ethology and psychoanalysis. Useful for further reading into the question of children's attachment behaviour.
2 Bruner, J. (ed.), (1976), *Play, Its Role in Development and Evolution*. A series of papers by different authors on play, some are technical others more generally readable.
3 Fraiberg, S. H. (1959), *The Magic Years*. Slightly dated, but still perhaps the most readable introduction to the psychodynamics of young children.
4 Millar, S. (1968), *The Psychology of Play*. As the title suggests, a straightforward text about play in animals and humans, and theories concerning it.

Chapter 7

THREE TO FIVE YEARS OLD

Observable Behaviour of the 3-Year-Old
As a toddler, even as a baby, a child will have been interested in other children without knowing what to do with them. The toddler's play was egocentric. Around 2 years old, he will begin to seek out the company of other children, but his games will still essentially be private. This has been called 'parallel play' or 'collective monologue' (Piaget, 1951). At this stage there is usually a lot of squabbling and fighting over toys, interspersed with quiet periods while children go separately about their own business.

At about the age of 3, the first group games emerge. Here children share ideas, and help each other. It is social in the real sense with comradeship and friendliness. This depends upon a child's growing capacity to feel himself as a coherent person in a world of other people, and this in turn is dependent upon his intellectual grasp.

In this intellectual sphere, bafflement about the world is still in the forefront of his mind. But now, having organised mental structures which take in more and more experience, he is beginning to be able to pinpoint puzzles in his mind and hence *ask questions*, which often go on from morning till night.

His skills broaden and become articulated. He will be able to ride a tricycle, probably actively keep a swing going. He begins to make recognisable drawings, scrawl 'pretend' writing and even write some recognisable letters. He will get absorbed in simple constructional toys.

Play becomes less focally concerned with learning how to manipulate objects. A child now enjoys things more for their ideational content. For instance, he tries drawing for what he can reproduce rather than for the pleasure of the feel of the pencil on paper and the sense of control that he is achieving.

Conceptual development
Now, with his ability to talk, a child can make plain to us the nature of his puzzlements about the world. The questions asked by a 3-year-old

show how far he has got, and yet how uncertain are his concepts. Let me quote a few examples of 3-year-olds' questions, taking representations and concepts of *space* first.

How big is a ship? Is it as big as the moon?
Can you hold a star in your hand? It isn't as big as an electric light is it?
Could I touch the sky if I stood on the roof?
Are clouds as big as a house?

He has a similar puzzlement over time. For instance, 'We did see Father Christmas yesterday' (said in late spring). It seems that 'yesterday' is often used for any time in the past, just as 'tomorrow' is used for the future in general. If you are a parent you have to be on guard not to promise a treat too far in advance. When you say 'next week' the child may expect it the next day and be bitterly disappointed.

Number is similarly undifferentiated to begin with. The 3-year-old can usually count up to two or more correctly if the objects are placed in front of him. Later if he can, say, count up to ten in speech he may nevertheless be unable to count this number of objects placed in front of him. He will forget which ones have already been counted and end up with a wild guess. There are great variations in this ability. Some children can enumerate quite young, but many are unable to count up to more than three by the age of 5.

The statistical norms or average ages at which these intellectual skills are developed have, of course, been studied by *intelligence testing* (Butcher, 1968).

At some time in the fourth year a child usually gets the idea that written words stand for speech and hence for things, actions or ideas. A few children can read and write by this age, but most content themselves with scrawling 'pretend' writing. They usually recognise a few letters and may be writing them in an unsteady way.

The child is also becoming more articulate in his representation of his own inner feelings and those of others. A few examples will show how intellectual and emotional developments are interwoven:

I don't like you, mummy, when you are angry.
'This Little Pig Went to Market', that is a sad rhyme.
David is cross because his mum smacked him.

These are all about inner feelings, but their conceptualisation and communication involve highly articulated intellectual processes.

Here the child is becoming coherent in his *empathy*. On the one hand, this is dependent upon the child's ability to recognise that he himself is a coherent individual who has a physical place in time and space and has inner feelings as well. On the other hand, he is recognising that other people also have their places in time and space together with their feelings. Intellect has played its part in the articulation of feelings.

Optimally, intellectual and emotional development go hand in hand. However, it is plain that the two can become split. Some clever adults and children are highly articulate in physical thinking, yet remain empathetically stupid. This can be seen from the difficulties they have in getting on with other people. Likewise, others can be very articulate and mature in their feelings, yet intellectually ignorant.

Children Playing Together

Even quite young babies of less than a year show great interest in others of their age. They may even be carried away in imitation of them, for instance, when they burst into tears at another baby's distress. They are also vulnerable to other people's moods, not only their parents' but also strangers' and particularly other children's.

Toddlers are more coherently interested in fellows of their own age. They often greet each other and want to be together. There seems to be a pleasure and relief in being with others who are the same size, whose faces are on a level with theirs, whose hands are as small as theirs, and who are puzzling about the same problems as themselves. But play is in parallel. When paths cross there is usually a fight, often because two children want the same toy. Towards the age of 3, however, children begin to want to play at the same game together. We begin to hear 'Let's play at houses', 'You be ill and I'll be the doctor', 'I'll drive and you be the conductor'.

Just as solitary play is of paramount importance in intellectual development so I, like many others (for instance Isaacs, 1933), suggest that the beginning of mutual play is a keystone in social development. It seems to be vital in the growth of humane morality but is also subject to gross perversions: war, for instance, has with justice been called 'the great game'.

What mental functions are involved in this mutual play? The most obvious is language. As already mentioned, Bruner and others have highlighted the non-verbal language used by animals to communicate intention to play. The human child can, of course, do more than this and use his speech not only to indicate intention to play but also in the content of the game drama itself. Incidentally, those who have had the opportunity to work with deaf or blind children will recognise the special difficulties that they have here, although they and other children can be very ingenious in finding special ways to communicate.

But as well as using language, mutual play essentially requires a child to *empathise* with others. He must be aware of them as human beings like himself whose needs must be recognised and accommodated to. There has to be a *sacrifice of egocentricity*. A child must have developed an ability to inhibit his own immediate impulse and whim for the sake of pleasure in communal enjoyment. One can hear this taking place in children's conversations: 'Oh all right, you get the water this time, I'll get it next.'

The ability to make this sacrifice of egocentricity at 3 years old seems to be dependent upon the formation of a coherently structured, if still rudimentary, social conscience or super ego. In order to play mutually, a child must be able to *enjoy* empathy with and *concern* for others. We have already suggested that this is associated with depressive guilt. And furthermore, in inhibiting his egocentricity, he must check the expression of that rage and hatred which naturally arise when whims are frustrated. In other words, persecutory anxieties have to be minimal at the time of happy mutual play. Social play depends on the working of conscience. And by thinking in a developmental framework, it is natural to infer that a particular child's internal structuring of conscience is dependent upon the long chain of earlier experiences with his parents of pleasure, love, frustration and neglect which we have described in earlier chapters.

It should also be stressed that a parents' task does not end when a child moves off into mutual play with other children. Because children have established rudimentary consciences within themselves, they can now generate simple *rules of conduct* amongst themselves. But these only encompass short spans of time and can easily be swept away by the surge of a child's impulsive whim. An adult needs to be around to mediate sharing and re-establish fair play. Children of 3 can be very aware of and sensitive to the fairness of sharing, but they have usually not yet developed the breadth of vision to re-establish it when it has been shattered.

The importance of the growth of mutual play for later life has already been stressed, but it can usefully be reiterated. In it can be sensed the germ of fairness and justice as well as social enjoyment amongst peers. It is a great step from dependency upon the autocracy of those early collossi, one's parents. It is the breeding ground of democracy. It is of note that throughout much of history in both East and West the step to mutual play has been left to children themselves. Children seem to have tended to be left to find their own games while the adults got on with their work. Development of fair play has thus been left to young children themselves or their older siblings; a few rich families will have supplemented this by employing servants, nannies and maids to act as supervisors. Serious consideration of this vital phase is only of recent origin. The pioneer playgroup work of Froebel, Montessori and Susan Isaacs is very recent history, and the formal recognition of playgroups and nursery schools is still incomplete in many countries.

So far I have been discussing the virtues of mutual play. As it is also subject to dangerous destructiveness, it is necessary here to refer back to the previous chapter. Here we noted that one fundamental motive for playing was stress and the experience of anxiety.

Although his contention is doubted by many, it seems that Freud (1900) made a very major step in our understanding of behaviour when he observed that *dreams* could be recognised as coded, symbolic repetitions of anxious situations. It seems that when an experience has not been put to rest in waking life it is 'worked over' in sleep. If the working over is successful we wake refreshed; we even sometimes remember a dream as having been a good one which resolved something in us. If the dreaming process is unsuccessful we are disturbed, often with associated nightmares.

It was later noted, particularly by Anna Freud (1928) and Melanie Klein (1932), that children's symbolic play bore similarities to dreaming. Play often seemed to be a symbolic repetition of anxious situations. Further play seemed to have a settling effect. Children seem to need, are even compelled, to play certain games for themselves. A good game worked through leaves a child calm and satisfied, like a good night's sleep. A disrupted game leaves a child in distress. Even though we do not yet fully understand the mechanisms involved it does seem that *both dreaming and play can be means of resolving distress*. Furthermore, if a stress-provoked game remains uncompleted even further distress is created and the game tends to need to be repeated in an urgently compulsive way.

We can roughly distinguish two sources which might prevent the satisfactory completion of a game. The first lies prior to the game as it were, when the stress may be so intense for the child that his central control system breaks down. In this case his experience is in such bizarre bits that coalescence into a game is impossible. This is not uncommon; a child can often be seen to be too anxious to play. On the other hand, he may intrinsically be less shattered than this but prevented from playing by the limitation of external circumstances. These circumstances will usually involve his parents, for it is they who order his environment. They may explicitly forbid certain games, order him or carry him off to do something else, or more generally they may simply provide a climate where playing is devalued and poverty-stricken. At all events, when playing is prevented for whatever reason it seems that this frustration in itself creates further distress with its attendant hatred within the child. The need to play then becomes compulsive with an underlying mood of tense fear and vengeful rage. Persecutory feelings have swamped depressive concern. Under these circumstances a child will not care about, or feel for, other things or people. He will want to use anything at whim; other children become playthings rather than playmates. This is very common indeed, as in the description in the last chapter of a boy who cruelly smacked his little brother after being beaten by his mother. Here a game was played *without concern for the object* of the game, i.e. little brother. It is perhaps useful to term this *ruthless play* to distinguish it from genuinely *mutual play*. It is important to make this distinction for, although both forms may have similar origins in a wish for mastery, they have very different consequences.

Naturally, just as with any symbolic play, this ruthless play does not end with childhood. The fantasies of ruthless play are readily detectable in adult life even though they may be covered by polite or diplomatic smokescreens. Ruthless play seems, for instance, to be rampant in all those engaged in imperialism, be it Roman, Islamic, Japanese or British. Its most ghastly emergence was in Nazism. On a smaller scale, it can probably be detected in any activity where one or more people use others for their own ends without consent. Intimately it occurs within families, particularly in the stalemate tortures of unhappy marriages and also by parents who treat their children like dolls. The multiplicity of forms this play can take has been stressed by Berne (1964). His book *Games People Play* is light-hearted, often to the point of flippancy, but his message is a very serious one. Laing (1970) has written in a heavier but similar vein.

It must be stressed that these ruthless personal games are usually enacted without conscious awareness of their theme, especially without awareness of personal hatred and its effect on others. Yet to the observer they are repeated with such consistency that chance or accidental occurrence must be ruled out. The theme of the game is unconscious; defences must be operating. Usually an array of splitting, projecting and denial manoeuvres can be recognised (such as when politicians adeptly lay blame on others for a belligerent war or economic catastrophe). But whatever the detailed manoeuvres may be, blotting out or *forgetting* of the original stress, its anxieties and the theme of the ruthless game seem to be omnipresent. This forced forgetting is termed *repression*.

Psychoanalysts have stresed that *unconscious* play is active in *psychoneurotic* symptoms. When suffering from these, the individual is not seriously assailed by the disintegration of the ego and loss of self-feeling as in psychotic anxieties. These remain relatively intact, but he appears to be compulsively caught in highly charged ruthless games locked within his own mind. These are either grossly enacted with other people, as in the case of hysterical personalities, or the dramatic themes may emerge less flamboyantly, and probably involving other people less, in the distorted form of hysterical conversion symptoms (Cameron, 1963; Fenichel, 1946), phobias and obsessions.

The Oedipus Complex

Let us briefly recapitulate the developments in the first three years. In the area of play we have seen a child begin with simple sensori-motor manipulations, and out of this develops symbolisation and the use of words. With this comes make-believe, which at first is a monologue linked at times into dual play with an adult. But during the second year a child becomes interested in and obviously feels affinity with other little children like him. The child now plays alongside or parallel with another. Only towards the fourth year of life has a child developed enough to engage in truly social or mutual play.

At the same time we have recounted the growing articulation of a child's relationship with his parents. In earliest infancy there seems no distinction in the child's mind between what is himself and what is not. Only slowly in the first year does he sense his being a different entity from others. But even then his mother is largely conceived of as an extension of himself. Likewise, conversely, in a deeper and more long-lasting way, he still feels himself to be a possession of his mother's. Nevertheless, differentiation is taking place, all being well. Especially from her 'Yes' gestures and words of love and 'Noes' of disapproval a child slowly has to accept that she has a life independent of his own. With this comes the pain of loneliness as well as the freedom of solitude. In times spent together, however, it is usually his mother who administers his world; and even when he becomes interested in things beyond the home it is she who interprets and explains it or confuses it for him.

A father seems usually to be experienced in a similar yet rather different manner. He has a different physical feel to him. In British society, at least, it is usually he who goes out into the world and comes back. He works for money, so a child must sense his mother's dependency on him for this. He is also usually bigger and physically stronger and this is sensed quite early, in the second or third year. Maybe there is frequently a triumph for the child in his discovery of a mother's dependency on her husband, something of a 'Ha, ha, you have ruled me, now I've found someone who rules you'. A child threatening his mother with 'I'll tell my daddy of you and he'll smack you' is a common utterance. But then this is easily contradicted in a child's mind if he hears his father being ordered about by his mother so that he seems to be dependent on her.

I hope the previous chapters have given some idea of what giants, if not gods, parents are to a child. They are big and complex and mysterious because he is small and immature. I think it is important to recognise that this is a given of the human child's condition whatever our conventions of rearing are.

I have already argued that a two-parent nuclear family has natural advantages for the rearing of young children. Later I will be investigating its weaknesses. To a child, even on the small scale of a contented nuclear family, parents are still mysterious giants. Add to this the frequent contradictoriness of most parents, and the family must at best be puzzling.

It may be argued that this is an overdramatised picture. A small, chuckling child shows no obvious evidence of his being baffled by his parents as complex giants. But we cannot expect a child to say everything that flits through his mind. Furthermore, what can be more enjoyable for a small person than to live in the safety of benign giants who love him? And to a child these giants are not always benign; if you cast your minds back to your earliest memories you will probably recall something of your anxiety and sense of mystery about them.

So far this book has discussed a child's general feelings about his parents. In these his bodily experiences, particularly the fantasies arising from erotic pleasure and frustration, have been stressed. This brings us to the controversial conception of the Oedipus complex, introduced by Freud (1913). This is centrally associated with *genital* excitement and I wish now to focus upon it. The subject can be introduced by a general formulation which I think would be agreed by most present-day psycho-analysts. It differs in some respects from Freud's own, which will be briefly discussed later. I hardly need mention that, although generally agreed as important by psychoanalysts and many other therapists, the notion of the Oedipus complex is vigorously attacked by very many other psycho-logists, therapists and psychiatrists. Here I will state the formulation as I see it and must leave each reader to decide about its validity for himself.

I have already stressed the child's experience of his body and of the particular importance of highly sensitive erotic zones in arousing vivid fantasy. We have also seen how a boy and girl begin to be aware of their sex or gender by about 2 years old, and of the similarity of their parents of the same sex. In particular, a child must become aware of his or her own genitals. This is not surprising because they are used for urinating and are also highly sensitive organs densely populated with sensory nerve endings. Their musculature has to come under control for toilet training and they are thus central in the pleasures and anxieties of early social control. Being highly erotic, they are highly evocative of fantasy and a source of masturbatory comfort. Furthermore, by being so erotogenic they are readily arousable but, to a degree, never satisfied.

To complicate matters further, as already mentioned, *genital arousal is associated with dreaming.* I have also suggested how important dream-ing is in working over unresolved tensions. Certainly, individuals chronically deprived of dreaming time feel themselves going rather mad.

The association of dreaming with the genitals on its own would make a child feel them to be vastly important. Add the other functions and we have a disturbing but most precious organ even for a child. But, apart from urination it has as yet *no social use* for him. A genital is physically and socially 'small' for a child, yet personally precious. It is exciting but has nowhere to go, and it is often invested with parental fantasy and taboos. Yet, even to us adults, the genitals often seem to hold the secret of sanity and madness. 'The best anti-depressant I know is a good fuck' is a common phrase. The genitals' association with vital dreaming suggests why this experience is so common. We, of course, cannot say that children feel them to be as important as this, but it is obvious to any close observer that they are puzzled and excited by them.

How does this genital excitation affect a child's feelings about his parents? In answering this, it is first important to distinguish the child's *inner sexual fantasies* about his parents from what parents and children actually do with each other. The former, the patterns of private fantasy, is referred to as the *Oedipus complex*. The latter, the social triangle, is usually termed the Oedipal situation or *Oedipal triad*. The two are clearly related but not the same. Secondly, early chapters have stressed how all parents relate to their children differently. Thus the Oedipal situation is different for all individuals. And, as also argued throughout the book, since social experiences affect inner fantasy, every child's predominant and pressing fantasies will be different from others. Each individual has *his own privately patterned Oedipus complex* of feelings and ideas.

However, we can define certain common outlines based on the bodily structure of the two sexes. Consider first of all a little boy. As we have said, in *general non-sexual ways*, he both loves and hates his mother for all the particular experiences he has had. He also is beginning to feel himself as physically different from her (and she, of course, feels him to be likewise sexually different from her). Now, any ordinary, vigorous little child wants to love and hate with *all* the organs of his body. This includes his penis which sticks out. So he wants to love her with it, as well as with his other organs, and also, in hating her, wants to attack her with it. As it is a sticking-out thing he wants to touch her with it, stroke her, get inside her and have it cuddled. And also, in hate he wants, in *fantasy*, to beat her and get inside to attack her with it. These are fantasies not often openly heard, except by a child when very excited or by children in therapy. Open expression of sexual fantasy is much less tabooed and more readily heard in an ordinary family today than it was a few years ago. But I cannot pretend that this description proves the omnipresence of a little boy's sexual fantasy. However it is hoped that the question has been introduced in such a way as to suggest that at least such fantasies could be important.

Let us now turn to a little boy's sexual ideas about his father. He, like the mother, seems to be loved and hated for all the child's past experiences. These, too, have the urge to be expressed with all the child's body, penis included. However, he tends to see his father as being like himself; both are male but his father is a giant compared to him. His father is bigger in every way including the size of the precious penis. So we have *rivalry* by son for father. This is the celebrated Oedipal or phallic rivalry.

Lastly, a boy experiences his parents being intimate with each other, both in love and anger. In particular they usually sleep together while he is shut out and *alone*. This proclaims to the boy that his mother is not his sole possession, sexually at least his mother is more intimate with his rivalled father than with him.

Being fraught with highly charged fantasy this situation of being shut out can rearouse past non-sexual feelings of being neglected, unwanted and scorned with their attendant-distastrous moods of depression, despair or hatred. It is because of its rearousal function that psychoanalysts stress the importance of this experience of being shut out when parents are together sexually. It is often termed the *primal scene.*

This exprience cannot really be a catastrophe in itself. But it can be fantasised as disaster on the child's part; then usually quickly forgotten and accepted as natural. What is more it has its recompenses for the child when he has had time to experience relief that his parents are fond of each other.

This being so it is absurd to suggest, as some psychoanalysts have done, that the experience of parents in bed together making love is a catastrophic trauma for a child. What we can say is that a child is *very sensitive* about it and thus he should be treated with sensitivity. Most people can forgive and are glad of their parents making love together. On the other hand, parents who ignore their children's feelings and indulge themselves without thought in front of them are not forgiven. Brash, exhibitionistic sexuality disturbs a child greatly and, in my experience, is a source of hatred and vengeful resentment for years afterwards. To counter this, in every culture, however open or naked the people are, there is *decorum*: and it seems right that it should be so.

Now consider the typical little girl with her different body structure to that of a boy. She, like a boy, loves and hates her parents non-sexually for her experiences with them. She, also like a boy, wants to love and hate both her parents with her whole body including her clitoris and vagina. (As one decent word for these organs does not exist, I will use the term genital which is a dull but gentle word.) This genital does not stick out but is inside her. She must see her father as physically different from her even if she has little overt knowledge of his having a penis. And she, too, wants to love and hate him with all her body including her genital. This means that as far as sexual love is concerned, she, in fantasy, wants him inside her genital to love and hate him, either to caress or crush him in rage. But, of course, like the boy this is never consummated, except in incest, so the urge continues until she finds a sexual partner in later life.

With regard to her mother, there is the same non-sexual love and hate arising from past experiences. However, physically and sexually she feels herself to be *like* her mother, but smaller than this magic giant. What is more when she sees her mother and father intimately together her smallness is compounded by realising she loses her father to her mother. Hence arises the little girl's rivalry and envy of her mother.

Like the little boy, she seems quickly to notice that her envied mother is smaller, physically less strong than, and often financially dependent on her father. This can accentuate one of two predominant fantasies. She can easily use this perception to deride her mother, as if to say, 'You think you're big but daddy is bigger than you and he specially loves me'. On the other hand, she can side with her mother by cooling her envy with the idea, 'My poor mother and I are like each other, enslaved by this gross, giant father'. This is readily generalised to dislike of all men. Here we have the situation of so-called *penis envy*.

This envy was considered by Freud to be central to a girl's sexual development. He thought that boys' and girls' sexual fantasy was similar until about the age of 3 when the little girl realised she lacked a penis and hence envied all males because she herself was deprived of one. My formulation is rather different from this and, as mentioned early, most psychoanalysts agree that Freud's interpretation of the girl's early sexual feelings was incorrect, or at least of limited application. However, this does not mean that his concept of penis envy, or more generally of envy of masculinity, is invalid. As my formulations make plain, and much clinical evidence confirms, it is a consuming passion with some girls and women.

Lastly, the little girl has a similar sensitivity to a boy about her parents' intimacy and love making together; to the primal scene.

This ends the general formulation about the Oedipus complex. From it, I think there is no reason to assume that parental sexuality itself causes neurotic disturbances, except where the parents' behaviour has insensitively aroused the child's excitement in ways with which he cannot cope. This happens, in my experience, when the parents have been brashly exhibitionistic or have intruded upon the child's *genital privacy*, as occurs in incest. I have instead pointed to a multitude of general experiences which arouse stress and produce inadequate methods of resolving it. However, the *Oedipal situation focuses* many old problems into one simple yet highly charged 'zone' of fantasy creation. It thus becomes an axis for future development or disturbance. The genitals are the gathering ground of the child's early passionate life. Because of this, the common habit of laughing at the concept as old-fashioned seems absurd. To consider the Oedipus complex as the only experience of importance is blinkered: to ignore it is ignorant nonsense. It is perhaps like any drama on the stage. To go to a play just for the dramatic climax of the last act makes a play essentially meaningless as the build up of tension is ignored. But to miss the climax and resolution at the end makes the play equally pointless.

What is highlighted by the Oedipus complex is the apparent impossibility of resolving its conflicts or internal double-binds when seen from the *impulsive* child's point of view. For instance, a little girl wants to love her father with all her body including her genital. But, quite apart from parental incest taboos, if she does actually experience him incestuously then the privacy of her genital with its sensitive use in essential dreaming is invaded, and thus probably grossly disturbed. On the other hand, if incest does not occur, as is usually the case, then her genital yearnings remain irritably unsatisfied. It seems a dilemma; it is a conflict or internal double-bind. The same applies to a boy with regard to the satisfaction of the urges of his penis.

How can a resolution, or at least partial resolution, of these apparently impossible conflicts come about? I have already pointed out the importance for sanity of a child's genital privacy because of its close association with dreaming. This being so, we can see that the age-old incest taboo, usually upheld by parents, is not simply an outworn prudish custom. It protects a child's sanity and hence his emotional and intellectual development. But, quite apart from pressures from parents, we can also detect that the child himself, as he develops, *wants* to surmount his erotic attachments to his parents. This is similar to the way we previously noted that a child reaches a stage when he himself wants to be clean and dry. To see how he comes to want to accomplish this second major feat of self-discipline let us first look at his general social and intellectual development.

Inhibition of Eroticism

We have noted the pre-school child's all-or-nothing spontaneity, his eager, engrossed happiness. We have noted also his propensity to switch on and off quickly from one interest to another. This was termed normal splitting or proneness to dichotomise. This enabled him to be deeply absorbed and learn about minutiae very quickly. But it also meant that when persecuted he felt totally distressed. The all or nothingness of his response also created confusion for him, both intellectually and emotionally. Thus, as he grew older and learnt more, new, wider puzzles were created for him as smaller one were solved. We have also noted the healthy child's urge to solve puzzles. Piaget (1953) particularly has shown this in his observations. A child even more than an adult is always attempting to make sense of phenomena into wider meanings; to link up incomprehensible data he tries to integrate continuously, otherwise he remains puzzled and anxious. I think that Piaget is right in stressing that this urge to integrate is fundamental, though it can very easily be disturbed.

We are thus presented with a paradox. The infant's proneness to split allows him to learn certain elements quickly, but by its nature it prevents integration of wider meanings. However if, after mastery of the elements, a child *waits* or stands back for a moment he finds that his mind can wander over a variety of phenomena and memories and hence is enabled to integrate them. The child discovers that *inhibition* of impulse is *rewarded by the pleasure of greater understanding* or meaningfulness.

Thus, in a child's growth from infancy onwards, there is a normal, continuous dialectic between impulsive zest and a spur to self-inhibited appraisal. It can easily be helped or disturbed by parental pressures.

We noted that this normally occurs in toilet training, but I suggest it occurs in many other developmental activities also. It seems to be very important in one particular instance. As a child grows up during the fourth and fifth year he usually finds pleasure in spending more and more time away from his mother in the company of other children. It has been noted that when young these periods of being enjoyably away from his familiar mother are short, but that as he grows older he seems to become aware of the advantages of self-contained independence. He may be anxious about the lack of his mother, but when this is inhibited he triumphantly finds himself free to enjoy new experiences.

Here, through inhibition, we have the resolution of the conflicts or double-binds that are consequences of impulsiveness and all-or-nothing splitting. With this, too, ambivalence tends to ease so that representations of parents become more strongly whole or rounded. Inhibition is frustrating and infuriating but it brings new freedom. In particular, this propensity for inhibition plays a vital part in a child's fateful steps out from his home into the wider, strange world, and especially to school. This is very important, so let us consider it further.

Latency, the Self-containment of Oedipal Feelings and School Readiness

If you compare a group of children of, say, 3 or 4 years old with children of 6, one noticeable difference is that the younger children are full of eager bounce but are easily given to tears and need to be hugged and kissed better. In the older group, on the other hand, they still show signs of bounce as well as tears but a subtle, more erect *dignity* has appeared in their posture. Their heads are, as it were, held higher, and they survey the world from a more *detached*, but still interested, point of view. This dignity, which involves inhibition, not only manifests the child's wish to integrate wider experiences, but is also a sign of being able to be alone away from the comfort of his mother and her body. The finding of this dignity is a sign of readiness for school. It means that a child is able to stand the puzzlement and anxiety of being in a strange environment for six hours or more at a time.

Going to school not only means being separated from home, it is also a journey into *new patterns of culture*. There is the culture of the classroom, itself presided over by the teacher. The child also meets and is called upon to relate to many other children who have come from the different cultures of their own families. Many of these will be like his own, while others probably come from different social climates and countries. Detached dignity seems very important in facing this *culture shock* (Toffler, 1970) more or less alone. As a child goes through the early school years one sees this detachment gaining strength. The period between about 5 years old and puberty, when this detachment is gaining strength, is often referred to as *latency*.

Looking at this dignity rather more closely, we have already noted that the child stands more erect, surveying with detachment the world around him. This posture is very similar to the one a child will have seen his parents taking up when they were being protective, dispassionate and thoughtful. It is a mark of good parenthood. Psychoanalysts, like myself, think that the child, in being dignified like his parents (assuming they have been), has not only found the stance for himself but also unconsciously gains strength by being like them. He is *identifying* with his parents, who will by now be felt less like mysterious giants and more like ordinary fallible and interesting whole human beings.

Recapitulating, this adoption of a parental posture, using identification, allows the child to be less swayed by switching or splitting from one impulse to another. It also allows him to need less immediate comfort when distressed. It helps the child resolve, at least for the time being, his proneness to the intense loves and hates which bind him to his parents.

In particular, we noted in the previous section that the child's accumulated loves and hates about his parents tend to focus themselves into genital fantasies about them, and that these, especially, have a baffling and pressing quality. Now, with his detached dignity, helped by identification with his parents, a child has some means, albeit tenuous, of resolving these conflicts. For instance, a girl in the throes of Oedipal feelings is swept by envy of her mother and yet loves and needs her too. When immature splitting prevails, this must seem an impossible conflict to solve. But with detachment the little girl can find that it is enjoyable to feel that bitter-sweet emotion of envy and love interwoven.

The forms of partial resolution of infantile and Oedipal ties to parents are multitudinous. Each child has his own pattern of loves and hates for his parents because of his personal experience of them. But also, the patterning of identification to find his dignity out of those conflicts is personal and idiosyncratic. Each child 'chooses' different aspects of his parents to both identify with and reject. Let us take a hypothetical example. A self-assertive man may have married a woman who tended to do as she was told. They may have, say, two daughters. For reasons no one was conscious of, the father felt an affinity with one daughter, perhaps because she looked like him, and she naturally responded to his closeness to her. The other daughter missed this closeness. The mother, on the other hand, felt equally close to both girls. Now it is possible that the first girl might well 'resolve' her Oedipal feelings by tending to dismiss her mother as dim, while being eagerly devoted to and modelling herself on her father. On the other hand, the girl less favoured by her father might well side with her mother, accentuate her virtues, and reject her father as a male, chauvinistic martinet.

This is hypothetical; it simply points towards how fateful the partial resolution of infantile attachments by identification can be. The form of the resolution must depend not only on the patterning of early experiences, and on the continuing stances of parents, but also upon the pressures put on a child by the environment outside his home. For instance, a boy prone to identify with his sensitive, artistic mother is likely to be hard put to establish a happy identification with her if he goes to a pugilistic, all-boys school.

Here are two brief histories which show differing patterns of partial resolution.

The eldest of three brothers was the son of a kind but rigidly conforming mother and of a father who was a footballer. The boy himself was rather sickly as an infant, and his inexperienced mother was prone to react with horror because of her ideals of good health. Later, when his brothers were born, their mother became more confident and easygoing than she had been with him. The boy felt he was the sickly horror in the family and was frantic about it. But he found his compromise. From the age of 5 or 6 he quite consistently chose the path of being the 'oddity' in the family. Everything that shocked his mother, and she was easily shocked, he found a pleasure in doing. Later, in his midschool years he loved to investigate everything that was 'different'. By 10 or 12 he was absorbing himself in oriental mysticism. In his teens he naturally espoused any activity, philosophy or cause that was different from Western conforming standards. He was erudite upon Buddhism, Taoism, Zen, Shinto, acupuncture and macrobiotics. Athletically he could not be a beefy footballer like his father and brothers, but he found athleticism with a vengeance in karate. This example, of course, does not exemplify identification with parents but rather a consistent life-style of rejecting them.

In her first years a little girl adored and was thrilled by her father. At work he was a carpenter, at home he was artistic and imaginative. However, he was irresponsible and tended to let the house go to ruin. The little girl's mother began to grumble about her husband and a chronic rift of bitterness grew up between them. By the age of 6 or so, the little girl had become convinced, from her mother's arguments, that men in general were no good and her father in particular was a useless mess. Later, in adolescence, she entrenched her sense of contempt for him. In the early years of her adulthood she consorted only with women who likewise held men in contempt. Later, when forced to work with men, she tried very hard to hold to her old beliefs. It was only with great pain that she allowed her good feelings about them.

which she had had as a very small girl, to find a place in her conception of them, herself and the world.

These were people from two countries in Europe. But the 'working out' of childhood family ties ranges much more widely and is a fateful question especially in cultures in flux. Here is a quote from China.

Mao Tse-tung, speaking of his mother and his family, said: 'She pitied the poor and often gave them rice when they came to ask for it during famines. But she could not do so when my father was present. . . . We had many quarrels in our home over this question.

'There were two "parties" in the family. One was my father the Ruling Power. The Opposition was made up of myself, my mother, my brother and sometimes even the laborer.' (From Snow, 1968, p. 132.)

This, of course, is not the case history of a neurosis fit only for an analyst's couch, for Mao is humorously yet convincingly recounting the origins of his life's political passion and explicitly relating it back to his family as well as the social economic conditions of his time. From our point of view, it stresses that personal Oedipal feelings may be fateful for an individual, even for a whole nation, but they cannot in themselves be reasonably considered as just neurotic or sick.

FURTHER READING

1 Berne, E. (1964), *Games People Play*. Not about children's play, but a highly readable exposition of 'ruthless' play in adults.
2 Fraiberg, S. H. (1959), *The Magic Years*. It is worth referring to this book again for its discussion of Oedipal fantasy.
3 Freud, S. (1915), *Introductory Lectures on Psychoanalysis*. This classic gives Freud's original thinking about the Oedipus complex.
4 Isaacs, S. (1933), *The Social Development of Young Children*. This is a classic text about children's social development and anxieties.
5 Richmond, P. G. (1970), *An Introduction to Piaget*. Useful to refer to for a clear exposition on concept formation from Piaget's point of view.

Chapter 8

EARLY SCHOOL DAYS

Family and the Outside World

The law in Britain requires that a child goes to school at the age of five. This means that for six hours a day someone outside the family, a teacher, takes responsibility for him. Probably for the first time in his life a child is formally under the orders, in the possession as it were, of a stranger. Until now, unless he has been to nursery school, a child's awareness of the world will have largely been filtered by his parents. He will also have attuned himself to their habits and morality and, since he knows no other standard, those standards will seem the only ones possible to him. Now he is in the charge of a teacher with different habits from his parents. The other children will also have unfamiliar habits and beliefs. Lastly, the child is in a classroom to learn intellectual skills: he will not have submitted to this in a formal setting before.

Here are a few memories which distil some of the shocks of this new situation.

We were Welsh-speaking, but had to sing hymns in English. I know what they mean now, but can still remember the incomprehensible jumble of words from those school assemblies.

I remember going to the medical room with a cut knee to have what I thought was 'flints' (lint) put on it.

I jumped on a see-saw to show off to the Mother Superior, who was standing near. The other end shot up and knocked her over. I was frantic because I thought I had killed a saint.

I recall going to a strange school and standing petrified as the other children bullied a boy with no hair. I can still see his reddish wig being thrown around and the boy crying with his hands covering his face.

I can remember my first day. I was all right but another child screamed when his mother left him. He must have been uncontrollable because he was put inside the wire guard around the fire, like a cage, and he screamed all the morning. I remember thinking, 'Is this what it is going to be like?'

D

The following memory from Nigeria highlights differences from these European instances.

There were few cars in our town and everyone wandered around and played in the streets. Most people knew each other. Yorubas are rather proud of being friendly, so you might spend the whole day out even if you were very tiny. Going to school was eagerly looked forward to because it was very important to be educated. There weren't any birth certificates so you had an extrance exam. All those wanting to go to school were lined up and told to put their right hand over the tops of their heads. If you could touch the lobe of your left ear you could go to school, and jumped up and down with joy.

The shocks of going to school are of course well recognised and most teachers take a great deal of trouble with the early months. Yet however ready he may be and however kind the school, a child is often susceptible to being torn apart in efforts to conform to and placate the multiplicity of people and expectations which he encounters. Let us briefly examine the three main groups in this: the family, the teacher, and other children.

Early Home Development and School
The child carries the ways of home with him to school. These may have been happy enough in themselves but can conflict with those of the school. This is particularly so when the national culture of the school is different from the child's own. Here are two instances of shock, one involving national culture change the other not.

An Indian girl spent her early years in India. She naturally attuned herself to living in the open air and to an easy-going 'timelessness'. When she came to England, the way that school life ran seemed strange, cold and machine-like. Precision and timing seemed almost to attack her. She made many friends at school and was well liked. But her school days and classwork were strained and unhappy. She appeared a dull, slow learner.

An only child was much loved but most of his time was spent alone. He felt happy in this for, from a very early age, he populated his imagination with people and things that he loved dearly. He was reading at 3 and this increased the scope of his imaginative loves immeasurably. He normally never played with other children. By the time he went to school he was very well equipped to deal with his lessons, but the presence of other children was quite outside his experience. They shook him out of his rich, solitary inner world of imagination. Because of his cleverness, he became a teacher's pet, and hated by his school-fellows who unmercifully bullied him. He never made a friend all through his primary-school years.

Many parents fail miserably to recognise for their children the importance of differences in habit between home and school. Parents who are strangers to a school's culture, as immigrants usually are, must naturally find it difficult to help their children with the change. But many parents without such handicaps display surprising personal lethargy and ignorance. For instance:

A mother was very worried about her son's health, and insisted he wear long black stockings throughout the winter when the other boys all wore shorts. He was teased about this by the other boys, but dare not go against his mother. Later he found acceptance of a sort by becoming the clown of the class, but says he never forgave his mother.

Teachers and Formal Learning

It is perhaps useful to discriminate two functions of a teacher. One is to introduce the ways of people outside the family to a baffled and anxious child, and the second is to preside over formal learning. The first task has been given much thought by infant school teachers in recent years, so that it is now often common for a child's introduction to formal learning to be slow and playful, with much intimate conversation between teacher and child. But, just as parents often fail to recognise the anxiety a child may feel about the difference between home and school, so often do teachers fail also. Children themselves are not sufficiently developed to resolve contradictions by themselves. Both parents and teachers are called upon to help them with the transition. Teachers and other professionals are often prone to attribute all blame for distress in a child to home circumstances, as it absolves them of feelings of shame and guilt. However, a child's anxiety must be a product of what he brings from home and the new environment. The latter may be just as inadequate for his needs at home, but such personal considerations can only be peripheral for most teachers. They are faced with a class of up to forty children, and their main responsibility is to foster formal learning, so many children have to be left with their troubles.

Unlike home, where a child is usually left to choose more or less his own games, school learning is work. Whatever means are used, the fundamental aim of schooling is to become disciplined in thought. Thus a teacher must inevitably be a disciplinarian, however subtle. She must expect to raise the antipathy that any inhibitor of self-willed fantasy evokes.

Old-fashioned teachers perhaps saw themselves as the enemies of self-willed imagination, and set out to destroy it early by the imposition of iron discipline and repetitive learning. More recently, most teachers have come to see that self-willed imagination lies at the core of every person's being and, if recognised, can act as a spur towards self-discipline. The teacher thus becomes an aid to the part of the child which wishes to master a subject rather than his enemy. However, there must be a part of experience which loathes any form of constriction. To this part of a child the teacher, however kind, must be antipathetic.

Old-fashioned discipline perhaps shattered a child's natural wish to discover for himself at his own pace. Modern methods do not commit this crime, but when the teacher is unwilling to face antipathy, then a child is left with inflated and unrealistic ideas unchecked (Holt, 1964). Free methods are obviously rewarding, but they also produce strains for now a teacher must steer a difficult path between enjoying the pupil's ideas and at the same time checking wild fantasy.

The Society of Other Children

As childen fundamentally wish to be enjoyed by their teacher as much as by their parents, I think there must naturally be an underlying competitiveness in any classroom. Poor performance relative to others usually leads to despair and listlessness in a beginner. Doing better than others can be equally unpleasant since a child places himself in danger of being envied and ostracised by the less successful. 'Swot', 'bookworm', 'teacher's pet' are often designed to distress the clever child.

Around these core experiences of competition in the classroom, however, a child has the opportunity to find himself in the special society of other children. This is often a crucial turning point for his later enjoyment of other people. Previously his companionship with others will have been mainly under the eye of a mother, but in the school playground and afterwards in the streets or fields, he will be alone with others of his own age.

Other children can be frightening because they may be strange, hostile and are less controlled and responsible than adults. As already stressed, children are fundamentally anxious and in fear of shame when they go to school. They will do all sorts of things to alleviate this sense of inferiority. On the positive side, they will be spurred to learn new skills, both in class and with other children. They will also bring less-creative defensive manoeuvres such as bullying, teasing and scorn into play. For example, a child who is upset because he cannot read a passage in a book will feel better if he sees someone else in greater difficulty. His self-esteem is temporarily enhanced by the comparison. This itself does not amount to bullying. For example, the private thought or even public comment, 'I can read better than Ann', might have scorn in it, but it is not teasing or bullying. But when a child actively repeats and repeats.

'Ann can't read, Ann can't read', until a little girl is in a paroxysm of humiliation, this is teasing, a verbal bullying. It clearly uses violent projection as a defence.

Togetherness in groups lends itself to projection. Teasing and bullying is then transformed into scapegoating, when children gang up and feel mutual enhancement and obliterate their own anxieties in the discomfiture of another. Needless to say this can become institutionalised; teachers can subtly encourage it and young children can eagerly side with an adult leader against a scapegoat.

For all the dangers of being physically or mentally hurt, the company of other children usually enhances that reciprocity of feelings and ideas which is hardly possible in the company of an adult. We have already mentioned the child's pleasure in being with another fellow-sufferer. He can identify himself with his companion, and feel him sympathising back.

Apart from the dangers of violent projection, the company of other children is a rich ground for enhancing reciprocity of feeling and democracy. A child can identfy with his companions as fellow-sufferers on equal terms in the treadmill of school. Such reciprocity also gives a unique opportunity to develop further that depressive aspect of conscience which is based on sympathy for another human being. The roots of this may lie in early family experiences, but now it can be exercised in a wider society. This stresses, as Kohlberg (1969) has pointed out, that the development of conscience does not end in early childhood.

The Development of Industriousness

As important as interpersonal developments, is a child's gain in skill and knowledge in the company of other children. A moment's reflection upon boys' and girls' games, conversations and hobbies makes us realise that children probably glean as much information about the world from informal conversations with friends and family as they do in the classroom.

As he grows through the school years his skills develop, and with them his awareness of *self-efficacy*. As this becomes more solid, the need for childish make-believe gives way to sheer pleasure in *industry* (Erikson, 1963, 1968). Here is a memory which illustrates this transition:

I used to do a lot of tinkering and carpentry. When I was young I can remember pretending to be a carpenter or engineer when I was mucking about. It was fun doing it, but of course nothing ever really worked after I had finished. One day the handle of my mother's iron broke and in examining it, I realised I could shape a new one if I selected the right wood from the pile in the garage. I did this, screwed it on, and my mother could use the iron again. I didn't have to pretend any more.

The practice of explicit make-believe play perhaps falls away earlier in girls than with boys. It is my impression that it is boys in their early teens who are still absorbed in make-believe games and hobbies, such as model aircraft, cars, and so on. Girls of this age may have as many make-believe daydreams as boys, but on the whole their skills are often more oriented to reality. They certainly tend to be ahead in schoolwork. This may in part be due to the fact that a girl is of the same sex as her mother and most of her infant and junior school teachers, whom she has seen at their tasks every day. It is thus easy for the girl to imitate and identify with them, and hence to develop her skill and sense of efficacy. A boy, on the other hand, is of a different sex from his mother and probably his early teachers also. He tends to become antipathetic to identifying with them at quite an early age, yet usually has only a transient acquaintance with the tasks of men like his father. With less opportunity to learn he may be less sure of himself and hence more prone to make-believe.

The School Child and His Parents

As a child gains more confidence to be alone he usually seeks out the company of like-minded children and turns away from his parents' conversation. It is often stressed that children no longer want their parents' company during adolescence, but I am sure this progress towards separation starts much earlier. Children itch for the society of other children, which has a life of its own, with many secrets hidden from adults. Older children also like ganging up together to scorn and giggle at the silliness of their parents or adults. This doubtless uses similar projective mechanisms to the scapegoating of other children mentioned earlier. During early school years it is usually transient, so that a child can be laughing at his parents one minute and crying to them for help the next. It is probably not until adolescence that the perception of faults in adults plays a central part in development.

The child's tendency towards separateness is only partial. A general consideration of these years makes us realise that parents' behaviour is still of overwhelming importance to him. The conscious focus of a child's mind may be directed away from his family, but fundamental decisions are mediated through it: he lives where they live, is fed and clothed according to their notions, and goes where they go at week-ends and holidays. Both economically and psychologically, he is incapable of independence. Children, by and large, are quite aware of this and accept the ways of their parents without open question or rebellion. This does not mean that the child acquiesces in all his thought and feelings. These will be kept in his inner world and may even be quite unconscious. At most, negative feelings will manifest themselves in nervousness or 'difficult behaviour'. His ego-functioning has not yet developed sufficiently for him to come out in open, self-determined rebellion. This must wait until adolescence.

FURTHER READING

1 Erikson, E. H. (1963), *Childhood and Society*. Of particular interest here is the discussion of the phase of 'Industry'.
2 Green, L. (1968), *Parents and Teachers, Partners or Rivals*. Just as its title describes it is concerned with the relation between home and school.
3 Holt, J. (1964), *How Children Fail*. A personal account by a teacher of his perceptions about children struggling with intellectual tasks.

Chapter 9

ADOLESCENCE

Introduction

In its broadest sense, adolescence simply refers to the psychological changes consequent upon puberty. As this means the attainment of the capacity to produce offspring, it entails changes in expectation by and towards a young person. Sooner or later after puberty, depending on his society, a person is expected to be able to take on adult responsibility. This is recognised universally throughout the world and is often marked by ceremony. For instance, one of our earliest, known written inscriptions, by King Hattusili of the Hittites in about 1620 BC gives the following advice from a father to his son of 13. 'Keep thy father's word and stay away from wine in favour of bread and water while in youth, but when old age is with thee drink to satiety. And then thou may'st set aside thy father's word.'

In Western culture at the present time the pre-adolescent child *expects* to be cared for by and be obedient to his parents in major issues. The post-adolescent adult in this culture and legal system cannot expect as a right to be looked after by his parents. Nor does he expect to be obedient to them.

As will be evident from King Hattusili's inscription the degree of an adult's expectation of care from and obedience to parents varies very greatly indeed from culture to culture. Although the start of adolescence is fixed by our biological clocks at the beginning of puberty, it is drawn out and made flexible in its duration by both cultural pressures and individual needs. In our present society, for instance, there seems to be an expectation that adolescence ought to be completed by some time between 20 and 25 years old. However, I will argue that the changes involved in actual individuals assuming self-responsibility does not necessarily fit this expectation. It may go on for many adult years in differing guises and is perhaps never completed before death. Adolescence is a process not a state; as such I think it is better to give it verbal form and refer to *adolescing*.

Adolescence and Life Crisis
As the shift from expecting adult care to self-responsibility entails
major changes in behaviour and attitudes towards oneself and other
people, it requires far-reaching shifts in personal psychic organisation.
The end product is in doubt, but changes for the better or worse must
occur. Adolescence is a normal crisis of life. The notion of crisis is a key
concept in psychiatric thought at present and widely used (Caplan, 1964;
Mayerson, 1975). Let us briefly consider a definition of life crisis, which
will set a framework for more detailed thought about adolescence and
can also act as a model for other life crises.

*A life crisis is a personal situation which arises when well-tried struc-
tures of adaptation and defence are no longer adequate to assimilate new
demands, which may impinge either from within or from outside the
individual. Loosening up with at least partial disintegration of thought
and feeling then occurs. This is accompanied by anxiety and perplexity
and often also impulsive action. Regression, or the re-emergence of
primitive fantasy is also manifest.*

A common term for these occurrences is 'going mad'. As I suggested
earlier in the book this should be regarded as a necessary, healthy process.
*Only when a person's previous structuring of ideas has broken into a
fluid state is he then able to test out his widest array of responsiveness
to the new situation. A person can then discover new combinations of
thought and action that are more satisfactory to his impulses, his conscience and the external world.*

When an individual is faced by a new situation and is *unable* to go
into crisis, then there is no breakdown but a limitation of personality or
restriction of personal development. Where a person goes into crisis
but is *unable to re-emerge* then it can be said that he has broken down
mentally. In such a breakdown, if the person remains fixed so that internal
fantasy is confused with external reality, then he is said to be in a
psychotic state. If, on the other hand, the person fundamentally maintains the differentiation between fantasy and reality but *fixedly repeats
his old ways* of relating self to others while trying to adapt to the new
situation, he is in conflict and is said to be in a *neurotic state.*

Where a person maintains fundamental differentiation between fantasy
and external reality but achieves adaptation to the new situation through
obliteration of concern for others, then his conscience or super-ego is
defective and he is said to be *psychopathic.*

This definition may seem heavy and overdramatic as a description of
the apparently light-hearted transitions of life that many people enjoy
even through adolescence. It must be recognised that this is a condensed
analytic definition; an actual crisis may last years, being slow, quiet and
in the main very enjoyable with hardly noticeable acute distress and

however, that for a crisis to be resolved, the
here have to be passed through.
to the child. The early teens seem to be marked
ological changes of puberty but also by very notice-
elopments. How they are inter-related is not clear,
ly interwoven and must both be recognised if we are
to un... ...escing, in our culture at least. I will briefly describe
the intellectu... velopments first, then proceed to puberty.

Intellectual Development

In this description I shall lean heavily on the work of Piaget (1950); in
fact it is best for me to give a brief resumé of his theory concerning the
later years of childhood.

According to Piaget, thought develops out of memory of sensations
and body movement. Distinct phases can be defined. The first *sensori-
motor phase* (from 0–2 years) has already been described. Here the
earliest months are characterised by the rhythmic repetition of circular
reactions as the infant's innate reflexes become extended by the impact
of his immediate environment. This proceeds apace, so that by the end
of the phase invention begins to be manifest, that is, coherent mental
representations of actions are used in combination in new circumstances
to solve simple problems. Insight is occurring.

In the *pre-operational phase* (from about 2–7 years) the child is, at
the beginning, only capable of integrating ideas about simple aspects of
physical objects, but by the end has a steady recognition of whole objects
in space and time. With the mental representation of *constant objects*
the beginnings, but only the beginnings, of systematic *logical thought* are
possible. Thus towards the end of this phase a child is not only able to
recognise similar objects as belonging to the same type or class, he can
begin actively to structure his ideas in terms of simple classification.
Intrinsic to this comes the child's ability to count, to add and subtract.

During the next stage of *concrete operations* (from about 7–11 years)
a child can systematically carry out thought operations about classes of
things that can be concretely presented (he can think about things he can
see, hear and touch). Most centrally from the point of view of the development of logical thought, he can think *arithmetically* which is concerned
with counting representations of concrete objects. But he *cannot* yet
really master *algebra* which, although resting on enumeration, is concerned not with concrete objects but with *abstract possibilities*.

By about the age of 11, intelligent children at least show a change.
They begin to enjoy thinking systematically about abstract logical propositions. This is termed the stage of *formal operations*. Algebra is the
epitome of formal mental operation for it concerns *abstract logical propositions*. In it we say, for instance, let x be any possible number and y

be any other number. We then go on to make propositions or definitions about the relation between x and y and then work out the implications of these definitions according to the abstract logical system we have thus chosen. Formal operational thought is *not tied to actualities*; we define abstract rules which can be as arbitrary as we like and then work out their abstract implications.

Formalised abstract thinking is deemed by many as the highest achievement of the human mind. It is certainly not approached by any other animal. It may not be tied to the immediate actualities of apparent reality, but its systematic use allows us to create new models of reality and then test them against observation. This is science. Newton and Einstein thought abstractly in algebraic terms but created quite new ways of looking at and thinking about actual reality. Since these fitted physical reality better than anything before, they have given mankind enormous real power. Furthermore, abstract thought is not confined to formalised algebra, it is obviously used in the less-mathematical sciences. Darwin changed our view of mankind by his abstract theory of evolution. Law and order also is fundamentally maintained by people who not only have a steady sense of abstract justice but also apply its principles to actual events. The deepest religious thinking is essentially abstract. For instance, 'Blessed are the meek for they shall inherit the earth' is an abstract proposition, if not highly formalised.

Piaget maintains that formal abstract thought is not possible without long exercise in the previous stages, thus, for instance, arithmetic must precede algebra. There is much argument about this theory and it is by no means universally accepted (Boyle, 1969). His timing of the stages is particularly open to question. However, his work has had widespread repercussions on educational methods. For instance, New Mathematics, where much concrete exercise is given before introducing algebra, is closely associated with his insights. I myself am not convinced about the timing of his stages, but I am convinced of his general theme that coherent abstract thought is dependent upon prior concrete physical activity and is thus only achieved later in childhood.

Piaget suggests that the beginning of formal operational thinking marks the transition from childhood to adolescence. The adolescent has an expanded time scale and thinks directly about the future. In being able to think and manipulate ideas unrelated to the immediate world about him, he can think about abstract possibilities. He can be an *idealist*. This has a paradoxical effect on the young person's relation to the real world. He is more realistic because he can well understand the relativity of differing viewpoints. But he is less realistic because he is readily imbued with the *omnipotence* of thought.

It seems that Piaget's description of adolescent thought applies fully to only a minority of highly articulate young people. Most hardly achieve such heights. But abstract argument and idealism is a very strong feature in the full working through of adolescence in the West and thus must not be brushed aside in our considerations here. How does it link with the undeniably universal puberty?

Puberty

This, of course, refers to the maturation of primary and secondary sexual characteristics. In girls in Britain, on the average, breast buds and pubic hair appear at about 11. Maturation is not complete until about 20 and the first menstrual loss occurs on the average at about 13 years old. The age of onset varies somewhat from country to country; in the USA it occurs a few months earlier than in Britain and in the tropics onset is probably rather later. At present the age of puberty is tending to get younger in Britain; in 1890 menstruation did not begin until girls were nearly 15 years old. This is at least partly due to less malnutrition and disease, conditions which are known to delay it.

In boys, pubic hair appears on the average at about 12, and the penis and testes begin to develop at about 13 and do not reach maturity until about two years later. The voice breaks at about the same time.

These changes are accompanied in both boys and girls by a spurt in skeletal growth. In girls there is widening of the hips, lengthening of body and change in body fat. In boys there is widening of the shoulders and increase in body length. In all these, of course, there are great individual variations (Smith, 1968).

Changes in Body Image

These physical developments naturally call upon both boys and girls to change the mental image of their bodies, not only with regard to structure but also their urges and function.

Let us consider girls first. The appearance of breasts and changes in hips are likely to be the first impacts of puberty. Depending on the cultural climate in which they live, the experience of this can vary from downright fun in exhibiting their bodies to knotted up shame and ungainliness. The greater sexual openness at this time in Britain must be welcomed, if only because it allows natural enjoyment at a critical time of life.

Genitally the fundamental shift comes with menstruation. This means not only 'the curse' but its consequence, 'I can have a baby'. This and the general development of the genital mean that a girl is now prone to be swept with sexual feelings. She cannot, from her past knowledge, have immediate means to deal with them; they are new, so some form of crisis must come upon her. She usually finds herself fleetingly attracted to boys and men but, being unsure, usually resorts to dismissal of them. She is likely to have done so earlier at school, but now it is perhaps with greater insistence. With this usually come accentuated *homosexual* crushes interspersed with bursts of passion for *part aspects* of men or other boys. A boy is distantly loved 'for his red hair, or 'his gentle face' or because of 'his firm voice'. This falling in love with parts is most publicly manifest in ecstasies about pop stars. In this psychoanalysts like myself, hear the re-emergence of primitive modes of feeling and *all-or-nothing* thoughts about simple aspects, parts or even bits of people. A similar sign of opening out into benign regression in the new situation can be detected, if less obviously, in a re-emergence of fleeting sexual feelings about parents. A father is quickly passionately loved then, equally violently, irritably scorned. A mother is bossily shouted at and then childishly made up to. Masturbation is likely to take on a new interest, and I will discuss this later.

With boys, too, the most marked personal feature of puberty is a genital excitability which they do not know what to do with. A boy is also usually swept by crushes on part aspects of girls, their breasts, hair, smile or posture. Not knowing what to do with himself, he usually takes to switching to boisterous mucking about with his pals and jeering at girls. Homosexual crushes burst out about part aspects of boys or men. Sexual feelings towards parents come up and, as with girls, are usually brushed aside with embarrassment. His body will probably have grown several inches in a year and he does not know quite what to do with it. He tends to be ungainly and irritably shamefaced.

In puberty there is a fundamental difference between girls and boys. Menstruation comes regularly and inevitably from inside the body; it is not under the control of the will. The parallel development for boys, ejaculation of semen, is controlled by the will and is played with in masturbation. It is possible that the boy's apparent psychological immaturity at this age is related to this difference. Menstruation cannot be the game that masturbation is. Boys can go on playing with sexual ideas in fantasy. Girls do the same in masturbation but the clock of menstruation insists that it is real. Girls are thus perhaps rather more serious at this age than are boys.

Puberty used to be a time of intense sexual curiosity. My impression is that this is not so concentrated now. A child's curiosity is stimulated, and partly answered, nowadays in the early school years of latency by television, press and conversation. So perhaps curiosity is not so urgent when puberty arrives.

Denigration of Parents

We now come to the central psychological issue of adolescence especially as it is experienced in the West. Our discussion here focuses essentially on the internal changes in psychic structure, on the major shifts in patterns of feeling and ideas that occur in the years after puberty. It follows fairly closely the thinking of psychoanalytic writers, particularly Blos (1962) and Erikson (1963, 1968), but the attempt to integrate psychoanalytic thinking with ideas about the intellect, stemming from Piaget, is largely my own and must be recognised as speculative. There is also a great deal of literature based on social psychology (Fleming, 1967; Mead, 1950; Reich, 1971; Schofield, 1965; Willmott, 1966). These non-analytic works describe and discuss how adolescents react to and interact with the societies of adults they are about to join. This is one vital side of adolescence which must not be ignored. But I shall say little about it here for it is well covered elsewhere. Rather the focus for us will be upon the changing structure of feelings and thoughts within the individual as he adolesces. Neither the psychoanalytic nor the social approach is complete in itself; the one complements the other.

It was noted at the beginning of this chapter that the major psychological feature of adolescing was the progressive *forsaking of a child's expectation of care from and obedience towards his parents*. Implicit in the childhood attitude of expecting care is an underlying *idealisation* of images of parents. This may not be overt, parents may even allow themselves to be humble slaves to their children, but, whatever the actual social situation, it seems that little children have to cling to a dream that adults have a sort of invulnerability which will enable them to go on being looked after. A child may even be consciously disillusioned with his own parents, in which case he often creates an illusion for himself of invulnerable, good adults to look after him somewhere else. Without such an illusion children would be desolated and frightened. Such childish fantasy is enshrined in wish-fulfilling fairy stories of prince charmings and fairy godmothers. And also in myths of benign deities.

The sexual changes of puberty force upon a child the recognition that he is now reproductive; he is thus close to parenting himself. In addition, his body is reaching the same size as his parents: girls are as tall as their mothers and many boys are physically stronger than their fathers. These changes herald a mood of rather *manic grandiosity*; of 'I am as big as they are'. It is termed manic because the big ideas have unrealistic elements. The young person has not been tested as to whether he can really function sexually, socially or at work. But he can be filled with fantasies that he can and masturbation epitomises this. The manic mood is not only grandiose about the self it is also *denigratory* or *destructive* of the psychological images of his parents and other adults.

This denigration is usually quite openly directed at the parents themselves, their beliefs, way of life and their discipline. It is infuriating and often most unpleasant. It seems, however, that, unpleasant as it is, this manic denigration must occur in some form if the child is to develop out of his childhood expectations of support from, and idealisation of, parental images. Acceptance of parents' belief has at least in part to be destroyed internally in order for a young person to work out his own values.

This mood can also be justly called manic because, in his grandiosity, the young person *denies* his own fears of incompetence, helplessness, and loss of protective parents. In fact, it is well known that adolescents swing easily from arrogant grandiosity to helpless dependence. This was epitomised by one 14-year-old who screamed at her parents, 'Do something you idiots, it's your job to look after me'. It may validly be called manic and then depressive, but it is still the beginning of a process which is necessary and, if completed, is healthy.

Much of this denigration is often accompanied by *acting* deeds which assert grand independence and potency. This is evident in slamming the door and leaving home, sleeping around, impressing others by making a lot of noise, and dressing to be seen a mile away. Grandiose assertion of power is also manifest in overt violence: and in taking frightening risks like 'playing chicken' or in drug trips which terrify their more staid and conservative elders. There is a paradox in this acting, in so far as it is impulsive it shows that primitive processes have the ascendance over more reflective and mature ones. On the other hand, without some definite action being taken, real testing of new powers can never take place.

Parents in Mid-Adolescence

In the face of this denigration and insubordination, which they have no real power to prevent, the parents themselves are often thrown into bouts of despair. If parents humbly accept the adolescent's criticism then his grandiosity is confirmed and this usually makes him more frantic. For he knows dimly that his arrogance is not firmly based. He is also likely to be swept with guilt about the hurtful power of his destructiveness which seems to reign supreme if his elders submit to him. On the other hand, if a parent insists on continuing to order his son or daughter about as if they were children, then they still become madly angry. They know they are not little children and are choked by parental condescension. The home climate is felt as unrealistic. The young person is left with the alternatives of, either accepting his parents' words like a sheep and continuing in the false act of still being a child, or alienating himself as completely as possible from home.

A solution to this dilemma seems only to be found by parents going over a mini-adolescence for themselves. They perhaps achieve this by talking to their children as intelligent human beings like themselves, while at the same time going over their own beliefs and conduct to find a new firmness for themselves.

Substitute Idealisation

A void is left by the adolescent's destruction of parental images. This is usually filled, at least transitionally, by finding substitutes as models to be copied and adored. Young people not only have crushes on other boys and girls and pop stars, they also become devoted admirers of older people, particularly of the same sex – uncles, aunts, teachers and young people's leaders. It can be more or less primitive with more or less sexual involvement. When the older person holds himself with interest yet a certain detachment it can be very precious. This is because, through their example, a young person can find the way to new perspectives of action and thought outside the limits of his family. Some day perhaps these 'uncles' and 'aunts', be they blood relatives or not, will be given the respect in our society that is their due.

We are, I think, these days much more the sum of our identifications with such people than just our parents. Parents, by definition, are our most primitive objects of identification. As such they probably remain timelessly within us as active memories ready to be used or even to take over the self in times of regression. The adolescent cannot really expurge his parental representations. What he can do is destroy his own habits of internal childish expectations, overvaluation, and idealisation of them. In this 'uncles' and 'aunts' can be invaluable. If this de-idealising is achieved in the end, without the young person being alienated from his parents, then he can feel them to be nearer to friends, equal and reciprocal. His inner world is less under the sway of the adult giants of childhood and his images of his parents are further rounded, ordinary and more whole. But this takes a long time and is never, perhaps, fully completed.

Depression
A further consequence of attacks on parents' images are feelings of emptiness at lost, old dreams with nothing certain yet to replace them. This creates depressive moods which particularly show themselves in the popularity of sad music about lost love. This theme of lost love undoubtedly echoes something deeply felt by young people. It may appear to be phoney because they do not seem to have had the time to lose any longstanding real loves. But they have: that towards their parents when they were children. Frequently a young person's sadness is quite consciously about old times past for ever. For instance, I remember myself returning at the age of 15 to my old home two years after the family had left it, and finding myself uncontrollably weeping. No one had died, time only had passed.

Awareness of Death
I would suggest also that the young person's great sensitivity to *death* is also related to this sense of loss and mourning. A young person is now thinking more abstractly in terms of possibilities on a longer time base,

as Piaget points out. This entails conceiving more consciously of the end of personal time: death itself. Furthermore, feeling nearer to being an adult, a young person recognises himself as closer to those who are old and about to die., Then these thoughts seem to be reinforced by the 'internal deaths' already experienced by the young person. I suggest that these are to do with ending the age of innocent dependence on one's parents.

Reparation
Destructive attacks, even if they are only in fantasy, evoke *remorse*. Young people often feel they have *hurt* their parents badly; they do not usually really want to return them to their pristine state of idealised protectors. But they often make great efforts to heal their parents' apparent wounds. One 16-year-old said, 'I have only two responsibilities, myself and my parents. I have a long future, they very little, I must look after them.' Such a sentiment is often spoken about in one form or another. Much adolescent rage is a fury at parents who will not recognise their child's attempts to wish them well.

The Self in Adolescence
As a limbo of uncertainty prevails for a young person, investing the image of the self with great importance acts as a *transitional security*, this is often referred to as *narcissism*. Being unsure of how and what else to love in safety, the self at least can steadily be attended to. The 'face in the mirror' is a solace and helpmate. Even so, the image of self is not only pleasantly at hand for scrutiny and affection, it is also itself in a great state of flux. The adolescent is neither a child, nor the possession of his parents, nor an adult. He is a bundle of fantasies of possibilities. He is not yet someone with a set appearance or with an identity which has been tested in the society around him.

As the sense of self is so much at the centre of questions for the adolescent, it is no wonder that he makes it a focus of preoccupation. It is often in an opened-out, regressed state. Thus he is readily assailed by strange doubts about his acceptability to others, about where he belongs, the presence of his body, the existence of his mind and the reality of the external world. These are worries of a psychotic nature; they are frequently transient and often go unnoticed by outsiders. To the youth himself they may be puzzling but carry no particular implications of great dread; they are part of everyday 'philosophical' thought.

Masturbation
Close to the comfort of preoccupation with the image of the self lies autoerotic self-stimulation. This has already been noted as a source of pleasure, stability and comfort in infancy. Genital masturbation like any

autoerotism seems to arise out of frustration and is close to moods of paranoid rage. As an activity it performs several functions as well as comfort. It helps the *discovery* of certain aspects at least *of one's own body* and brings its image closer to images of other bodies (Schilder, 1935). It thus acts as a step towards heterosexuality. It is also wish-fulfilling, being a flight from the painful reality of physical frustration and loneliness.

So here we have another paradox. Masturbation helps to discriminate the body and maintains mental stability under stress. It is thus conducive to reality discrimination. But also, in wish-fulfilment, it is conducive to denial of reality.

It is also important to recognise that the patterning of an adolescent's or adult's masturbation fantasies rests on a long history of anxiety, frustration and attempts at self-gratification in childhood. In masturbation, the young person draws fantasies from many zones of his body into the focus of the genital. And as the genital organ has a particularly satisfying quality it is very possible for particularly insistent fantasies to become entrenched there (Laufer, 1976). These fantasies from other parts of the body, although fed by genital excitement, may be about biting, beating, sucking, urinating, defecating, whipping, laughing or many other activities. And masturbation, often being triggered by angry frustration, can be a private orgy of sadistic as well as otherwise perverse dreams. A person may remain solitary in such gratification or act them with a partner taking various roles. When entrenched as a life-time habit they are referred to as perversions. Adolescence is often considered to be a critical period for the entrenchment of perversion. This is because, with the newly found genital orgasm, a young person may become very satisfied with orgasm centred on perverse fantasy. Then, however miserable these make the rest of his own and other people's lives, they are very hard to shift. They have an addictive quality. This, however, does not militate against my early argument about masturbation as a transitional comfort, stabiliser and body discoverer.

Withdrawal and Creativity

Investment in the self and one's own body involves withdrawal, albeit transiently, from zestful love of external objects and people. This entails an at least temporary ascendancy of regression into primitive feelings which stems from when the self and outside world were less differentiated and when all-or-nothing splitting held sway. Because of this tendency to split (especially into idealised all-good and all-bad), and to withdraw into self-preoccupation with its psychotic-like anxieties, it is often said that adolescence is a *normal schizoid* crisis of life (Jaques, 1970). This does not imply that adolescence is an illness but rather that, because self-discrimination is so vital to its progress, the primitive schizoid forms of splitting and withdrawal are necessary to enter into for its resolution.

It also does not mean that the adolescent is perennially withdrawn. This is obviously not the case, rather, if all goes well, he moves back and forth, withdrawing to regain a sense of himself as unique and then opening out again to find new, enjoyable ways of relating to friends, the natural world and institutions.

In this movement between withdrawal and turning outward there is often a sense of gazing in two directions, half inward, half outward. It has a poetic quality to it and in it may lie the key to much creative activity, especially in the arts. Articulate adolescents are often very creative. However, they are usually not yet in the position to be uniquely devoted to one medium. They have not had, and probably should not have, the opportunity to spend long hours and months in refining *techniques* to communicate their visions in the economical forms demanded by 'high' art. Good creativity is after all 'ten per cent inspiration and ninety per cent perspiration'. If the adolescent does narrow himself down he is impoverished in his explorations and will have little richness of experience from which to draw for his ideas.

One direction of this adolescent gazing both ways is outwards with a nakedness to the sensory world. The young person quite often can experience sudden mystic feelings when things are seen very clearly in a flash of great beauty. One young person said:

The things around me were of great beauty, they had no yesterday nor tomorrow, just now, without time, there was no urgency, they were just there very open and clear. I suppose it was how a dying person sees things.

Or it might be added like, perhaps, a new born child sees them. Psychadelic lighting and sounds could be attempts to stimulate these flashes of clear, pure vision; drugs certainly are. My impression is that neither method of induction has the pure satisfaction of the mystical sense of beauty experienced in the natural course of life, for both psychadelics and drugs have a forcing quality about them.

Certainly the first profound and self-conscious aesthetic experiences occur in adolescence. This is not to say that younger children have no sense of harmony or beauty of form; many very obviously have. But the young child is not intently self-conscious and is not interested in abstract harmony. During adolescence, there seems to come the first self-conscious realisations of *possible inner-harmony* and centred awareness of *self-disharmony*. Parallel to this flows concern with the harmony of the external universe and its disharmonies. Einstein, for instance, reports that he had his first intuitive grasp of his theory of relativity at the age of 16. As well, there is deeply felt, if ill-thought-out, concern for the world of living things and its disorders, and yearning for general beauty or peace.

Here again the adolescent seems to be gazing both inwards and outwards. But he is at the same time being very *abstract*, his ideas are about generalisations and possibilities.

This adolescent, abstract consciousness of harmony seems to match Piaget's observations concerning formal, logical operational thinking. Piaget (1950) describes the criteria by which fully logical operations can be defined. I cannot enlarge upon this here, but roughly they concern the ability to think abstractly about *closed systems*, and the parts of closed systems are by definition harmonious with each other. I think we can see most easily the coincidence of aesthetic and logical harmony in the close relationship between music and mathematics. For instance, an acquaintance once pointed out that the particular pleasure of Bach's music lay in its stability. Well-defined harmonies moved out and back, reversing themselves about a central note. What is more, the left and right hands could invert themselves and return. There was reciprocity of theme which gave the whole a clear, coherent, yet beautiful form. All these criteria could also almost be definitions given by Piaget for some of the characteristics of logical operational thought. My acquaintance contrasted Bach with Delius whose music was beautiful but disturbing because it was not stable; its themes were not reversible about a centre but wander off and get lost. It is, perhaps, in regions of abstract form like these that the schizoid experiences described by psychoanalysts come together with the intellectual operations described by Piaget.

Looking back over the last few pages it may be noticed that two sorts of mental process have been laid alongside each other. Both are seen in healthy adolescent thought. The first process is that of nakedly being open to immediate experiences which suddenly strike. Either from inside or outside, the young person is smitten by realisations. In these there is no particular experience of self (that comes after such experiences); they are just experienced as very beautiful or very frightening, as perhaps a baby feels things. This is the line that mystics are interested in.

The second, very active process is that of *drawing together* experiences and trying to create coherent meanings. There is comparing, contrasting, ordering, thinking abstractly in systems and harmonies. This is the line that Piaget and logicians are interested in.

Now let us consider for a moment creative works that have beauty in them. I am not referring only to works of pure art, but also to those deep and penetrating perceptions in ordinary conversations that have a moving of unforgettable quality about them. These have much more relevance to the helping professions than does a rare work of pure art. In both sorts of art there is, I think, a movement from immediate naked experience to the abstract and back, so that the two enrich each other. For instance, several centuries ago John Donne was struck by an immediate experience. He heard a church bell toll. This reminded him of many ideas culminating in

No man is an Iland, intire of itself; every man is a peece of the Continent, a part of the maine; if a Clod bee washed away by the Sea, Europe is the lesse, as well as if a Promontorie were, as well as if a Mannor of thy friends or of thine owne were; any mans death dimishes me, because I am involved in Mankinde; And therefore never send to know for whom the bell tolls. . . . (*Devotion*, XVII)

These are abstract thoughts which have a logical sequence to them. He then shocks us into an immediate experience, smites us as it were, with the words 'It tolls for thee'. It is a line which is hard to forget. It inter-penetrates between immediate experience and abstract thought which generalises, so that each time we hear a church bell ring we are likely to be stirred into thought, the wiser for Donne's reminder.

This may seem a long way from our not-so-poetic experiences in every-day life, but I am not so sure. Any creative discussion seems to involve the participants in opening themselves to a certain nakedness of feeling with each other. This nakedness in itself may be fun or shocking, but it usually has no more lasting quality by itself than the colours of a firework. For unforgettable, moving conversation there has to be an interpenetration of abstract ideas which arise out of the naked experience. This aids the detachment of thought into general possibilities. Primitive openness is involved; at this level of experience the self is of little interest. Thence egocentrism and self-conceit are broken. Self-gratifying prejudices are transcended and new insight is gained. One is opened and extended. Dif-ferent points of view can be explored. Such moods are probably vital in any serious personal change of direction or social planning. These are not easy to attain because they evidently require *both* an ability to be open to experiences and also an ability to be coherently abstract or logical.

This movement from immediate experience to abstract thought is often vividly displayed by adolescents. It is, I think, one reason why older, more stale, mortals can find them so moving and refreshing. It also serves as a warning not to deride these adolescent urges in ourselves, for in them perhaps lie the seeds of our own useful creativity.

Conscience

We are now in a position to draw some of the strands of this chapter together. I suggested that the changes of puberty provoked a somewhat grandiose tendency which involved denigration of parental images. With this comes depression and also the throwing into doubt of precepts and beliefs received from parents. Important aspects of the person's super-ego or conscience are thus thrown into disarray. A young person is likely, then, to feel depressed and agitated at the loss of this old inner stability and finds some solace in masturbation, self-love and withdrawal. This makes him acutely aware of himself, but his ability to think abstractly is also active so that he is prone to feel deeply about the world at large as well and his *effectiveness* in it. There is thus an acute sense of self interpenetrating with immediate awareness of the outside world. These are drawn together with wide, sweeping abstract ideas, some of which are infused with remorse and personal responsibility for parents as sufferers. Such perplexing experiences are likely to provoke a young person to search for, argue about and try to forge what he himself believes to be moral and just. In such process as this we see the articulation and self-conscious strengthening of his *own personal conscience*.

It has already been stressed (particularly in Chapter 5, in the section on primitive guilt) that the roots of conscience probably lie in depressive feelings of concern about the childhood self's effect on others. If this sense of effect on others is depleted, then one dimension of *being realistic*, both morally and intellectually, is impaired. Only by facing experiences of guilt, without the depleting trickery of defences, can a person be in a position to *test out his effects on others*. Thus the capacity to be realistic, both socially and intellectually, seems to depend on the operation of conscience. Conscience is not an isolated moral issue; real working effectiveness depends upon its formation.

Summarising, we can say that the more mature young person is not so much under the sway of his imagined omnipotences nor of his fears of adult giants as is the child. Rather he experiences himself as having some effectiveness in a world of ordinary, interesting, 'whole' people. Likewise his internal voice of conscience is ordinary, measuring him as an ordinary person affecting and being affected by other ordinary, fallible human beings.

The ideals of conscience may be shared by others but need not be blindly received from them. Its final form may have a fundamental closeness to the beliefs of his parents, but if it has been hammered out by the young person himself, it becomes his own and the source of his *integrity of character*. Kohlberg (1969) points out that individuals with such highly developed consciences are statistically in the minority. His is an American study but I suspect the results would be similar in other Western countries. In which case, it would highlight a gloomy fact that the number of people who have successfully worked out that fundamental issue of adolescence, finding their own conscience, are few.

We have now passed through the acute internal questions of adolescence, the next chapter concerns itself with turning to the external world and testing the self in work contributions and sexual love.

FURTHER READING

1 Blos, P. (1962), *On Adolescence*. A highly technical psychoanalytic text. It is nevertheless a readable standard text on the subject.
2 Caplan, G. (ed.), (1969), *Adolescence*. A series of papers by specialists; nevertheless many of them are very readable.
3 Erikson, E. H. (1963), *Childhood and Society*. Again is valuable to refer to about this stage. Erikson is at his most authoritative when discussing adolescence.
4 Fleming, C. M. C. (1967), *Adolescence, Its Social Psychology*. A good general book with a social rather than psychodynamic viewpoint.
5 Laufer, M. C. (1974), *Adolescent Disturbance and Breakdown*. A brief and simple, but searching description.
6 Smith, A. (1968), *The Body*. A very interesting section on the physiology of puberty.

Chapter 10

WORK, IDENTITY AND LOVE

Testing the Self by Making Contributions to Others
Let us now turn to the young person's testing out of himself and his effectiveness in the adult world in work and love. Naturally my sequence of adolescent internal crisis, followed by going out to work, and lastly falling in love, does not take place in this neat order in actual fact. All three are concurrent and interweave. Even so, the order has some meaning for I am arguing that the breakup of childhood patterns of obedience, the acute adolescent crisis, must fundamentally precede the finding of a solid work identity if the latter is to be felt as freely chosen and deeply satisfying. Likewise, I will argue that a person in our culture must have found an assurance about himself, to be alone and self-sufficient (through work particularly) if he is really to esteem himself as worthy of the lasting commitment of another's love in marriage.

The main stream of school makes demands which have much in common for all pupils. But when young people leave it, and if employment is available, each individual finds a place and kind of work which demands its own, specific form of skill and presents its own satisfactions and burdens. Young people find themselves in a less-homogenous setting than school presented. It would be inappropriate to examine any of these specific work situations in detail here as there is ample literature on the subject (Carter, 1966; Friedmann, 1961; Herzberg, 1966). I will confine myself to some general considerations as they affect any individual.

Testing of ourselves in the adult world takes place largely through the *effective contributions* we make to others. A young person is faced with a variety of situations: his friendships, hobbies, sport, home, loves and work. He has to assess intuitively his contributions to and satisfactions from all these in shaping the style of his life. This is done only half-consciously, probably in a blundering fashion, and is naturally often seriously avoided. But facing an assessment of our contribution is centrally important; it takes *courage*. If this fails a person is left flitting in self-deceptions, with a very shaky sense of self-esteem and integrity. These contributions involve effects on others, so the scrutiny of conscience plays a central part in this process of testing.

Of central importance in this array of situations is work itself because it provides *money* earned by oneself. And self-earned money gives *freedom to choose* one's satisfactions. But work also entails loss of freedom, of time if nothing else; to gain some freedoms, *sacrifice* of others is inevitable. Making *compromises* is essential to working out any adult style of life. Here are a few examples of older people reflecting about this in conversation.

I am a cowman of course, and it's good enough work. But politics is what stirs me. I wouldn't like it as a job, but it and the job go well enough together.

In doing social work, I at last found I was happy. It was me. I felt pleased with myself for what I was doing and people liked me. I couldn't imagine doing anything else. I relaxed, I suppose, in the evenings, but the middle of me was being a social worker.

In those days football and motors were my life. I wanted to become a professional, but my dad said I must really help in the shop. Being in a village with no one else to do it I could see his point, so I said, right I'll do it, but Saturdays must be mine for football, and it was agreed. Later, I ran a taxi from the shop and everyone hereabouts came to me if their cars wouldn't go.

As well as time – sacrifice – work entails varying degrees of skill and differing forms of mastery of anxiety and use of defences. For instance, a dustman has to master his disgust, a spiderman vertigo, and a teacher has to master class discipline. A lorry driver must keep anxiety within bounds but maintain enough to be vigilant. And amongst many other controls, a nurse must restrain her fear of causing death while still having it available in her caring; needs to be friendly but to check her sexiness; must be immaculately clean but not give way to disgust or nausea.

Repetition, Creativity and Responsibility
When a person settles into any job he will find varying degrees of *repetition*, together with opportunity for *creativity and responsibility*. Let us consider some of the personal strains and satisfactions involved in these.

All jobs entail physical or mental repetition, some more than others. The epitome of such repetition is in conveyor-belt assembly. It is not the sole prerogative of manual workers. Perhaps the most repetitive are copy-typing, costing or filing in offices. Industry and commerce have an omnivorous need for the mechanical capacity of the human body allied to the minimum of creative intellect.

The essence of repetitive work lies in speed of movements carried out time and again without variation. From the personal point of view, *choice of action* is excluded once the skill has been mastered. This seems to constitute the drudgery of repetitive work more than gross physical toil. Just as a child's does, the adult mind seems to need exploration and variety for its satisfaction. When a task cannot be invested with imagination, intolerable boredom is likely to set in.

The means by which those involved in repetitive work find variety often have to be ingenious. Some people slightly alter their mode of carrying out a task from time to time. Music is another way. In listening, we can play in imagination while the body carries on with something else. Daydreaming is a common outlet, so is talking, but this is only possible when the noise level is low. Using such means, many people find it easy to submit themselves to being mechanical for long periods. Perhaps the fact that anxiety is reduced to a minimum in repetition helps here. Incidently, Arendt (1969) has made a fundamental distinction between *labour*, which is essentially repetitive yet tied to the essential cycles of life, and *work* which is not. She suggests that when repetition is in the service of an essential cycle, as in agriculture, it is not necessarily intolerable but becomes so if alienated from it. Work, on the other hand, is enjoyable only with skill, choice and creativity.

Much work fortunately requires a great degree of choice. Thus a fitter has more choice as to how to go about a task than a conveyor-belt operator. The greater the freedom of invention, the more *skilled* does the individual have to be. This entails self-disciplined sacrifice of idiosyncratic whims. For, like a mother with a newborn child, the worker has to submit himself to the limits of his tool and material. But after perhaps years of self-discipline, he, his body and his materials have formed a sort of unity. His skill will then be a pleasure to perform and a beauty to watch, and his products of high quality. It is of interest that skill in the West tends to be placed on a lower plane than verbal intellect. In the East it has tended not to be so; here the highest levels of enlightenment have often been regarded as only attainable through physical skill.

Art, like skill, starts with a person becoming 'at one' with his object and materials. To be good he must lose himself in them. This recalls the 'immediate naked experience' referred to in the last chapter. And then, as also mentioned there, the creative artist tries to allow a personal abstract vision to arise which he reproduces. It is usually only after years of devoted practice, when he is master of himself with his materials, that this is possible.

Skill and art are, of course, omnipresent in anyone's everyday life. It is often tainted, however, because most of us cannot be bothered or have not the time to devote to gaining mastery, so we have to make do with unsatisfactory, botched-up jobs. We are amateurs at most things.

Good artists have, I think, a deep conscience which works in a way that is baffling to many people. They feel a fundamental responsibility to their art, to purify their abstract vision and its communication to others. They are not so deeply concerned about their everyday effect on other people and can be indolent and thoughtless about it, hence, perhaps, their reputation for irresponsibility.

For most people, however, responsibility means concern for others, directly or indirectly. Let us examine this, for it is this responsibility that is, I think, a keynote of *adult maturity*.

It will be remembered that both repetition and creativity were exercised in school, so they will not be new to the working adult. But full *responsibility* for a task upon which other people depend will be relatively new.

Responsibility for a task means being entrusted with its successful completion. You will remember how the infant first needed to trust his environment and then began to trust himself. With this he began to be self-responsible for his own functioning. By adulthood this has come full circle. Other people expect to put their trust in him. They become infants, as it were, in his hands during the period of the task. Thus passengers need to trust their driver, housewives their plumber, or patients their nurse.

The individual's sense of responsibility involves knowledge of the task to be carried out. It also requires other functions. His *conscience* must be operating so that he recognises the existence of others and feels *concern* about his effect on their well-being. This operates to inhibit impulsiveness or withdrawal from the reality of the task. It requires *continuity*, sticking at the task no matter what personal impulses arise. Lastly, it involves *anticipation* of possible trouble and disasters. The responsible person must be able to tolerate anxiety about possible *faults*, both in himself and in the situation in hand. Only then can he realistically watch over it. The exercise of responsibility has great satisfactions. The individual is master of the situation and is also being *parental*. But it also involves burdens of personal anxiety and guilt. To be responsible, a person must use his feelings without being overwhelmed by or being carried away in egocentric fantasy.

Each task provokes its own particular anxieties, so that some people can bear its responsibility while others could not. For instance, an individual may find that anxiety about heights is too much to contain, so he would not make a good airline pilot. On the other hand, his anxiety about vomiting, death and damaging others may easily be under control, so that being a doctor would be quite tolerable.

Many tasks involve no direct responsibility for other people's well-being. But all jobs involve it at least indirectly. Thus a man making spare parts for washing-machines is not directly responsible for other people's lives. But if he fails in his job, a housewife may be affected months later and miles away.

This description of responsibility will probably make it sound pedantic and dull. I make no apology for this. The essence of responsibility does carry a necessary solemnity and sameness which is dull. It entails conserving and is thus, as it were, conservative. And in many ways it is antithetical to romantic exploration and personal creativity. It is this, I think, which makes it loathsome to many people, young and old. They seem to associate responsibility with dullness and dullness with dead depression. They are frightened of guilt and the depression that goes with it, so hate responsibility.

In addition to being dull, a person apparently weighed by responsibility can also, often quite unconsciously, gratify his yearning for omnipotence by playing covert ruthless games. For responsibility does carry with it power over other people's lives. National leaders, particularly, are notoriously prone to become corrupted into playing ruthless power games even though they frown with the burden of their immense responsibilities. So are doctors, teachers, parents, businessmen, directors of social services and psychoanalysts.

But some people can carry their responsibility with a quiet naturalness. It is not flashy but it can be deeply enjoyable. Its steady working, with self-scrutiny to watch out for insidious ruthless games, is essential to the good working of our, or any, society. It is a 'must' in parenthood unless we are unconcerned about shattering the growth of those we have brought into the world. It ought to be, I think, a 'must' in politics too. Self-scrutinising responsibility is the keystone of helping professions; here it needs cherishing because it can easily be swamped by histrionic or paranoid games play. Perhaps the helping professions also can give a lead to our society in responsibly cultivating a climate of understanding.

However, if adolescing, with its regression, romance and madness, is not kept alive throughout our lives then we neither have the strength to change ourselves, nor can we provide the environment for others to change. We become either very dull, shrunken people unable to face crisis, or arthritic martinets, self-satisfied with power and unable to be either humble or flexible.

Identity

We have just been considering the young person facing the various situations of work, friends, family and leisure. Here each specific activity can be considered as a role. At any time a person has a multiplicity of these. When, and if, he has found a *personal patterning of roles which together give him inner satisfactions, he then usually experiences a sense of wholeness and well-being.* This integration is often referred to as *adult identity.*

It is essentially idiosyncratic and private to each individual (Erikson, 1963, 1968; Lynd, 1958).

I have been stressing that the honest scrutiny of our *conscience* is essential in finding this *integrity*. For it is by self-scrutiny that we assess and balance the responsibility for enjoyment of our own life with that towards others. As has been pointed out in earlier chapters, this conscience seems to be born in our earliest experiences and is readily shattered, distorted and impoverished by them. It is for this reason, perhaps beyond all others, that psychoanalytic therapists are often so concerned about the early years of life.

Residues of Childhood

Even though a person assumes the responsibilities of being an adult, and his childhood-dependent attitudes slip into the background, this does not mean that they have died within him. The childish parts of himself may remain active, often unconsciously. Introspection will probably make it plain to the reader that there are parts of himself which continue, either in thought or behaviour, from his own childhood. Here are a couple more illustrations.

A young boy was brought up in the country. His father ran a progressive boarding-school which was regarded with some suspicion by the local people. The boy's mother cared little about this, and ran her family with a back-to-nature philosophy. Her pigs, goats, hand-loom weaving and home-made pots were unusual and were laughed about in the neighbourhood. The young boy grew up isolated from the local children, though he went to school with them. He was baffled by them and envied their conventional toys and games, so that he rarely felt at ease to join them.

When he grew up he became a schoolmaster like his parents. His resemblance to them seemed to end there, for he went to work in a city and was more conventional in his ways. He was respected and very well liked, so that quickly became head of a department. However, as soon as he cast off his professional mantle he was crippled with shyness. He could not bring himself to be at all intimate with others in the neighbourhood. When not at work, people outside his family seemed like a race apart, who would look askance at him just as they had done years before.

A boy, many years ago, was one of the elder of many children. He was very fond of his mother, but each year brought another birth, so that he had but little of her company. He took this stoically, and in fact became particularly admired by his family for his bravery both at home and in childhood exploits. His mother died when he was 10 and his father struggled on alone to bring up the family. Two years later the young boy said he wanted to relieve his father of one mouth to feed and was determined to join the navy. His father gratefully accepted this further demonstration of bravery.

When he was 18, after six years at sea he fell ill and was invalided home from the East. In the ship on the way back he seems to have gone through an acute adolescent crisis. He became aware that he had no future in the navy, and could see no way of life that would fulfil him. He wondered whether to throw himself overboard and finish it all. Then 'a radiant orb was suspended in his mind's eye'. He exclaimed, 'I will be a hero and confiding in providence will brave every danger'.

Later in adult life this is just what he did. As Lord Nelson he became the brave hero not only to his family, but to England at large and to succeeding generations of schoolboys.

Compromise and Adult Identity

Throughout adult life, demands to *conform* to other people's require-ments are continually impressing themselves upon the individual. At the same time, he has his own inner wishes, so that conflict becomes inevitable. If a person is to maintain an *integrity* of his personality, he has to make *compromises* between his own wishes, his conscience, and demands of the outside world. I would argue that integrity is lost when chronic splitting occurs, so that one set of interests obliterate others for any length of time. Fanaticism is one instance of this, and a person preoccupied only with himself is another. So, too, would be someone who surrenders himself totally to other's demands. For example, compare these two men, both bank managers.

Mr A was highly esteemed by his superiors and customers. However, his whole life was consumed by his bank life. He had no hobbies. People were invited to supper on the basis of their business connections. His family life was invaded by ideas and strictures about the bank. He would say to his wife, 'You mustn't wear trousers in the front garden because customers pass'. Or, 'You should order your groceries from Jones's because they bank with us,' and so on. In submitting to the bank he was unable to enjoy either his own bodily functioning or the inner lives of his wife and family. He repeatedly fell sick and his wife, failing to make an impression on him by ordinary means, soon found herself turning into a chronically hysterical individual. Although esteemed by many, he had failed to go through the agony of making an integrating compromise between the various demands of his situation.

Mr B was actively interested in athletics, music and literature when young, but went into the bank to earn a living. When quite an old man he said, 'I often thought I would leave the bank and do something that directly interested me more, but I fell in love and decided that getting married was the more worth while. And to do this I had to stay in the bank.' However, he did not forget the expression of his inner life. He continued to be a reader, talker and musician in his leisure time. 'The bank was satisfactory in a way. It was secure, and looking after people's affairs was interesting. But everyone knew my heart was in other places as well, and because I wasn't married to the bank I didn't get far up the ladder.' Here we see evidence of making compromises, but not of losing self-integrity.

We see in Mr A a form of fanaticism. He was obsessed by ambition and conformity to banking. Mr B, on the other hand, tried to evaluate the various aspects of his life and sought to compromise between them. Because of this he may have suffered the fate of being thought ordinary, but no one would say he was a nonentity, and many were glad to have known him. While Mr A compromised himself, Mr B made compromises. The course through adult life seems to be a continuous compromise between conflicting issues. As new situations arise, so the individual is called upon to develop new patterns of thought, to find new compromises which will maintain his own and others' integrity.

Continuity of Adult Identity
Some writers seem to think that once an adult identity has been found, in the mid-twenties say, this should now normally remain set through life. Even Erikson, the originator of the term, often seems to imply it. It may have been true when life was short and societies relatively static. But even a cursory glance at lives today points to the many shifts of role, often of a fundamental kind, that individuals have to develop through life. A woman, for instance may leave school, genuinely find her independence through being a secretary, then fall in love, marry and forget all about her previous work in engrossing herself in mothering. When the children go to school and grow away from her, she may find herself dissatisfied with married dependency and seek a new, paying career which offers more personal creative satisfactions than a secretarial office. So she becomes a student again, trains and gives herself a pattern of responsibilities she has not known before.

All these require change and development of adult identity, and each change is likely to be a life crisis. This being so, I would argue that the individual must expect to proceed through a breakup of old patterns, loosening into regression and testing new modes of competence of a similar form to that of adolescing. These later crises can often be even more searching than the teenage shifts. It is for this reason that so much time was spent on adolescence; its form can be repeated, wtih modifications, at any time of life.

Falling in Love

In our society, when the subject of sexual love arises the question of marriage is not far away. But for the time being I shall ignore marriage, leaving it to the next chapter.

Turning our minds back to previous chapters, the whole sequence of the history of erotic development through life will be recalled. First came the baby's erotic love for his mother and the necessity for harmony between them for healthy physical and mental growth. Then came frustrations of this love, easily evoking experiences of extreme distress and hence mad rage. At this time, also, intellectual events were readily accompanied by gross physical reactions. Thus the whole complex web of meaningful enjoyment, puzzlements, frustrations, rage and despair that a child felt, with his mother in particular, was intervoven with his eroticism. In other words, meaningful love and eroticism have roots in the mother–child relationship. This was continued in conflicts over social and bodily control in the second year of life. And then, though less obviously, the joys and conflicts of the child about his parents seemed to be sensitively focused upon genital urges and fantasy. This was epitomised by the Oedipus complex. With growth into relative independence and going out into the company of other children, the child seemed to be less erotically attached to his parents and assumed a certain detached dignity; latency had set in. Though easily arousable and sexually curious, there were probably few major upsurges of sexual feeling until puberty. At this point the arousal of the genitals and body growth insists that a child is a sexual being like his parents. This acted as the trigger to the adolescent sequence which, if successful, culminated in the ending of dependent expectations about parents.

The first directly sexual feature of an adolescent's turning away from parents is crushes on other people. These tend to have a disconnected and primitive all-or-nothing quality about them. They are passions for parts of people or abstracted physical characteristics: firm mouth, mellow lips, welling breasts, or the way a head is held. They are physical attributes, but I think they usually also symbolise *personal characteristics*. For instance, firm mouth reminds the adoring one of 'determination', mellow lips suggest 'sensuousness', welling breasts evoke ideas of 'generosity', and so on. They are primitive metaphors, rather like dream symbols in which physical attributes also frequently stand for more general functions. This is supported by the fact that physical attributes are not the only things adolescents fall in love with. Psychological characteristics of a person are often quite explicitly felt as objects of passion. Here are one or two examples of young people's reflexions about their loves.

I am in love with Jacques more than anyone, it is I think because he, like I, is half in love with death. (15-year-old)

I love Dean, he is nothing but pure kindness. (14-year-old)
I only fall for hard men. I think it is because they are the only ones who could stand my violent temper. (17-year-old)

Why are these abstracted parts of a person's character fallen for with such deep personal meaningfulness? The girl who gave the last example gives a clue. She sensed she needed someone to control the rages she could not manage herself. She *fell in love with a characteristic* she felt *deficient in herself*. This tallies well with the age-old saying of 'Falling in love with your other half'. This stems from Greek mythology, which held that man had originally been happily whole, but later one-half of the soul had become separated from the other. Thus mortal men were always incomplete, searching for their other half.

If at least one aspect of falling in love is towards a characteristic we feel deficient in, then we would expect that a person would feel extremely humble compared to his adored one. Idealisation would be a facet of love. This is certainly the case. What is more it is experienced in an all-or-nothing way; it is primitive and readily ruled by splitting. This being so, we would expect even slight misunderstandings to lead a humble lover to switch to violent hatred at being betrayed. This is certainly likely to happen with immature crushes. They are *unstable*, what is more, since idealisation of the loved one tends to *deplete* self-esteem; a lover readily becomes explosively envious. Only when the idealisation is reciprocated does this self-depletion receive a counterbalance.

Obviously this is not a complete unravelling or understanding of the crush. The girl quoted above who was in love with Jacques, for instance, said she loved him because he was *like herself* 'half in love with death'. Here she had found a comrade in her suffering, the two, alienated from the rest of humanity as they saw it, could understand and comfort each other like babes in the wood.

These are just two positive lines of inquiry into the riddle of why one person falls in love with another. It is certainly not exhaustive but is, I hope, at least a start.

At this stage we have simply discriminated some types of characteristics that may be fallen in love with, and of course they could belong to a person of either sex. In adolescing, apart from social pressures, movement of love for a person of one sex to love for the other is usually fluid, at least at the level of fantasy. But we have so far described only the crush, the first stage of being in love. Let us proceed to the second where the fantasy crush generates a real two-person relationship. We shall consider homosexual choice first, and then heterosexuality.

Homosexual Love

First it must be recognised that a love choice has its negative as well as

E

positive side. A love choice *towards* one sex is also away from or *against* the other. There are elements of rejection, and hate at a primitive, unconscious level, towards the discarded sex. In other words, a male's homosexual choice seems to involve positive revulsion against sexual love of women. Likewise, a female's lesbian choice is positively against sexual love of men. It is a common clinical finding that, in this revulsion, fear, hate and paranoid feelings about the opposite sex are active (Stoller, 1968).

Here is a brief description of a homosexual love choice. It is anecdotal, but may suggest wider lines of inquiry.

A young man had, since earliest childhood, been preoccupied with the necessity of pleasing people. His father said he seemed very happy and very clever when a little boy. If there was anything wrong it was that he was too good! He got on well with his father who was sensible and quiet. He doted on his mother who histrionically lavished adoration on him. This was matched by the company of many old ladies whom his mother also looked after. He was precocious intellectually and hence quickly became something of a teacher's pet at school. Perhaps because of this he tended to be very frightened of the jealousy of the other children and, being small, had no means to assert himself physically. He yearned to please them. Going into his teens he became readily acceptable as a clever boy, but was still obsessed with the need to please. At this time he began to consciously dislike his mother, feeling that she overwhelmed or ate him up. He also began to be aware of how ruthless he could be and noticed that he often dreamt of being a despot, like Caligula for instance. But he was in fact effectively unassertive, and awareness of his ruthlessness doubled his wish to be nice and liked. In his late teens he tried a lightning affair with a girl but was thrown into a chaos by her flighty histrionics and discreetly retired from the encounter. Thereafter he went on liking women, and had many as friends, but sexually he kept his distance.

Then he fell passionately in love with a brash, ruthless young bisexual man who was apparently socially more outstanding and successful than he was. The Caligula of his dreams had been found, in actuality. The young man was enthralled. The ruthless man seemed to find kindly innocence appealing, so they fell into a passionate affair. The ruthless man, however, soon tired of this and found another *amour*, leaving the young man hurt and bereft, determined to give himself to gentler lovers next time.

In this we see many elements. No only a *revolt* against 'good' practices, together with a dread of being *overwhelmed by women*, but also a *hunger for the character of the loved one*. In overt homosexuality this hunger for another's character seems to take a physical form. It is wanted physically, even to incorporating the loved one's body, and penis in particular. The loved one's penis may be wanted inside and this can be achieved in anal intercourse. Or it may be wanted as something to fondle and worship in mutual masturbation. Both these are, of course, common in homosexual intercourse.

This one example cannot validly be extended to general conclusions about homosexuality. But I think you will find the features mentioned here are quite common.

Secondly, here is a description of a lesbian love choice:

A young woman had been brushed off, when a little girl, by her mother who inordinately doted on her older brother. He was a rather soppy crybaby, bitterly envied and yet held in contempt by his sister. Her father was rather distant but loved by the little girl, however he was careless about the home and was openly denigrated by her mother.

When grown up, she liked and was liked by both men and women. But when close to men she found herself overwhelmed by hate and contempt for them. Being unsure of herself in intimate relations she began to feel very lonely and yearned to be fussed by a woman, as her mother positively had not. She met a colleague who was openly contemptuous of men but warm and affectionate to women and also wanted to be soothed by female affection. They naturally fell for each other and lived together for a long time. However it was not entirely satisfactory. One young woman loved children and wanted a baby, the other was hungry for the company of women with strength, definiteness and power so that neither was very fulfilled.

Here we have a pattern that is different from the male homosexual; there is *envy and contempt for sexual men* and a yearning to be *fussed over in a motherly way* by women. This again is only an anecdote, but it shows themes which can be quite common in lesbianism (Cameron, 1963; Rosen, 1964; West, 1960).

At this point it must be emphasised that I have described only a few of the vast multiplicity of feelings and fantasy that are set loose in sexual arousal of any sort. Many involve projections of the self into another, or fusions of another into the self. Others involve being of the opposite sex to what one physically is. These fantasies are thought of as perverse by many people and hence repugnant. I would suggest that the primary feature to note is not that homosexual and lesbian fantasies are objectionably perverse but rather that they are *unstable*.

This instability has great values; the shifting of identification of self from one sex to another in imagination, for instance, is essential for sympathy with the other sex and for creative breadth of vision. It is also intrinsic to certain areas of learning and work. For instance, if a man is to learn how to nurse babies, or if a woman is to model herself on male teachers to develop competence in her work, then both need to enjoy mental identifications with the opposite sex. It is, I think, one of the social achievements of recent years that prejudice against this cross-sex identification has begun to relax.

However, where actual homosexual or lesbian relationships occur, certain instabilities and impoverishments do seem to be inevitable. The young man I quoted, for instance, did not find a relaxed use of those feelings which made up his ruthlessness when he fell for a ruthless young man, he simply got hurt. And the young woman could not satisfy her yearning to be engrossed with a baby by lesbian intercourse. This raises the question as to how heterosexuality compares with them, so let us turn to this now to continue the argument.

Heterosexual Love

As in homosexuality, perverse fantasy is usually embedded in hetero-sexual love, but there is something else as well. I have just been pointing out that in both male and female homosexuality there seem to be severe persecutory and paranoid feelings about the *opposite sex*. These are particularly felt when in close physical contact, which is usually avoided. These persecutory feelings of fear and hate are strong enough to swamp and then freeze heterosexual urges. A person who can turn to hetero-sexuality cannot be ruled in this way by paranoid fears; they must either be milder or strongly defended against.

Whether it be a homosexual or heterosexual love, a young person taking the momentous step from pubertal crush to an actual approach to a boy- or girl-friend opens up the possibility of sexual reciprocity. I referred to reciprocity in the early chapters when describing those mutual contributions to each other's self-esteem which can occur between parent and child. Then it was one-sided, the parent really held power, now the reciprocity can be more equal. The idealising lover can be loved back so that he not only feels humble but, by being idealised in return, he is made to feel wonderful as well. He probably comes to feel, and be, more vital and colourful than he was before.

Where this reciprocity takes place with someone of the opposite sex the two, obviously enough, physically fit like jigsaw-puzzle pieces. The man's physical ecstasy with its particular form fits with and affirms the woman's ecstasy with its different shape. As their body shapes complement each other, so too does much of their fantasy which is closely tied to body shape and impulse. And, since thought patterns are fed by fantasy, so there is the likelihood that more intellectual functions can be felt as working in harmony too.

It is this mutual body acceptance that can give a blessed inner stability and peaceful harmony to young lovers. At best, unlike homosexuality, there are no loose ends. There are, as it were, no penises with nowhere to go, no unused vaginas or breasts that will never give milk. This is important, if only because it is neglect of these parts of the body that can give rise to violent, painful, even uncontrollable, destructiveness. These parts are somewhere felt as part of the self, even if unconsciously, and I have argued that when a self feels neglected it is hurt and easily becomes destructive. It is this harmony, rooted in physical intimacy without loose ends, that homosexuality and lesbianism seem to miss. Having said this, it is as well to recognise that heterosexuality can itself become a chronically perverse defensive trick. For instance, it can be used as a flight from depression while at the same time being swanked about as the 'height of normality' to less fortunate creatures. Naturally this is a subtle but unpleasant form of cruelty.

We are usually not satisfied to rest with physical harmony which, even though it may give rise to intellectual enjoyment as well, is often transient unless there is a deep, reciprocal appreciation of *character* as well. When this occurs, for instance, a person may have some ability which he believes in but is unsure of, and deeply wishes for it to be affirmed by a lover. If it is not noticed a person can feel just as hurt as if his whole soul and body has been spurned. The 'chemistry' of characters in interaction is as important in love as that of bodies. This interaction starts with idealising crushes which, as mentioned, seem to involve a falling in love with aspects of character. But for lasting enjoyment something of the following process must also, I think, take place in reciprocity.

A lover may idealise and want the characteristics of his loved one, but then sense that if he had them they would be antipathetic to him as a whole person. When this occurs, the individual may be glad of a partner with these ideal attributes, so that he can possess them at one remove.

Here is a simple example. The characteristic used is a part of the body, but it could apply to any part of bodily or mental functioning. A man may particularly idealise and dote upon his girl-friend's delicate, expressive hands. In one case it might be that he simply wants expressive hands like hers for himself. He may yearn to be a beautiful musician, but feels he could never be one because of lack of dexterity. In this case he will simply feel his own lack, and his loving idealisation may turn to corrosive envy. In another case the young man might equally feel moved by his girl's delicate, expressive hands. It might equally be that in *part of himself* he too would like to have such delicate hands. But, at the same time, he is proud of his own heavy, muscular hands, and delicate heavy hands just cannot go together in the same person. So as a *whole person* he does not want delicate hands. But he is very glad that he can 'possess' them at one remove in his loved one.

Likewise his girl might want, in part of herself, to have strong hands, and yet be proud of her own delicate ones. She reciprocally will thus dote upon his strong hands, while being pleased by her lover's appreciation of hers. Both partners are happy. This is a trivial example but the notion can be applied to many more complex characteristics.

I have argued here that, because of complementary sexual body shapes, heterosexuality is *potentially* the more satisfyingly stable and harmonious form of love. This does not mean that homosexual attachment is less creative of ideas, on the contrary I mentioned that homosexual feeling and imagination are necessary for breadth of vision and sympathy. What is more because it is potentially more satisfying this does not mean that heterosexual chemistry is less explosive. The fact that primitive feelings, with violent splitting and projection occurring, are opened up makes a love affair bliss or hell. A slightly more detailed consideration of this must wait until the next chapter.

FURTHER READING

1 Brecher, R. and E. (eds) (1967), *An Analysis of the Human Sexual Response*. A collection of articles arising out of the work of Masters and Johnson, together with a discussion of attitudes to sexuality.
2 Carter, M. (1966), *Into Work*. A general test on this subject.
3 Davies, D. R. and Shackleton, V. J. (1975), *Psychology and Work*. One of the 'Essential Psychology' series giving a straightforward introduction to this subject from the academic point of view.
4 Erikson, E. H. (1968), *Identity, Youth and Crisis*. A series of papers, particularly about youth and the concept of identity.
5 Fisher, S. (1973), *Understanding the Female Orgasm*. Also arising out of the work of Masters and Johnson but with considerable discussion of the interpersonal issues involved. I wish there was a companion to this about male sexuality.
6 Fromm, E. (1957), *The Art of Loving*. A very popular book. Some readers will find it rather solemn and old-fashioned, but this is perhaps its great virtue.
7 Storr, A. (1960), *The Integrity of the Personality*. Although some years old, this is still one of the best introductions to psychodynamics generally and to identity and integrity in particular.
8 West, D. J. (1960), *Homosexuality*. A general introduction to the subject.

Chapter 11

MARRIAGE

Reciprocal Appreciation
In this chapter I am going to include under the term 'marriage' all varieties
of bond where sexual partners agree upon a *continuity* of relationship,
whether until death or not. *Legal marriage* with its personal and social
implications will be considered towards the end of the chapter. I realise
that this definition is arbitrary and such terms as sexual partnership or
pair-bonding are appropriate. But they do not evoke the same psychological meaningfulness as does the word 'marriage'. And when two people
commit themselves to each other with legal ceremony or not, it is a very
real psychological event.

The last chapter spelt out what is obvious: that when two people
sexually fall in love, whether they go to bed together or not, there is the
opportunity for expansion to their lives with a harmonious stability that
has not been known since childhood.

In finding reciprocal appreciation much more than sexual feelings
are released. Because the reciprocity is sexual it is close to dreaming and
is thus rich in fantasy, primitive, deep and very personal; but intimate
friendship can be found as well. The intellect also seems to become more
vital; the chapters on early infancy suggested that intellect is born of
personal body fantasy; this seems to repeat itself when adult mutual
love is found. And with steady appreciation the couple's shame at expo-
sure of personal absurdities seems often to melt away. The comfort of
companionship has been found, defensiveness with its egocentric arrogance seems to matter no more, at least when the two are alone together.
With humble selflessness in the ascendant, one's conscience often glows
with a love for all creation.

And, because of the mental closeness of lovers, communication comes
with quick intuition. The two can find themselves growing into *being a
team*, moving efficiently together as one unit to solve problems.

It is a wonderful, stabilising magic, but also explosive. Lovers live,
whether they think so or not, in a social matrix. Their relationships with
others are affected. Work, other friendships and family ties may become

dimmed. What is important to one lover may be of no interest to the other. Habits of one may jar on the other. Sooner or later some sacrifice of personal idiosyncracy, which can be freely enjoyed in solitude, must be sacrificed in a partnership. But this is a partnership where primitive feeling and fantasy, stemming from those of a little child, have been loosened. This primitiveness entails splits of all-or-nothing feeling, things can be loved with consuming adoration or violently hated. Add to this the loss of self-discrimination, so painfully developed through earlier life, which may arouse anxieties of a psychotic intensity, then the outcome can be very explosive indeed. Lovers' quarrels are usually comic to an outsider, but to the participants who are defending their own precious selves against threatened invasion it is not funny at all. Only later, if they can look at themselves with the detachment of a third person, will they be able to see the humour of it. I would suggest that the lovers' quarrel encapsulates every facet of an individual's *early problems of social control*. Thus every form of personal habit, from meticulousness and untidiness to more general lack of care, comes under attack, sometimes with lavatorial obscenity but more often with simple disgust and contempt. On the positive side, the healing nature of laughter after a quarrel shows how precious is the ability to detach from the strident defence of self and, in imagination, see oneself as others might.

Courtship
Since a love bond is so magical and yet potentially explosive most people warily test each other out, slowly trying to discover whether the rewards are outweighing the sacrifices. This is courtship, and is as intrinsic to post-adolescent reality testing and is the finding of other contributions in work, leisure or friendship. The traditional form of courting in our society, overshadowed by the prospect of legal marriage vows, assumes that non-sexual testing of mutual interests, companionship and fondness comes before the final commitment of sleeping together. Many people nowadays turn this sequence on its head and, like the Trobriand Islanders described by Malinowski (1916) in his famous work, seek to test out sexual compatibility first and then, reasonably assured of this, go on to discover whether wider meanings are shared. Naturally the traditional method was the better of the two when the risk of pregnancy was high. Now, with contraception, the latter may be just as logical. However, long-lasting sexual compatibility seems to be just as dependent upon the wider companionship of ideas as vice versa (Gorer, 1971). Physical sexual aversion sets in deeply for many people, for instance, when they see their partner's preferred life-style or morals as alien to their own. So it is as well not to pontificate that the second procedure is universally the better. Perhaps, so long as children are not born of these tentative explorations, there is no reason why it should not be a matter of personal preference.

What can be said more dogmatically is that if a person values the quality of his own and his partner's life, then serious testing of each other must go on before commitment to living together for any length of time. We are usually capable of knowing consciously so little about ourselves, even less about others, and are so susceptible to rationalisation and self-deception, that this commitment usually contains gross errors of judgement.

Being in Love and Adult Identity

In the context of commitment to love and its errors of judgement, it is important to refer back to Chapter 10 on general work and leisure identity. When a person has found that personal patterning of roles in work and friendship which gives the sense of wholeness called identity, then he is in a good position to measure his losses and gains in these, as set against the values of a passionate love commitment. If, on the other hand, these are still amorphous or ill formed, then he has no such steadying measure. He then plunges into a relationship with little self-esteem or stable sense of what he is contributing. He is thus caught, tied to a relationship which is likely to be based on infatuations with parts of another person's character and which highlights any weakness felt in his own. In time, this probably must become a depleting experience. Then, struggling to find the integrity and self-esteem of adult identity in other pursuits, he tears at his love relationship as if it were a prison. If the loving, or rather now hating, couple had originally agreed to only a temporary commitment neither would suffer much, except perhaps that both would be inevitably thrown into loneliness. However, if they have committed themselves to lifelong marriage, and even more if there are children, the consequences can be dreadful. This is not just an abstract piece of theorising. It is known, for instance (Bernard, 1972), that teenage marriages are much more likely to become unsatisfactory and break up than are those contracted during or after the mid-twenties. Later in the chapter I will argue that it may be a woman's lack of opportunity to find an adult identity before marriage that makes for the greater preponderance of women unsatisfied by matrimony as compared to men. Erikson (1964, 1968) particularly, has stressed the importance of finding this identity before commitment to marriage. This time sequence is important, of course, only where the question of long-term commitment is concerned. It does not mean that satisfaction in work must be found before embarking upon love affairs, and for most people these happen concurrently.

These considerations about identity stress one further point. To find one's identity it seems centrally important to be *able to be alone*. Not necessarily alone socially, but alone with one's conscience, clinging to no one's opinion in order to carry out one's evaluations. This will sound a high-flown demand upon ordinary people. Most of us are just not capable of such self-discipline, but I am sufficiently convinced of its importance to stress that it merits serious thought.

Legal Marriage

Legal marriage is vowed in the presence of a few witnesses in a few minutes, yet it deeply binds for life most people for better or worse. It is obvious why this should be. Not only is marriage usually born of romantic love and reciprocal appreciation tested out over months, but it is also a public act symbolising a profound personal psychological event. Each partner is moving further out of his own family to become also a member of another, as well as creating a third. Added to this, friends, fellow workers and the state formally recognise the change. Thus, quite apart from the partners' personal attachment to each other and the feelings of conscience and responsibility that this entails, enormous external forces work towards the couple being surrounded by expectations and assumptions that the marriage vow will be kept until death.

Yet this is all based on the decision of two young people who can hardly know what is in store for themselves let alone their partners. They can only have a fleeting, second-hand knowledge of the demands of later life, the turbulence of child-bearing, the boring repetition of home, the burdensome anxiety of wage earning, the yearning for new lives in middle age and the restrictions of infirmity. It is almost strange that it works, more or less, or does it?

A question like this is statistical and sociological because it concerns a legally recognised cultural institution shared by many people. But, as it has such a deep and personal bearing on individual development, I must be an amateur social historian for a few paragraphs to outline the social setting individuals find themselves in.

The institution of monogamous marriage for life based only upon the decision of two partners who are romantically in love is of course not universal. There is polygamy, polygyny, polyandry, patriarchy, endogamy, exogamy, matriarchy, patrilocality, matrilocality, and so on. Each one is considered as quite moral in its own society. What is more, the criterion of romantic love for a marriage decision is of fairly recent origin even in the West.

In times past, probably because economic survival depended upon the extended family, formal marriage, if it occurred at all, was often more a matter of the convenience of the two families than of individual fulfilment, so that leading relatives were the deciding judges. This is not to say that individual romantic love was unrecognised. For instance, the Greeks recognised it in their idea of searching, for 'the other half', but this could be homosexual as much as, or more than, heterosexual love. Other considerations seemed more important, however, when contracting a marriage.

There are a few tales of romantic love in the Old Testament but these are rare compared to arranged marriages.

The New Testament says little about marriage and romantic love; however their origins can be traced to it. North-west Europe found a new stability and relative peace based on the growth of feudalism in the eleventh and twelfth centuries after centuries of turbulence in the Dark Ages. Possibly because of this social softening and stability there arose at the same time a new religious emphasis on Christ's gentle humanity and suffering. From this grew a gratitude to and worship of his mother, the Virgin Mary. Until then she had played only a small part in doctrine. This Mariolatry originated in France, but spread fast and is now enshrined for all to see in the great cathedrals of north-west Europe. It was paralleled by a secular movement in the cult of the troubadours. The knightly ideal that they celebrated was that of a man who would devote his life to his lady, content to carry out her commands and earn her favours. It was for the *lady* to decide whether he was worthy of her. This is a development of historic importance.

But the relationship celebrated by the troubadours was still irrelevant to marriage, even often adulterous. The romances perhaps provided an escape from the harsh realities of the marital customs of feudal Europe. However, the idea that a woman is no longer a chatel, that she has the power to say 'No' to the man's advances, is seen here for the first time. This can be seen as a step away from male dominance, and certainly the whole courtly ideal contributes towards our present-day aspirations concerning the relationship between men and women. What was originally an ideal, standing in time and space outside the ties of marriage and family, has been grafted onto the main stem of marriage and child-rearing. How far this can work is another question.

In Elizabethan and Jacobean writing the idea of mutual love is widely expressed. It is perhaps only then that reciprocal appreciation, of two lovers *equally* concerned for each other, came to be expressed. This is particularly apparent in the poetry of John Donne. But it was several centuries before those ideas could be solidly confirmed in social reality. Seventeenth-century divines played their part in enjoining men to honour their wives, but a primary factor in the change must have been economic. With the Industrial Revolution, people became mobile in their search for work, the nuclear family tended to replace the extended one as the social unit. When this occurred individual men and women had to find their own partners to start a family, separated perhaps by hundreds of miles from their kin. Furthermore, industrialisation meant that women came to be employed in large numbers outside their families, and being independently employed they could say 'No' to their suitors without fear of family repercussions or destitution.

And that might have been the happy ending of woman's rise to equality with men in marriage, but it is not quite. How do women fare in marriage compared to men today? The statistical and sociological evidence cogently amassed by Bernard (1972) suggests that women still do badly out of the deal. Married men, for instance, tend to live longer, are physically healthier and less prone to mental disorders than are bachelors of comparable age. Married women with children, on the other hand, tend to have shorter life expectancy and suffer very significantly more from mental disorders than do childless women of like age. Thus the worse affected are those who have been *mothers* of families. Married women who have not had families fare better. Bernard's work is predominantly American but seems to be supported by findings in Britain.

Logically this draws us to the inference that sex difference in marital satisfaction has something to do with the social expectations, still prevalent, that a man should find and maintain his independent work identity and subsume his marriage under it. This is a fundamental way in which men differ from their spouses. Married women are symbolically expected to throw away their identity by changing their name on marriage. They are not expected to have 'found themselves' before marriage, nor to maintain identity other than as wife and mother after it. 'Wife and mother' is obviously honourable enough, but it does mean that she is likely to be financially dependent on her husband for many years. This financial dependence must, for many, encourage fixation upon old infantile dependencies. We know that mental disorders involve the sterile repetition of infantile patterns of function. And it is predominantly mental disorders that Bernard reports as the fate of wives and mothers. Women often *wilt* into wives.

These are very serious social questions and we must be indebted to the polemicists of the women's movement for drawing attention to the problem in the first place. They are matters of long-term social policy which I am not equipped to argue about in detail. Social policy affects individual growth, but the two should not be confused. We are primarily concerned with the latter, that is how two individuals make a life together.

As a social institution legal marriage for life may eventually entail for many, even the majority, more shrinkage or burden than joy. However, the yearning for *continuity* in an intimate sexual relation is near universal for women as well as men, and, as we have seen, it can have deep rewards in happiness. I have already argued that it is optimal for the rearing of young children. So there are many things vitally worth preserving in marriage. What is more, we are here not social policy makers, but concerned with the inner processes of individuals who are married. There is a very large body of literature on the subject, not only sociological but also psychological, psychiatric and psychoanalytic (Blood and Wolfe, 1960; Dicks, 1967; Dominian, 1969; Skynner, 1976).

We have noted,, only broadly, how marriage involves a loosening of self-boundaries. Some individuals change, not necessarily for the better, in the formation of a married team. It is thus a crisis of life, not usually felt as such at the time because of the happiness of new-found love. Later, however, extremely painful and violent crises can occur very frequently indeed. It is my, perhaps over gloomy, impression that marriages without long periods of crisis, or without lapsing into sterile deadlock, are the exception rather than the rule. I realise that this seems to contradict more optimistic statistical finding such as those by Gorer (1971). But these are usually based on what people consciously say about their marriages and do not explore the subtle shrinkages of experience that so often seem to occur.

This raises a vital question for most married couples. What is in the ascendant when couples are in harmony, as compared to when marriages break into crisis which may then sink into painful sterility? I will introduce a few general points about this in some brief descriptions of married couples.

Mr and Mrs A

The report says:

I have never seen any show of love on either side, there was no kiss goodbye or welcome in the evenings. They seemed to have nothing in common, and therefore no subject to discuss jointly. His work and hobbies were his only topic of conversation. These bored his wife, and she spent more and more time with her mother, who came to live with them.

There were rows over Mrs A's mother. He resented her interference but, instead of telling his mother-in-law to mind her own business, he told his wife to speak to her. Naturally she didn't or couldn't, and there were more rows. So the family split; he went his way, she went hers. Eventually the grandmother died and the children left home but Mr and Mrs A stayed the same. They considered living apart, but decided that this would not be possible economically.

Mr and Mrs B

One day Mr B outlined his reasons for seeming so depressed. He talked for several hours saying, 'I can't talk to her and she doesn't seem to understand'. On another occasion, Mrs B gave a long account of hours spent locked in the bathroom crying into a towel. I asked why she need hide her feelings and she said, 'I wouldn't let him see me so upset'.

They never used words of endearment and Mrs B said they all ended on the wedding day. Her husband is charming to women. In company he would say to his wife, 'Why can't you look like that?' This might have gratified the other woman but hurt his wife terribly. Finally,

Mrs B started an affair with a neighbour; her husband wouldn't believe it even though everyone else knew what was happening. They have separated now.

Mr and Mrs C

Mr C was a lecturer at a college and gave a lot of time to the drama society. His wife felt left out and neglected; being very pretty she soon attracted other men, but he spent more and more time in rehearsals. The climax came when she slapped him on the stage one evening in front of all the students. Her parents encouraged her to leave him and return home to them. She did this and was soon having an affair with another man.

Mr and Mrs X

Mrs X is a driving sort of person and her husband much quieter. But if she wears the trousers it is because Mr X is content to let her do so, and she enjoys it. They have endured considerable hardship together, especially when he was out of work. But this seems to have made them more united. Now in middle age they still show all the outward signs of being in love. They say that they have few major quarrels and most decisions are reached amicably. One suspects that she makes most of these while he acquiesces, but when there is something about which he feels particularly strongly she would not attempt to argue.

The whole family is doted upon by both sets of in-laws. They have helped them out financially in the past, but do not seem to intrude.

Mr and Mrs Y

In many ways husband and wife are very different. Her liveliness can at times be overwhelming. He is quieter and seems to find her liveliness attractive. His quietness seems to counteract her boisterous nature in a way that is comfortable. They often have different opinions and argue, but one senses a tolerance and respect for each other's views.

They say they hardly ever have a row. When they are on the point of one they say they go to each other and swallow their pride until the bad feeling subsides. He is interested in her clothes and ideas; he likes to talk about his work. Both are rather eccentric and vague, but in different ways, so that between them they get things done efficiently. They are both loyal to each other in every sense of the word.

Mr and Mrs Z

Mrs Z is gay, dramatic and untidy. Her husband is critical and can be rude; he is something of a snob. One might not think they would mix well, but they seem to have an inner respect for each other. They appear to me as a couple and not as two individuals trying to keep their own side up.

When he is insulting or flies off the handle, she will stand up for herself and tell him he is wrong if she thinks he is. Rows do not seem to last; perhaps they just have a sense of proportion. Mrs Z says that he upsets her at times, 'Sometimes I could throw him down the drain, I don't know why he says the things he does, but then there must be things about me he hates. I know I wouldn't really change him.'

The cases of Mr and Mrs A, B and C show an underlying *splitting* of feeling occurring. Each tends to see the other in black and white terms. each openly hates the other. All appreciation has gone, so they are gripped by feeling their partner is just bad to them. They see themselves, on the other hand, as poor sufferers struggling to keep their end up. Faults are reeled off, resentments of long ago are unearthed and chewed over inexorably. Primitive, paranoid mechanisms predominate in the partners' feelings about each other. This, however, does not necessarily extend to other people outside the marriage. They do not manifest themselves as generally paranoid characters, and are enmeshed in these feelings only in the intimate partnership. Malign *regression* has occurred. We have noted that this can happen to anyone on all sorts of occasions. But various factors conspire in marriage to encourage such tendencies. There is its intimacy, its dependence, the loosening of taboos on eroticism, and the loss of boundaries in becoming a team. It has often been stressed in previous chapters that such regression is vital for full-bloodedness and deep developments in mental functioning. But it also means that there is a proneness to violent splitting and projection.

It is also noticeable that the *partners' parents* were often intrusive with the A, B and C's, but not the X, Y and Z's. For whatever reasons, the former group do not seem to have dissolved their childhood ties to their parents and have been unable to form autonomous adult identities to take to their marriages. Parents often play very active and malignant parts in the splitting processes which occur in marriage. One partner turns back to his parents to be all 'good' to them, while the other is rejected as bad.

Turning now to the X, Y and Z's, we see that splitting into good and bad has not solidified into a way of life. This does not mean that hatred is never experienced. To re-quote Mrs Z, 'Sometimes I could throw him down the drain, . . . but then there must be things about me he hates. I know I wouldn't really change him.' Here anger emerges, but close after it comes *depressive concern* ('There must be things about me he hates.'). This is followed by appreciation. The splitting has not taken hold, but rather an integration of feelings and ideas creates perspective and a sense of proportion. This has succinctly been described as 'containing hatred in a framework of love' (Dicks, 1967). In happy marriages, partners are *kind to each other*.

It must remain an open question why benign processes such as these occur in some marriages and not in others. Certainly, individuals bring propensities from their childhood. But just as important must be each person's choice of partner and their intermingling of feelings as they go through life. Those who strike a note of appreciation and protective sympathy for each other, develop an underlying *respect* which is emphasised in Mr and Mrs X, Y and Z. When this key is not maintained couples tend to retire hurt, bitter and disillusioned, and paranoid splitting becomes entrenched. Dicks (1967) particularly stresses the omnipresence of mechanisms like these in marital breakdown.

FURTHER READING

1 Dicks, H. V. (1967), *Marital Tensions*. A well-known text on marital therapy, but its introductory chapters on the psychodynamics of marriage are of more general interest.
2 Dominian, J. (1969), *Marital Breakdown*. A general introduction to the subject.
3 Gorer, G. (1971), *Sex and Marriage in England Today*. A very readable report of a social survey of this subject.
4 Mead, M. (1950), *Male and Female*. Although a good many years old this is still the most comprehensive study of male and female attitudes in different cultures.
5 Skynner, R. (1976), *One Flesh, Separate Persons*. Fundamentally a compendium about family therapy, but its introductory chapters are generally valuable for their discussion of marital and family dynamics.

Chapter 12

PARENTHOOD

Parenthood as a Developmental Sequence
We have now come full circle and return to pregnancy and the early years, but are looking at them from the parents' point of view. Parents still carry their own childhood experiences with them, but are now responsible for bringing up the next generation. It will be useful to browse again through the early chapters of this book to recall what this responsibility entails. Because my thesis is as follows: *As a child grows, so it is necessary for a parent to change in emphatic responsiveness to his/her child. This entails not only being intuitively aware of himself at equivalent ages to the child, but also being aware of their own and their child's separate lives with differing present-day problems.*

In ways like this a parent can assist the child when he cannot act for himself, while allowing him to be free when he can. If a parent fails in this at any stage, he either does not assist him when needed, and the child is distressed, or he chokes initiative. Both have detrimental consequences for development. Parents are called upon to develop in parallel with their children.

This is the point of view implicitly taken by many writers on bringing up children (Kelmer-Pringle, 1974; Winnicott, 1964). It is most explicitly stated by the psychoanalyst Benedek (Anthony and Benedek, 1970). Naturally every parent fails to live up to these criteria to a greater or less degree. They have their own lives to lead and cannot be aware of everything about their child. What is more a child cannot develop independence if scrutiny is overwhelming; *thoughtful neglect* is not only inevitable but also necessary for a child to be unspoilt. But, if childhood is to be deeply enjoyed by both child and parent, then the parents must take these criteria, and the responsibilities they involve, seriously. Quite apart from anything else, it is only when being responsible that each parent will deeply enjoy himself. But it is exhausting and limits many other activities that invite and press themselves, especially today. Let us briefly consider the social situation of parents.

Parents in Society

In societies with little technology high fertility is balanced by high mortality. This was certainly the case in Britain until a century ago, when death was common and a child could hardly expect to live until old age. People then tended to be fatalistic and life lay in the hands of God. Although many parents loved their children much as they do today, they could not be so hopeful in their responsibility for them. Probably partly because of this, there is much evidence that neglect, exploitation and cruelty, especially in Europe, was rife (de Manse, 1974). However, non-technological rural living and extended families meant that children could extend in space; they could wander and homes of relatives would be nearby. Responsibilities of care could be spread.

In modern urban communities families are hemmed in by lethal motor traffic, if not cooped up in high flats. Parents are under continued stress to make provision for these. What is more, isolation from relatives gives freedom from interference but throws parents on their own resources. They are strained by the knowledge that they have only a few hours in which to relax or be ill, for there may be no one else to help (Gavron, 1966).

Medical and dietary knowledge, making for increased life expectancy, means that parents can optimistically throw themselves into the enjoyment of bringing up children. But the price for this is greater pressure of responsibility on parents; there is heavier guilt if anything goes wrong. The predicament of parenthood is epitomised by birth control itself: there is greater freedom to choose but the parent must then bear anxiety and guilt for its consequences himself.

In our present society it is mothers who bear the brunt of this most directly. As we saw in the last chapter, mothering is a high-risk occupation for mental disturbance and debility. It can also be devalued. When asked who they are, many women do not expect to be honoured or admired but apologise with, 'Oh I'm just a mother'. Yet it is largely upon them that the vitality of any society and its future rests.

It has been cogently argued, particularly by the women's movement, that much can be done to free mothers from this burden. Certainly many fathers will have to become more engaged in their families if the burdens of mothering are to be lightened. And other institutions, particularly when considering hours of work, need to change their practices if the isolation of mothers is to end. But I have argued in earlier chapters that the nuclear family provides certain optimal conditions for the care of children, especially when very young. So that, whatever other rearing means are experimented with, this unit is precious to preserve. What is more, it is mothers not fathers who are pregnant and lactate; it is women who go deeply and enjoyably into maternal preoccupation. So, if a mother is really to enjoy herself, not to mention the child, she must expect to lay aside other ambitions at least temporarily and engross herself in parenthood. As we have seen this puts her at risk emotionally, but many women will agree that this is worthwhile. Let us consider the sequence of mothering in more detail.

Fantasy and Reality in Having a Child

Primary maternal preoccupation has just been recalled (Winnicott, 1958). It is a life crisis where old modes of adaptation and defence are loosened so that a woman tends to withdraw and regress. The baby inside the womb is likely to become the focus of vivid fantasy and feeling. A mother is prone to dream of things for her child that she herself has missed, or to dread that her own bad experiences and unwanted characteristics will re-emerge in the new life. As the baby is inside and part of her, it tends to become part of her own inner world of affect-laden imagery. At the same time the infant is a new creation, an entity of his own who is not just a fantasy in the mind of his mother. These two, fantasy and reality, are in continuous interplay in the mind, not only before birth but long into later life.

The closeness of a baby to his mother's inner world of feeling and fantasy means that her exchange with him is usually warm, deeply emotional and colourful. But it also means that she must be continuously, if subconsciously, testing her fantasy out against the baby as he really presents himself before her eyes. For instance, a mother may at a glance catch a glimmer of resemblance between him and her own father. He may then be endowed with feelings that rise up in her from ideas about her father. But next the baby turns his head and looks like her mother-in-law and this arouses its own particular imagery. Then the child laughs in his own special way and impresses himself upon his mother as a conscious living person in his own right. The mother's fantasies may well emerge again, but now altered slightly by her realistic perceptions so that a coherent representation of her baby slowly integrates itself.

Such a close investment between the inner and outer world means a delicate balance between the two which is readily thrown into disorder. Thus maternal breakdown in infancy is not uncommon (Lomas, 1967; Deutsch, 1944). Sometimes this takes the form of a gross breakdown in differentiating in her fantasy from external reality as in a *puerperal psychosis*. Of more frequent occurrence are puerperal depressions. Here, unlike psychosis, a mother usually experiences a flatness because she cannot endow her child with enough fantasy from her inner world. Transient depression of this kind seems to be almost inevitable and must be regarded as part of the normal crisis of early mothering.

Some mothers do not break down in their functioning, but unself-consciously turn their children into the playthings of their fantasy in a chronic way so that it becomes a life-style. Here are a couple of examples:

A woman, whose own mother had become pregnant two months after she herself was born, produced several children and tried to keep them as babies as long as she could. She seemed, through them, to be trying to have the gratification of a long babyhood which she had herself missed. She lost interest in them as soon as they began to walk.

Two parents lost their five children in a fire. They then had five more children, who turned out to be of the same sex as the first. The children were given the same names as those who had died. When the fifth was born the whole family with great rejoicing emigrated to a commonwealth country, just as the parents had planned to do just before the disastrous fire of years previously.

Psychiatric literature is full of other instances (Anthony and Benedek, 1970; Bell and Vogel, 1968; Laing and Esterson, 1964; Lidz, 1963). It must be stressed, however, that by the nature of parents' fantasy this is not just a question for psychiatrists. Every child is in some measure the sport of his mother's madness; it is part of the fate of being a child dependent on adults. But where a mother continues to match fantasy with an awareness of her real child then the experience can be rich for both.

Multiple Responsibility in Mothering

The business of mothering is a continuous *to and fro* between mother and child. Her life is acting and reacting from dawn to dusk, so that both she and her child are enjoying each other, yet are self-willed, tired and angry. When a mother loses this responsiveness, then the child is *left alone*. Children are glad of this in small doses, but if prolonged it becomes unbearable. As a child grows older the areas of activity where this 'to and fro' is required become wide and various.

Perhaps the most common stereotyped idea of a mother is that of cuddling and nursing a young baby. This may seem too trivial an oversimplification even to mention. But many young women are so enthralled by this idea that they envisage little else. When their children are no longer babies, they may find themselves at a loss and become lethargic, bored and depressed. The children for their part are then left understimulated, drifting about lonely and disillusioned. This pattern is frequently reported by despairing health visitors and social workers. Fathers also may tend to limit their ideas to this fantasy of infancy. Being unable to envisage other responsibilities for a mother they irritably dismiss their wives' work as trivial. Years after their infancy, many young people complain bitterly that their mothers could only see them as babies and not as they really were. It seems to be endemic as a source of family fiction.

One mother epitomised the essential quality of mothering as *multipli-*

city. If we cast our minds back to the previous chapters on infancy to adolescence, we shall recall how complex the patterning of activities was in those years. A mother is called upon to watch over all these and respond to them as her conscience dictates. This is the responsibility of mothering.

Changing Responsibility with the Growth of Children

As a child grows up, a mother is called upon to *develop her responsiveness* to match. This entails continuous, new intellectual learning and articulation of feeling. Let us recapitulate some of the salient features of earlier chapters to clarify this.

The first months of life see a mother preoccupied with attuning her body to the physical presence of a new living being. Later in the first year a child is beginning to recognise his mother, and wants to discover his and her boundaries by playing with her. With the second year he is mobile, and a mother finds her will clashing with his. Personal and social discipline begins to become a crucial issue.

As a childhood progresses the young person begins to talk and explore. When a mother has time and inclination, she can spend hours in friendly investigation and explanation which is deeply satisfying to both. If she has neither, they can both lapse into irritated boredom.

By the age of 3 or so the child will probably be seeking out other children. This means a mother must broaden her horizons to befriend other mothers and be liked and trusted by their children. For this to happen she has to extend her modes of thought in order to be able to talk to several children at once. The breadth of response must be even wider if a mother has several children of her own of different ages. It is only necessary to be at tea with, say, half a dozen children of different ages to see how exhausting this can be.

Coming out of infancy, the child becomes a sexual person. Sexual feelings towards their children are often dim and little talked about but most mothers are privately aware of these and discipline themselves to cope. For instance, mothers often find that they have no trouble in cuddling and kissing their children of both sexes alike until they are 3 years old or so. Some then find themselves being slightly disgusted by too many caresses from their daughters while still enjoying the kisses from their sons. Both sexes want these caresses, and the daughters get hurt if rebuffed while brothers are favoured. One mother, equally fond of all her children, said she found herself rather guiltily cuddling her son in secret when her daughters were in another room.

With school age comes the question of following intellectual progress and finding a working relationship with teachers. Soon after this the child tends to turn towards the private company of his friends. Then begins the long process of losing intimacy with a child as he proceeds into puberty. In adolescence all a mother's old ways of doing things are likely to be called into question. It becomes a day of judgement for her years of motherhood, so that she may be fraught with worries about her failures.

In so far as a mother has kept in touch with her child, recognising his independent existence, however much she may muddle along the way, both of them will probably have found life profoundly worth while. The one-sided parent–child relationship may recede, but the friendship, begun years before, in the cuddling and chatter of infancy is likely to remain.

Going to Work
When technology was limited and life short a young woman could expect the rest of her life to be taken up by nursing children and domestic economy, that is if she did not need employment to earn bread. A great deal of intelligence had to be exercised. Technology has given women more time to enjoy their children and also many years when mothering is no longer full-time work. It has thus made the apparent burdens of motherhood less obvious. I have already mentioned that there seems to be a prevailing climate of disrespect for mothering. This is not only amongst men, as has been the tradition for millenniums in the male-dominated West, but now also more stridently from women engrossed in their own professional aspirations.

Under these pressures from outside, as well as from their own wishes to find a worthy identity and a need for money, many mothers are torn, from pregnancy onwards, between their family and work.

The argument of this book has been that, if a woman is to fully enjoy being a mother, she must reckon to put aside other work completely for the first months of a child's life (unless she can work at home). This probably needs to continue until at least social control with her child has been well established so that he has enough independence to go to nursery school at about 3 years old. Even then, full-time employment is not really possible unless a father can take part-time work or another consistent person is available. However, after a child has been at primary school for some time, there is evidence (Davie, Butler and Goldstein, 1972) that children positively benefit from both parents having the wider experience and freedom which is provided by other work.

These injunctions may sound severe and many women, not only those living without husbands, find them impossible to meet. This is especially so for those in the full spate of realising their professional ambitions who are faced with two possibilities. They must first seriously question themselves and perhaps decide not to have children at all. Or they must accept that they will not be their child's mother in the fullest meaning of the word, for others will have taken over many of a mother's functions. This may not be disastrous for a child, there is a lot of evidence that it often is not, but the mothers themselves may feel unfulfilled. It is for each person to decide their compromise; one cannot have one's cake and eat it.

On the other hand, if a woman has steeped herself in rearing children for years of her life, there is no easy solution either. She is left with school-age children who do not need her every attention and are in fact often choked by it. She is likely to be understretched, fundamentally bored and with no identity to ensure her self-esteem. If she stays at home she is prone to wilt into indolence and parasitism. If she seeks work she is likely to be at a disadvantage compared to those of her age who have continued in careers. It is another life crisis which must account for much of the reported mental disturbance in women who become mothers.

The other side of the balance sheet is provided by evidence that second and third careers are becoming more acceptable. Prior experience of being a mother, for instance, is often recognised as invaluable in many jobs, especially in the helping professions. Furthermore, mothers who have devoted themselves to mother, have had the opportunity to enjoy something which no others, men particularly, can possibly have had.

The Father in Modern Society

Just as for women, modern society has begun to transform expectations about fathers in a family. This has been less acute than for women, for a man's work identity can still progress consistently even though he has a family. But machines have diminished the ascendancy of the male's superior muscular strength and women have proved that, when prejudices die, they can do most jobs demanding intelligence as well as men. The male dominance that has characterised Western culture for all recorded history is cracking. As a consequence, there is an underlying unsureness about male functioning, especially in fathering. This has been but little singled out for special study and is usually only included in consideration of the family as a whole (Mead, 1950). But comments like the following are very common indeed.

I think we men fall over backwards to avoid being authoritarian like our fathers, but when we try to be democratic and discuss things, our wives complain that we are being soft.

My grandfather was certain of himself in his narrow confines. But my father had the whole of his world crash about him when he was a young man in the First World War. I don't think he has ever got over it. The only thing he can talk about with pride is the war. I am a bit luckier, but I do wonder where we go from here.

This is perhaps reflected in recent psychological literature. The first decades of this century were full of discussions, particularly by Freud, of childhood ideas about fathers and their importance in the growth and pathology of the individual. In the past forty years the pendulum has swung to interest in mothering. Very few writers have thought it necessary to consider as a central issue fatherhood and the problems it poses for the individual. The work that has been done on this often stresses the point made here, that there is uncertainty about fatherly identity (e.g. Erikson, 1963).

Technology and modern knowledge have exposed the delusions and tricks of male dominance so that patriarchism is not viable in a modern family. Here the co-operation of the independent intelligence of husbands and wives working together as a team is required. But this democracy is not firmly established either in law or in general social expectations, so that men particularly are unsure of themselves.

The Biological Circumstances of a Family in the
Early Months of Childhood

Repeating a familiar point, in order to be viable a mother must, at least in the early months of children's lives, have outside financial support. If she has three children spaced two years apart this means that she will be fundamentally dependent on others for up to ten years of her life. Either another individual or an institution must finance her, or she must look to others to care for her children while she works. If a woman is dependent upon an institutional structure, neither she nor her children are likely to reap the benefit of quick and easy communication which, as we mentioned, grows in the intimacy of marriage. So, in general, if mothers want to enjoy being full-time mothers, they need working men to provide for them.

Thus during the early child-rearing years, the man still 'stands at the door of the cave' just as has been expected of him through the ages. The period during which his breadwinning functions are crucial has been reduced. But the burden of a father's responsibility if anything rests more heavily than in times past, when he could count on more extended family support. After hearing many men feeling most deeply about their families, I think that it is useful to conceive of a variant of Winnicott's idea and talk about *primary paternal preoccupation*. This would not, of course, be rooted in pregnancy and lactation like maternal preoccupation. But, so long as it is not shattered or avoided, it can be deep and long lasting. It has many and various shapes.

A father must look two ways at once, outwards towards the world of work and inwards to the family. If his wife is to relax his work must be, in a sense, primary. When a man will not, or cannot work, then, as we have said already, the family loses its autonomy. Other agencies must be called in to provide this interest of fathering. If, on the other hand, a father takes no other interest in his family apart from providing for it through work, then at least it can remain an autonomous unit where its members respect themselves.

Probably because of this, much of most men's zest and opportunity for public esteem is in their activities outside the family. Men are geared to competition, mutual praise and support from their friends in ways that often seem absurd to women. Furthermore, very many of the skills demanded of men concern technology or large groups of people; they are impersonal and lack intimacy. But when they turn to their families quite different qualities are demanded.

A father will have had no formal education about family matters and, in contrast to a woman, he is unlikely to have learnt very much about them from male conversation or literature. For instance, women's magazines are full of articles about personal problems in a way that does not occur in magazines for men. Many forces seem to conspire to take a man's interest away from thinking about intimate family questions. Yet these will be his main concern as a father. Let us now consider them.

Family Environment

The place where a family settles is usually determined predominantly by the nature of a husband's work. Yet his wife and family will be the first to be affected by where they settle and by the housing that can be afforded from his wages. Thus in this, at least, a man will almost inevitably be held or feel responsible for shortcomings.

The predicament of work and housing is seen most poignantly with immigrant families, who move to alien environments because work is available. As often as not, accommodation can only be found which imprisons a wife and stunts the children. Even amongst those who can afford to pick and choose, housing is a very frequent source of a wife's misery and resentment, and hence of her husband's shame. But the house or flat itself is only one consideration. The social climate of the neighbourhood and the availability of schools often turn out to be of paramount importance to a mother and her children. Yet these are often difficult to estimate without living in the district first. Perhaps only a minority of mothers find themselves in an environment where they are deeply contented, and many fathers feel at least some burden of guilt.

Looking after a Mother

When he turns in towards intimate interplay with his family, a father is perhaps least prepared by his previous learning from other men. In the family he is first of all a husband, so that our earlier considerations about being in love and marriage still apply here. But with pregnancy and primary maternal preoccupation he is also called on to increase his vigilance when his wife has slackened hers. Just as she mothers the baby, so his *maternal* feelings arise around his wife. When a father fails to develop this, his wife is left alone. In an extended family she would probably have female relatives to turn to, but in our society there is likely to be no one to take her husband's place.

A mother needs to be *held* both physically and psychologically by her husband (Winnicott, 1965). The most frequent instances of this holding will probably not occur in fraught situations, but simply in day-to-day conversation when a mother wants a second opinion for her ideas about the children on routine matters. To a great extent, opinions will be gleaned from other women during the day. But when intimate and crucial questions arise, a husband will be wanted because he is expected to know the nuances of his family situation better than neighbours.

The most usual time for such second-opinion conversations is in the evening after children have gone to bed. Both husband and wife can then relax and off-load their feelings on to each other without hindrance. This is probably the primary reason for the convention of packing children off to bed at the beginning of an evening.

A husband's failure to hold his wife's urges and anxiety is a frequent cause of complaint. For instance, you will often hear such words as, 'Oh, him, no sooner is he home than he's out in the garden', 'When it suits him he'll be as sweet as pie to the children, but help me with them, never', 'He always lets me do what I want but I never know what he thinks about it all', or 'He doesn't know what I have to cope with, he just comes in and criticises'.

Fathers no doubt react to their wives' anxieties according to their own characteristic modes of defence, which have been built up over the years. Some husbands, for instance, tend to be scornful by nature. If they care about their wives, they will probably adopt a mode of chiding which can be gentle and helpful because it absorbs worries while being appreciative. But scorn can frequently be used as a defensive means of ridding the self of emotional involvement, at the same time as shattering a wife's self-esteem. The martinet husband and frightened mouse wife are not uncommon.

This is not the only way a husband may fail to hold his wife. A reverse pattern is quite common in the henpecked husband. Here he may be very attentive to his wife, but frightened and in awe of her. Hence, having no independent strength of his own, he fails to contain his wife's impulsiveness, which can then turn to anxiety. Such a henpecked husband is perhaps epitomised by the man who said with admiration in his voice, 'My wife and I are of one mind, hers'.

A Father in Direct Relation to His Children

Earlier in the chapter I described how a mother is called upon to keep in touch with her children through each stage of development. The same applies to a father, and if he fails in this he himself has lost something of the pleasure of fathering, whatever happens to the children. In early months he is unlikely to be as intimately involved as his wife because he is probably out all day. Likewise his children will not invest so much passion in him, but he is usually deeply wanted for his own particular style of living. As children grow older the relative importance of fathers and mothers evens out so that he may be more sought after than his wife. But if he has not been in tune with them from the beginning he will inevitably be ill at ease and something of a stranger. He and his children will have missed a very deep pleasure.

Earlier chapters stressed the importance of fathers to their children. Having two parents makes it easier for a child to integrate his ambivalent feelings. Quite early in life a father becomes important as a separate person in his own right. He is of a different gender from his wife, so that boys and girls find their own sexual identity both by watching father and mother together and by the subtle ways in which each parent separately relates to them. A father is also likely to be the representative of the outside world, while still being an intimate family person. Parents vary, but it is very often a father who explains and demonstrates the mechanics of the more distant world to children.

Modern urban society presents one particular problem with regard to this learning from fathers. Children rarely see what he actually does at work. In days gone by most children could be with him in the fields or in his workshop. Such an opportunity is now rare. Fathers disappear at 8 a.m. to do something incomprehensible until 5 or 6 p.m. A man can say he works in a bank, an office, or factory, but verbal reports are usually meaningless to a child. One has only to see a boy working on a farm with his father to recognise that an experience is lost in urban life. A farmer's son of 7 or 8 can go with his father, watch him and then do things with him, so that at a very early age he is actually doing useful work himself when on holiday or after school.

Children of a father who works in an office can watch and copy him only in his play, tinkering with the car or in the garden. They cannot experience his primary fathering function of working. It has been suggested that this gap in learning about father's work has contributed towards the devaluation of fathering in Western society (Danziger, 1970; Mitscherlich, 1969). What is more, these paternal models, however fully presented by adults, will be near to useless if a child feels personally unrecognised by his father. He will probably be so consumed with hurt anger at being unnoticed that he will be destroying the models his father presents, however useful they might be in principle. Thus a father needs to attune himself to his children and appreciate them just as a mother does.

Many men assume that they can safely ignore their children in early infancy, but I am convinced they are mistaken. A father who has mingled with his children from babyhood will not only have the pleasure of seeing their growth, but will also know them intimately in all their non-verbal idiosyncrasies. Only when he intuitively knows their modes of thought will be able to be a teacher when the time comes to import new knowledge. If he has not known them in their early days he will come to them as a relative foreigner, speaking a language which is unfamiliar and imposing disciplines which will seem arbitrary. This painful experience is often reported in clinical studies.

Just as mothers have difficulties at different stages of development because of the intrusion of their inner fantasies, so also do fathers. The avoidance of infancy just mentioned is one point. Another is reluctance to participate in toilet training. This probably matters little except that a mother can then rarely have time to herself.

Some fathers find discipline easy and provide a useful backstop for a harassed mother. Others find it nerve-racking and impossible to apply consistently. For instance, it is commonly reported that a father has identified himself with his children against their disciplinary mother, so that he has connived in undermining her authority.

Fathers, like mothers, often find themselves troubled by sexual fantasies about their children. They may enjoy cuddling and kissing their children until they are 2 or 3 years old. But after this they can shy off such shows of affection, particularly with their sons, often apparently because of fear of homosexual feelings.

These are generalised anxieties, but a father also has his own personal fantasies which attach themselves to his children, just as happens with a mother. When these are flexible and allow room for him to recognise his children as they really are, they give vividness to his children's life. However, when a particular system of fantasy remains entrenched, it can stunt the growth of a child or at least embitter him. Here are a few examples:

A father was brought up in a severe religious faith. After many rebellions he saw the light and became strictly religious himself. However, his ambivalent feelings about it seemed to get attached to his two sons. The elder was a lively and rather naughty boy, so that the father became convinced he had no good in him. The younger son, on the other hand, was seen as a shining light of innocent virtue. The two boys then reacted in character.

The elder espoused unconventional causes and became a militant atheist, taking every opportunity to torment his father, whom he loathed. The younger son was obedient and tied to his parents. He was quite talented as a musician but could only play church music. By his early twenties he had few friends of his own, and had never taken a girl out.

A girl bore a strong resemblance to her mother, who died when she was quite young. The father doted upon her, but seemed fixed upon the image of his dead wife. When she had grown into her teens he would still take her on his knee and say, 'Your mother will never be dead while you are alive'. As a woman she was often invaded by feelings of being like her dead mother, and was overcome with bouts of depression.

A father felt himself to be a failure just as his own father had been. He was determined that his son should escape this fate, so saw to it that he was well educated and encouraged him to choose a career that he would throw his heart into.

This itself created few difficulties, but the father also felt a failure with his wife, and encouraged his son to take his place with her, just as he did over careers. Thus he would ask the boy to mediate between him and his wife, and also to care for her in ways in which he had failed. The boy felt proud and triumphant, but also very disturbed. He remained tied to his parents for many years, at least in part because he felt guiltily responsible for both of them, and unable to leave them to their own devices.

These are just a few suggestive examples. Others may spring to the reader's mind.

Because his functions are very diverse and lack the consuming intensity of motherhood, it is rare that a man breaks down mentally complaining that he is unable to father his children. Our society at present seems to make it easier for a father to opt out of his responsibilities towards his children than it is for his wife. This means not only that a great burden tends to be placed on a mother, but also that many serious problems between fathers and children continue unrecognised.

Later in childhood, fathers have problems that are very similar to those of mothers about schooling, puberty and the rejection of their ways by adolescents. They are also called upon to let their children go, and not to infantilise them into their adulthood.

Mothering Functions in Being a Father

Earlier we noted that men probably get little information about the intimate personal aspects of family life from other men. We have also noticed that these intimacies are called for in the modern family perhaps more than at any time in the past. The young man will have had his first and most important experiences of intimacy from his own mother in infancy and after. He will have learnt about them literally at his mother's knee. For instance, a young father taking his baby out in a pram and chatting to him will have done it all before. He will in all likelihood have seen his mother doing it with him, and then have copied her when he was a toddler by trundling a trolley about with dolls or teddy bears inside. Boys, when young at least, identify just as strongly with their mothers as do girls. But, for boys, these identifications are with someone of the opposite sex and we have noted before how children are vehemently conscious of their sexual identity.

By the time they get to school age, boys are usually prone to reject the ways of their mother and sisters as 'cissy'. This is enshrined in our society, at least in later education and in the attitudes of men together.

We could summarise this by saying that there is a tendency to reject, or at least feel anxious about, cross-sex identifications. This seems to be particularly the case with boys and men. It is also noticeable in women when they are shy of doing things they feel are not in accord with their sex. Some women refuse to attempt to drive a car or mend a light fuse saying it is 'too masculine'. I am convinced that such prejudices in both men and women serve to do nothing but stultify their own and others lives. Bernard (1972) streses the same point. Such prejudiced people fail to discriminate between their sex, with its particular male or female harmonius functioning, and mere symbols of 'masculinity' or 'femininity'.

When a man comes to marriage and then fatherhood, many of the functions he learnt with and from his mother are called upon to be exercised to the full. In many ways it might be an advantage that he has had little education from other men about such matters in his youth. He can be free of indoctrination to make his own discoveries and find his own best modes of caring and intimacy. But it also means that he has little support from other men, so that he is lonely, ashamed and unsure when faced with personal or family problems.

What is more, cross-sex identification creates its own problems. A father can turn into something of an 'old woman'. He can fuss and care too exclusively, so that his wife is deprived of his male romanticism towards her. She is then likely to become depressed or disgruntled because her sexual femininity is left unappreciated.

Mothers and Fathers Together
Most of this chapter has been taken up with consideration of each parent separately relating to their children. But it has been noted earlier, particularly in discussion of the Oedipus complex, that children need to integrate their experiences of their two parents into a harmony in their minds. A child who experiences violent splits between his parents can feel very disturbed indeed. Not only does he fear for his home's security, but his internal representations of his parents will not marry or function together so that it is hard for him to use them.

Some parents seem to be so sensitive to this that they vow never to disagree in front of the children. It is probably a good rule not to indulge in rows in front of children because they are not only frightening but also confusing. But when the appearance of agreement is carried to the length of falsehood this creates its own confusion. For children are very sensitive to moods, weaving solitary fantasies about them if nothing is said. Open expression of disagreements, recognising the other party's point of view and phrased in terms that a child can understand, is more likely to calm a child out of his confusion than is forced appearance of solidarity.

Even more striking, in my experience, has been the neglect and hurt imposed on children by some parents who have continued a 'chronic love affair' with each other. By being only interested in utter devotion to each other, they often seem to set up a barrier of indifference to their children, who grow up hurt, bitter and with a deep feeling that they as people are a nuisance. Romantic love seems to be a pre-requisite in providing the impetus and stability to rear children today. But great lovers probably do not make good parents. Romantic love is necessary but not sufficient.

Parents Separating Out
Throughout marriage, with stresses at work, changes in home, bringing up children and getting older, both parents will have been torn in many different directions. Each will have been through many, at least minor, crises by the time the children are well into school age. By then a mother will have to find a new work identity for herself or, in all likelihood, wilt. A father on the other hand, with his work to the forefront throughout, will perhaps be differently stressed but have to change in his own particular way. Under such circumstances, it would seem mere chance if both still find easy harmony together. However devoted and kind a couple may be to each other it seems inevitable that, in certain ways at least, they must separate out to find their own identities.

As this need to separate out is largely a new cultural phenomenon, it must be lonely and distressing for everyone going through it, bringing with it enormous blunders and mistakes. At the beginning of such a crisis, even if a person recognises that it is happening, it is virtually impossible to know what the outcome is going to be and plan for it.

All sorts of permutations have been proposed as solutions. Naturally, with their children's welfare in mind, many parents who are not deeply antagonistic or too ambitious for themselves find a fruitful reconciliation which they do not regret. Because of the enormous stresses involved for all members of a family when it breaks up, I feel that such reconciliations are precious and most worth striving for. Parents who break up a family home often seem to ignore the time and leisure that they need with their children in order for to be happy themselves, quite apart from their children's needs. Psychoeconomics are as important in families as material economics.

However, there are not only many couples who do find life more fruitful after divorce, but there are probably more who can be seen to plod on in a sad, holy deadlock who might have been better off apart. Marital counselling and psychotherapy cannot yet be reckoned as the universal panacea for partners' differences in personal 'chemistry'.

With this in mind there are strong bodies of opinion that suggest that legal marriage for life should be replaced by more limited contracts between couples, with longer contracts being demanded when children are conceived. I myself feel that this merits serious consideration, and am doubtful of the value of any legally binding contract until children are planned and conceived. This book, however, cannot enter deeply into these considerations which are well argued elsewhere (Bernard, 1972).

Here it is important to note that, even when happy reconciliation is impossible, there are other alternatives to total divorce of the parents. Divorce has the apparent virtue of simplicity but is often catastrophic; one parent must leave the children so that he (or she) and they are depleted. The other parent is usually then overburdened with responsibilities and hence often deprived of other opportunities. What is more, divorce is often more apparent than real for, whether they like it or not, parents are still tied. Even if they have opted out of everything else, they are tied by guilt, for it is they who brought their children into the world.

Other alternatives involve finding ways for each parent singly to gain his own freedom in ways that are compatible with both parents having continuing, enjoyable contact with their children. This can only occur in an environment where the children are at home with friends of their own. Children find contact in a strange environment lonely for them. Some financially lucky parents manage this by having two homes close by; others live under the same roof while going their separate ways. Although there are many different combinations that can be considered, I have never known any that were not very painful, at least in the early stages. But it is surely better to work things out with care than to act on impulse ignoring vital issues however 'natural' or 'honest' it may seem.

When parents are trying to work out what to do and are worrying about the effect on their children, they might find this very oversimplified list of priorities for children useful.

(1) A child needs to be happy with his mother and see that she is enjoying herself.
(2) He needs to be happy with his father and see that he is enjoying himself.
(3) He needs to be happy with his friends in an environment he knows.
(4) He needs to see his parents enjoy themselves together.

Optimally all these require very frequent contact with both mother and father *in a familiar environment* until adolescence at least.

The fourth requirement, parents enjoying each other, seems the one that is most often intractably ruptured. It is my impression that *if the other three requirements are well met*, then it is sad for a child but need not be catastrophic. Unfortunately I can find no statistical studies to confirm or dispute this contention. There are many studies about the children of divorced parents but these do not usually differentiate the several ruptures which occur simultaneously in most total divorces. My list of priorities also suggests that under some circumstances it might be better for a child to enjoy being with each of his parents as separate con-tented people, than to be burdened with two stressed people who keep together unhappily for want of working out alternatives. Fundamentally it must be the responsibility of each parent to decide the way that seems best for themselves, their spouse and their children.

In summary, I have argued that separating out between husband and wife as children grow older is probably essential. But this can take place within a continuing marriage if humility and kindliness are valued.

FURTHER READING

1 Anthony, E. J. and Benedek, T. (eds.) (1970), *Parenthood. Its Psychology and Psycho-pathology*. A compendium of technical papers of varying quality and lucidity, many of them highly technical. But this is the only work I know that consistently identifies questions of parenting from the parents' point of view. The sections by Benedek are difficult but undoubtedly the most useful and interesting.
2 Bernard, J. (1972), *The Future of Marriage*. A provocative yet scholarly book by a sociologist. Of particular interest concerning husbands and wives 'separating out' and on women's identity crises.
3 Gavron, H. (1966), *The Captive Wife*. One of the books that first brought the plight of isolated mothers to attention. Gloomy but provocative.
4 Kelmer-Pringle, M. (1974), *The Needs of Children*. First mentioned in the chapters on childhood but can be referred to again from the parents' point of view.
5 Lidz, T. (1963), *The Family and Human Adaptation*. A short and little-known book, but a classic of its kind about the stress of family living.

Chapter 13

BEING ALONE

Maturity and the Capacity to be Alone

Bernard's observation that married women, mothers in particular, suffer disproportionate disturbances compared to their husbands, has already suggested to us that finding, keeping and being accepted for one's independent identity is crucial to well-being. Her argument also suggests that it is possibly even more important than ongoing sexual intimacy (Bernard, 1972).

Extending this beyond marriage, I have suggested that the *capacity to be alone* is very important for growth into maturity. Maturity seems to involve not only responsibility, but also uncomplaining and dispassionate reflectiveness about issues where one is nevertheless emotionally involved. In other words, the capacity to be alone is necessary for wisdom. Looking back over the course of a life from birth, we can detect a continuous ebb and flow between intimate intermingling with other people on the one hand, and self-contained, even solitary thought and action. A baby, in particular, usually spends hours alone, looking, listening, sorting things out and trying new ideas. Without such solitary exploration a person can be little more than a cypher, an echo of others. With it well established, he can return to the company of others with his own ideas to contribute. In continuing chronically alone, however, a person must remain withdrawn, creating limited ideas about his world. These stay untested and lack the richness and depth gained from intercourse with others. It seems that growth can only come through an interplay between sociability and solitude.

Winnicott (1965) noted this when he stressed the importance of a mother and child being alone together in the house going about their separate businesses. But apart from this, there seems to have been remarkably little interest either by psychoanalysts or more academic psychiatrists and psychologists in the value of solitude. This is probably because it cannot, of course, be observed in a consulting room, nor is it easy to carry out experiments about it. Likewise the social sciences, being concerned with socialisation, have not been very interested either.

Yet it is common knowledge that really original scientific and artistic work is generated largely in solitude. Moral and religious thinkers, too, have known of its necessity for thousands of years. Moses went up Mount Sinai to commune with God alone before bringing down the ten commandments. The Buddha meditated alone under the Bohdi Tree until his enlightenment, and Jesus went into the Wilderness before resolving upon his mission. So, both in the West and even more strongly in the East, there is a long tradition of meditation. Perhaps because of this moral tradition, aloneness has been largely neglected in the theories of scientifically minded psychologists. Those with a more existential approach to life have not neglected it in the same way, perhaps because of existentialism's roots in theology (Tillich, 1952). But existentialists tend to be regarded as quirky by the scientifically orthodox. Because solitude seems to be undervalued in many other writings I am going to stress, perhaps over-stress, it here.

The importance of self-appraisal in maturation has shown itself time and again throughout this book. A person needs to copy, listen to and learn from others, as well as experience his effects on others. But, when each new crisis arises and a person is called upon to find a new integrity of his thoughts and roles with others, he must not only loosen his habits but also turn inwards to dispassionate observation of himself in his multiplicity. Only then can he evaluate the variety of his ideas and form resolves which lead to a new identity. It is particularly important in youth when a person, at his best, is challenged to find his own personal conscience. But it is also necessary in each crisis throughout later life.

The ability to retreat into the self does not, of course, require the life of a hermit. Engrossment in solitude is lop-sided, a whole life-style is then devoted to one side only of the necessary to and fro between solitude and sociability. What really seems to be important is the ability to maintain one's solitary mode of thought in the presence of others, and to recall others' points of view when alone. Some people may find it helpful to go off alone for long periods of time to think, others can make do by maintaining their own way of thinking in the ordinary course of social life. The capacity to be alone is important, whether in the presence of others or not.

Aloneness is frightening to a great many people, for it easily moves from enjoyable freedom into painful loneliness. It seems that it is fear of loneliness that makes many people avoid like the plague the very solitude that is necessary for growth into integrity and its peace of mind.

Why should loneliness be so frightening? A lonely person cannot be assured of physical comfort or have bodily contact; this is enough to frighten some people. But more than this, he usually has few means of distraction from the insistence of his own imaginings. Fantasy wells up with nothing but the resources of his own mind to check it. No other person is present, so that those prone to find comfort by projection of their unwanted ideas into other people have only nothingness to act as a receptacle (M. Klein, 1952). What is more there is no checking of ideas by others. Then we are like Robinson Crusoe with only the hills to echo back our own cries. Not for nothing is solitary confinement deemed one of the worst of punishments. But also like Crusoe, it is only through being alone, looking inwards and outwards, that a person can be in a position to know what thoughts he contains, and hence move through to self-containment and the dignity of knowing that he can look after himself in a physical and also mental way.

Many people seem to avoid loneliness by taking to promiscuous sexuality; they perhaps use eroticism as an anti-depressant. Others avoid it by jumping from childhood dependency into marriage. If my argument is valid, their integrity is likely to be depleted by this. Certainly it is my impression that many people do in fact shrink into petty narrow-mindedness after years of marriage. This applies to men, I am sure, as much as women. Women may react with more overt signs of distress to the depletion, whereas men can perhaps more easily slip into complaisance. It could be said that some married couples become spoilt, in the same way as over-indulged children are spoilt as characters when they are not left to find their own way enough.

Apart from the chronic painful quarrelling and unkindness which must be the worst that marriage has to offer, this dullness highlights its most negative aspect. It may, perhaps, give some comfort to those who have never married. Let us consider this by a brief comparison of the two states.

Staying Single

A person who has not married has not only never known consistent adult sexual companionship, but he has never been through the labour (to use Arendt's term) of producing and rearing young. This is fundamentally biological and shared, in their way, by the lowest of animals. Most of those who have been through it will testify that it is very deeply satisfying indeed. However, if a person is really to enjoy rearing children, many other pursuits have to be limited; there is just neither the time nor money available for them all. A single person can have more leisure to devote himself deeply to wider social and cultural concerns.

There is still something of an unspoken prejudice amongst the married that relegates single people to the position of failed, second-class citizens. It is as if many people vaguely feel that single people have not only missed something vital in life, which they often have, but that there must also be something wrong or immature about them. This is surely not necessarily the case. Bernard, for instance, makes the point that it is often dependent and immature women, not the self-reliant and thoughtful ones who seem attractive to men because they present little threat to their egocentrisms.

What is more, when it comes to the general exercise and enjoyment of responsibility for human lives, it is an open question whether a single person must fall behind the married. For instance, a school teacher who has helped hundreds of children into adulthood has probably made more contribution to future lives than a parent who has had and reared one or two. Many deep enjoyments of parenthood can be enjoyed just as much by a spinster or bachelor as by mothers and fathers. A few centuries ago, particularly when the Catholic Church held sway, the celibate state was held in higher esteem than the married. Then, in north-west Europe at least, the pendulum swung the other way. Perhaps this social attitude is now beginning to melt, so that people will feel freer to choose the life that seems most fruitful to them without the fear of scorn if they wish to remain single.

As things stand, however, perhaps in the face of social attitudes that devalue them, some single people do seem to shrink in open mindedness as they grow older. I have no formal statistics to support this contention, but the single person's shrinkage often seems different from that of complaisant married people. Un-sexual bachelors easily seem to become prey to fussy impatience and mysogeny. They seem to identify their whole selves with an anti-sexual part of their consciences. Others, of a more philandering nature, seem often to protest too strongly about the pleasures of not being tied down in life. They seem to be seeking solace from loneliness and depression in sexual athleticism. Middle-aged spinsters are, of course, the subject of many myths. They are suspected of prudery and overvaluing senseless correctness. From this position, they can be subtly destructive in denigrating both men and mothers who do not meet up to their arbitrary rules of decency. My impression is that this is not just a myth; many spinsters do feel sexually and parentally very frustrated. Some seem to get over this disappointment by feeling superior and subtly denigrating other more libidinous people. However, some unmarried people openly recognise their loss and are, I think, the richer for it. These are people who command respect, for having learnt to stand their loneliness and to be self-sufficient they have a dignity which is very fully human.

They can, perhaps, also provide a model to married people. This is because, for a marriage to work over the years, each partner must proceed through several, if not many, life crises. These, as we have seen, must in essence be personal, private and hence solitary, however close a person is to his partner. If a marriage prevents the progress of these lonely crises it is doomed either to break or sink into emotional sterility. Happy marriages seem to rest on each partner maintaining his own integrity alone (as some spinsters or bachelors can) while allowing it also for his partner.

Only then is sharing what is fruitful together a freely enjoyable experience.

Therapeutic Conversations

This chapter has stressed the value for growth of the capacity to be alone. Periods of aloneness seem necessary for integration, especially in times of crisis. However, it has also been noted that withdrawal into the life of a hermit is hardly a solution; it seems to act as a defensive posture against anxiety when relating to other people. Yet compulsive sociability can also be a posture to avoid loneliness. If the arguments throughout the book have any validity, sterile defensive postures seem to be a bane of life. But we cannot rest content even with this conclusion. For I have argued in previous chapters that defensive avoidance of anxiety, confusion and pain seems to be necessary for conscious equanimity. However, they can easily become self-gratifying and sterile habits which impede development. For growth to take place, many old defensive postures have to be broken. In some crises this can, no doubt, be achieved largely by a person himself. However, because the postures are largely unconscious the intervention of another person, who is involved but dispassionate, is often necessary to break them.

A conversation which leads to the breaking of a sterile, defensive mental posture can be termed a therapeutic conversation. These can occur informally at any time between parents and children, husbands and wives, and between friends, colleagues or lovers. What is necessary is that the two or more people are sincere and trust each other. They must also be intuitively in tune with each other's ways of thinking and be aware of the issues involved. These are times of 'talking straight'.

Informal conversations such as these have, I am sure, been used throughout history in the resolution of critical personal problems. They provide the moments of *creative insight* which I stressed when discussing adolescence. However, defences may be so chronic that they escape the capabilities of ordinary sensitive conversation. For these eventualities, the disciplines of casework and the psychotherapies have been recently formed into bodies of professional expertise.

These professions have numerous and often conflicting viewpoints. But I would suggest that all, with varying degrees of success, aim towards the breaking of defensive postures and then usually attempt to provide a setting for a person to test out new patterns of thought and action in sympathetic company.

The behaviour therapist, for instance, takes trouble to diagnose a person's pathological habits (defensive postures) and then carries out retraining procedures to break these and establish more fruitful ones. There is much evidence to show that this works in many instances.

The psychoanalytic therapist, like myself, has a rather different approach. Here a person's spontaneous mental activity is regarded as of central importance. A person is thus left as free as possible, within limits set to prevent disturbance to other people, to say and feel what rises up in his mind. By listening to these thoughts the therapist hopes slowly to become aware of the person's sterile, repetitive postures of thought and behaviour. He usually notices that these seem to be *repetitions from child-hood* and of patterns which have continued on into adult life, distorting his perception of himself and the outside world. These repetitions are technically referred to as *transferences*. They are likely to affect much of waking life, but can also intimately be experienced in the actual therapeutic relationship. The therapist attempts to initiate a break in these repetitions by calling attention to their occurrence. Because the repetitions are usually encrusted by long usage, a person often finds these observations unpleasant and may defensively reject them as ridiculous. But even so, an opportunity has been provided whereby the fears that gave rise to the repeated defensive postures can be seen for what they are, often many years old and now invalid. This is an *insight therapy*. It is a long-term, systematic and disciplined extension of the informal therapeutic conver-sations which have probably been used throughout history.

Therapists of other disciplines argue that it is time-consuming, possible only for a favoured few and not necessarily effective in its results. Here I must rest content to agree that these arguments are partly true. There are many forms of therapy nowadays (very often stemming from psycho-analytic ideas) which, though accused of being rough and ready, often seem to be effective in helping people to grow out of old encrusted postures. However psychoanalysis is the oldest of the insight therapies and, through the many forms in which it is applied, is the most widely established. What is more, its practice has accumulated a pool of know-ledge about the internal conditions of human suffering and happiness which have not been known before in the history of mankind. For this, it is worthy of care and respect.

Chapter 14

MID-LIFE

Introduction
There is a noticeable sparsity of literature about the sequences of individual development in the adult years of life. Much has been written about childhood and adolescence, some about marriage and parenthood, but not a great deal else until old age. There is a voluminous literature of general adult psychology about work, through social attitudes and behaviour to studies of stress, and then vast libraries about psychopathology and psychiatry. But these cut sections across time and are not specifically concerned with the movement of internal events as a person goes through life. Perhaps, the sparsity in this area is due to the fact that in childhood it is possible to detect processes of development that are more or less common to all children of a certain age. However, in the adult years people change more idiosyncratically. There may be general sequences of development, as in childhood, but they must be spread out over many years as different people arrive at a stage at very different ages. Thus general patterns are hard to detect. But I do not think this should allow us to ignore the fact that each individual must go through highly personal, complex developments in the whole process of his life. We have seen something of this in parenthood; it must be true in other areas but we know little about it yet. There is, for instance, a small but growing literature on career development (Rapoport, 1970).

However, quite a lot is known about one aspect of development in later years: this centres upon a person's changing awareness of the *time he has got to live*. Let us consider this.

The Individual's Awareness of His Life Span
From infancy until death, each person has something of a sense of his own age relative to others around him. This has far-reaching ramifications. In early chapters I stressed the child's pervasive sense of smallness and incapacity. Later we noted the adolescent's sense of being at a threshold. In his twenties a person establishes himself as a contributor, but is also a learner and servant. In his thirties he usually wishes to be recognised

for his contributions, and is less ready to relate to others as a humble learner. He is also usually in the middle of being a parent. Throughout these years he may frequently look back, but is still predominantly looking forward to the future. Then, somewhere about the age of 40, he often begins to realise that life is half over for him. When a person looks equally back and forward, he is aware of middle age. We can detect various threads interweaving in his mind to give him his own particular experience of age. Few of these are very pleasant in themselves. There is the awareness of a younger generation who are thrusting forward and will be alive when he is dead. There is also recognition of physical ageing in his body organs. This deterioration is the basis of mid-life, as much as growth was in the earlier years. We shall not enter into details of its physiology, but it will be repeatedly mentioned in the following chapters (Bromley, 1966). Physical deterioration takes us to death. This sets the end-point of our existence. Hence *ideas about death set a boundary to the conception of oneself, and are central to the individual's sense of identity*. Such ideas are critical in mid-life, but have much earlier antecedents. Let us return to childhood for a moment and trace these.

Development of the Idea of Mortality

It was noted in earlier chapters that ideas about death arise very early in childhood. Certainly children of 3 and 4 openly express concern about dead things. Usually with puzzlement, awe and worry they will investigate and ask questions about dead animals and birds. They will similarly ask with anxiety about the death of relatives. The sequences of the discovery of death have been well documented, particularly by Anthony (1971).

The worried emotions children show suggest that they have some dim idea about the implications of death. It cannot be said that they understand what it is like to be dead, for no one knows this for certain. Yet a child feels deeply about dead things. What moves him to this? Remembering our earlier discussions about childhood depression, perhaps something of the following occurs.

A person, a child particularly, sees a dead thing and notices that something he expects to be active is not so. It is *non-responsive* in every way to its environment and within itself. Such an external perception perhaps echoes *inner experiences* of unresponsiveness, so that death is understood in terms of the individual's own inner feelings. Such inner experiences are frequent, as when one 'feels dead inside', 'cut-off', or ways of relating 'die on us'. I have mentioned the 'death' of relationships at separation on many occasions from infancy onward, and noted that they are usually accompanied by depressive feelings. These small deaths are painful but a natural part of living and give it depth and richness.

The small deaths that are continually taking place physically inside the body itself have not been mentioned. These occur acutely in illnesses of every kind which every child experiences. They also occur in the general wastages of the body cells. Thus every child has dim awarenesses of breaks in responsiveness, if not from splitting and repressed feelings about broken relationships then from the illnesses of his own body. It is my suggestion that anxieties about all these focus themselves into dread when a dead thing is perceived.

It might be argued that a child's dread is simply a social imitation of adults, and certainly they must reinforce it. But it is so spontaneous in children and arises so often when adults feel little anxiety themselves, that this seems an insufficient explanation.

Children's conscious personal worries about death are usually expressed in terms of fears about losing their parents or grandparents. For example:

People die at 70, you are 35, mummy. So you won't die for 70 take away 35 years, what's that? Thirty-five years, oh, I'll be 41 then. Granny is 65. Well, she won't die yet. (6-year-old girl)

Children have inevitably experienced fears of being left by their parents, so the most important idea of a death is the loss of these much-needed people.

The child's own death must usually seem such a long way off that it is most frequently disregarded or *denied*. However, quite young children do think about it. For example:

I don't think I want to be a soldier when I grow up, because I might get killed. (4-year-old boy)

Children who have nearly died are often preoccupied with worrying about their own mortality when still quite young. For example:

I was 7 when I was knocked down by a car and was unconscious for a week. I remember being preoccupied with ideas of my death through my school days. I had a pervasive feeling of living on borrowed time, as if I ought not to be alive. Soon after the accident we left the country where it happened, and it wasn't until I was 19 that I could return. When I did, one of the first things I urgently needed to do was to return to the crossroads where it had happened.

For children who have not had such close escapes themselves, it may be some years before personal awareness of death comes home to them. Even a child of 9 or 10 will readily be filled with fear that death could happen to him when a neighbourhood child dies or is killed. Such thoughts, though, are usually very quickly put aside.

When a young person comes into the teens, his capacity to deny his own mortality usually melts away considerably. This is an intrinsic part of the adolescent's growth of adult identity. The transition is usually gradual. An example of this could be seen in the Second World War. Children in their early teens or less were often blissfully unafraid of the bombing, at least as far as being killed themselves was concerned. The evidence for death was all around them but was denied. By the late teens young people were more often quite openly scared. For instance:

I myself remember being frightened of being killed in an abstract way during the war when I was 17. But when a bomber dived straight towards me, I remember staring at its black shape, and within a few seconds thought, 'This is going to hit us. Somebody is going to get killed. I might get hurt, but I am not going to die.' My capacity for denial was still working. Three years later exactly the same thing happened again, but this time I was very frightened and thought I was going to be killed. I suspect I was a late developer over this, but something of this transition happens to most people at some time or another.

Nowadays, when immediate death is not present and dying people are usually nursed in private, perhaps this recognition of mortality is more difficult to achieve. However, the question is evidently still present, for young people's songs and talk are often full of ideas about death.

Ideas about mortality come quicker to some than others. Certainly the immediate and personal experience of death is the most convincing teacher. Nurses, doctors, and soldiers in wartime probably mature in this way sooner than others. However, many adults keep up their denial of mortality even after many experiences of danger. The behaviour of some drivers on the roads shows us this by the way they place themselves in absurdly dangerous positions. Perhaps being encased in the familiar shell of their car fosters an illusion of invulnerability.

Even in a country at peace, the evidence for personal mortality is inexorably placed before the individual in his own dangers and the deaths of friends and relatives. By one's twenties and thirties the idea of personal death has usually taken firm root in the conception of oneself. As I have mentioned, this is an intrinsic component of a realistic sense of one's identity. In it the individual recognises that he is finite, and is a humble being like all others. It is frightening but refreshing, because a long-standing denial has been thrown off.

With the sense of mortality included in his awareness, an individual is often spurred to clarify the things he would like to do in his life, and also to divest himself of dreams that mean little to him or are impossible.

By the age of 40 or so, awareness of mortality develops into the sense that life is half over and there is not much time left. Naturally people vary in the quality and time of life of this recognition, but it is sufficiently widespread to be discussed as a general phenomenon in both men and women. It is at heart a *depressive* experience with much anxiety. This is because it is concerned with loss, not necessarily real losses but lost hopes. With a long future in front of him the young man can assuage the sense of his own failures with dreams of the future. But by his forties a person's contribution to adult life has been largely delimited by work and family. The future is restricted both by these and by the physical reality of an ageing body. The old methods of looking to the future to deny anxiety no longer suffice; a new equilibrium has to be found. This is the *mid-life crisis*. Let us consider men and women separately before finally drawing the threads together.

Middle Age in Men
Naturally the external pressures on a man in our society will depend largely on his work commitment. This has usually been fundamentally delimited when he was quite young. The situation of a man in mid-life will largely depend upon his work commitment when young. A young man who has found his identity in an occupation that involves fast physical co-ordination has little to look forward to in middle age unless he can develop to new functioning; he must change large areas of his identity. Such changes are inevitable for footballers, athletes, racing drivers, soldiers, sailors and airmen. The fast co-ordination upon which these depend deteriorates noticeably from the late twenties onwards.

Most young men who take up these careers are well aware that the centre of their lives must be transformed in their thirties or forties, and prepare themselves for a two-career life. The second career may grow out of the first, for instance a middle-aged team manager must have been a footballer first. It is not likely to be as glamorous a career as the first, for this glamour depends on physical articulation which is on the wane. In the transition from one career to another the individual must mourn the loss of his old skill, and at the same time find new investments. If later careers are self-satisfying, they are often essentially parental rather than glamorous in nature, using past experience to contribute to others. This can be seen, for instance, in management, organising or education.

On the whole, a person who has a highly developed intellect is less likely to be faced by such an acute career crisis as is the physical performer. Intellectual functions deteriorate more slowly than speed of body movement. However, the swift manipulation of concepts falls off in a way which is rather similar to that of physical dexterity. Thus where speed of thought counts, young men and women are at an advantage. For instance, mathematicians have usually done much of their original creative work by the age of 40. But where speed is less important than the balanced assimilation and organisation of large bodies of information, the individual probably does not reach his prime until he is 40 or more.

Men who have committed themselves to work that requires depth and breadth of experience may hardly start being independently productive until they are 40. The same applies to other less intellectual occupations which require steadiness of judgement. A racing driver, for instance, is old at 40, but a bus driver is least accident prone between 40 and 55.

Something rather similar happens in literature. Poets often blossom young and continue into old age. But many novelists and playwrights only reach mastery of their craft by middle age. One can detect development, for instance, in Shakespeare's style as he grew older. His later plays show much more flexibility and originality in the use of language than his earlier ones. Jaques (1970), in particular, has described these mid-life changes in creativity.

The vesting of authority in older people is not just an outworn quirk of our society. Balanced judgement must rest on the assimilation of relevant information. In many spheres this can be done when young, but in others it may take many years to amass. This is particularly so where knowledge of people is concerned, for this requires face-to-face interaction with many different individuals. Thus physicians, psychiatrists, social workers, administrators and statesmen probably only reach their prime in middle age.

On the other hand, older people easily slip into stereotyped thought behaviour. Young people are not only revolted by subjection to the rituals of the old but also have life in front of them and are ready to welcome change. Then in exasperation they challenge older people to the familiar generation wars. When this happens the older person, with his settled identity threatened, is only too ready to shrink into a shell of outworn habits.

Although the middle-aged person's slower body must play a part in such a tendency to conservatism, it is due more I think to emotional investment in old modes of thought. In them he seems to cling to the fantasy of the adult identity which he discovered in his youth, and in doing so he often denies doubts about its viability in changing times. That this is psychologically rather than physically based is suggested by the increasing number of people who are able to rebel from their old ways during the middle of their lives. It is not only married women who are fundamentally shifting their way of life as their children grow up. Mature male students also often find that they are keener learners than their younger fellows.

When learning anything with freedom and zest a person is humble and romantic. To do this it is necessary to regress and to allow childlike parts of the self to re-emerge. It is a small crisis. An older person often finds this frightening and humiliating, for his self-esteem has developed out of the things he has mastered and he need no longer feel childlike. When an older person can loosen himself and still show this eagerness and use it, he seems to take on an ageless quality. It is as noticeable in some very old people as it is in the young. People having this facility seem to find little difficulty in communicating with any generation. When an older person has kept the child alive in himself, he can not only empathise with younger people but also learns from them, and in this way is also naturally acceptable.

Middle Age in Women

Some of the main problems of middle age for women have already been discussed in Chapter 12 on parenthood. I have already stressed the plight of mothers who, having engrossed themselves in their families, find themselves, with much life ahead of them, largely unneeded by their children and financially subservient to their husbands. I have also noted that, whereas many women find this pleasant with plenty to do, others find it deeply unsatisfactory and strive for a new work identity and hence a changed relationship with their husbands.

Compounding this crisis is the menopause, though I think the identity crisis usually comes before it. For a long time the menopause has been considered a critical period for emotional disturbance. Its marked hormonal disturbances often evoke very distressing physical symptoms. More than this it marks the end of a woman's childbearing, and impresses on her, perhaps more forcibly than on a man, that her life is irreversible and finite.

It is my impression, unsubstantiated by statistics, that many of the disturbances ascribed to the menopause are also symptoms of the older woman's identity crisis. For instance, many women have pointed out that having enjoyed bringing up children and then having found the enjoyment of a new identity, the menopause is not particularly depressing; it is even a relief as there is no need to worry about getting pregnant any more. What is more sexual life need not end with the menopause; although known for centuries, this is a new discovery for many women. Naturally this affects men too, for husbands often readily slip away from sex if their wives have gone off it. When this happens a man's virility seems no longer to be centred on his penis; he often seems to turn paunchy, taking on rather old-womanish characteristics. Women also seem to lose the centredness of sexuality in their genitals. When this happens they often develop rather heavy, even mannish 'battleship' features. The sight of other men and women of the same age maintaining their youthful vigour suggests that this disintegration of sexual centredness is not a biological necessity but rather a psychological phenomenon.

Women who are particularly disturbed by 'the change' seem often to be those who have not found their way to conceiving of anything else to do except rear children. They are dissatisfied and frightened of the future. This is an identity crisis, not just the menopause.

However, another group of women who do more directly feel deeply depressed about the menopause are those who have never had children. To them it is a time of real loss of biological fulfilment and sadness. It is not the same, either socially or psychodynamically, as the identity crisis just mentioned.

Let me end this particular discussion with a word of warning. I have tended here to stress the importance of the identity crisis rather than the menopause itself. Even though the identity crisis is not necessarily intimately tied to the change of life it is still fundamentally linked to biological ageing. It is part of the endless cycle of life and death. What is more my argument in understressing the menopause may seem to encourage the attitude that it does not matter. Quite a lot of people brush the menopause aside denying the underlying feelings they have. I think that it probably affects every woman and always has a depressive note of loss to it which it is best to recognise. My main argument suggests that if recognised it is sad but can also herald new freedoms.

Middle-aged Parents and Their Children

The dramatic problems experienced by parents with their adolescent children have often been noted by psychiatrists and others. I suggested during the discussion of adolescence that parents themselves often seemed to need to go through a reworking of their own adolescent questions, in order to break their old preconceptions and find their own beliefs rather than parroting outworn ones.

Not only are middle-aged parents' beliefs explicitly challenged by younger people, but they also have many distresses of their own which are aroused by their children's youth. Parents' envy of their children's vitality is one. This often seems to arise when a parent feels he was cheated out of a full adolescence himself, and then resents it in his children. This can be compounded by the menopause where a mother becomes preoccupied by waning and not having a second chance. Less often mentioned but equally insistent is the converse of this envy. I have noted how often parents seem to be tied to their children in a depressed way. They are not so much clinging to or envious of their children, but rather preoccupied because they feel, realistically or not, that they failed to give something which was vital to their children's upbringing, and their children will be incomplete without it. This is often most painfully felt by parents of handicapped or disturbed young people. They feel they have not completed their job properly. Sometimes this is clearly a neurotic fantasy, but for parents of handicapped children it is a very real worry. They often can never have the satisfaction of letting a child go with the assurance that he will manage on his own. Detailed discussion of this is outside our province here, but the question does highlight that it is not only children who want to grow up and away from their parents. Parents, when they are enjoying themselves, are also really glad for their children to grow away from them. Not only has a burden been lifted, but they have the pleasure of seeing that they have done a job well enough.

The Mid-Life Crisis

This is a term in general currency given to those crises which, in at least an underlying way, arise from a person's awarness of the ageing of his body and of the passing of half his life. It has been particularly stressed by Erikson (1963) and Caplan (1964); a very searching description is given by Jaques (1970).

It is stressed by these writers that mid-life is at root a normal crisis arising out of the inevitable ageing of the body and the recognition of the growth of a younger generation. This awareness may be defended against, but change in old ways of life must occur for better or for worse sooner or later. As in any crisis, chronic pathology does not arise simply because inevitable anxiety or depression occurs. Rather, pathology arises either when a person frantically clings to old patterns of thought and behaviour which are no longer viable, or, having given these up, he can find nothing new to take their place and sinks into regressed despair.

The crisis is essentially concerned with the experience of *loss*: loss of hopes, loss of old, enjoyable capacities and loss of capacity to procreate. Its progress is thus marked by *mourning* and its resolution is found in *renunciation* and finding *sadness*. Feelings about death are never far away. This is partly because it is stirred in the first place by recognition of one's own future death, but also because it concerns the death of old hopes and pleasures. These in themselves rearouse unconscious, primitive childhood experiences of loss and distress. With these come fears of the shattering of the self (as described in Chapter 4), which is a dreaded 'death of the self'. Fundamentally it must assail both men and women but, as we have seen, owing to differing physiology and social pressures, the timing and forms it takes tend to be different for both sexes.

Jaques has pointed out that it is essentially a *normal depressive* crisis, whereas adolescence is a *normal schizoid* one. He makes this differentiation to highlight that mid-life is a crisis of *loss*. In adolescence, losses occur but they are not the essence, rather it is a crisis of *finding* an adult integrity of the self. Because differentiation of the self is at its essence, with the psychotic anxieties that this entails, it is called schizoid.

However, although this fundamental distinction is, I think, unassailable, we should also remember that the mid-life crisis can involve finding, partially at least, a new identity. This is particularly so for many women at the present time. In which case, many features of what is often thought of as adolescing occur in mid-life.

It is for this reason that I stressed adolescence as a model for future crises and argued that adolescing does not necessarily finish for good in the early twenties. Many aspects must be reworked as new identities are found.

Jaques has also pointed out that mid-life is not simply a time of loss and renunciation but rather of change. In creative people this can be seen as a movement of style from the lyrical one of early adulthood, through tragedy, to the more serene and rounded one which characterises later life. An examination of art and literature shows how often this is borne out. At the same time, mid-life, being a time when many people are particularly aware of tragedy, is also one of urgency. Desires which have hitherto been vague must be brought to fruition. Thus middle and later life may be a time of great creative energy and sense of purpose.

It is a common assumption that the impatient innovators of change are all young. This may be true when considering people in the mass. But the organising centres of innovation and change, either socially or in ideas, are very frequently individuals in their later life. Taking extreme examples, the major political revolutionaries of history have mostly been middle-aged at the time of their fruition. Lenin is a case in point. Britain's major revolutionary organiser, Oliver Cromwell, is another outstanding example. He was probably fired with Nonconformist zeal as a boy by his schoolmaster. But it was not until he was in his late twenties that he became deeply committed to religious puritanism. In his thirties he became politically active, and he was over 40 before he moulded himself into a military leader and vital political organiser.

A more peaceful but poignant example of the recognition of mortality as a spur to self-organisation can be seen in Guiseppe di Lampedusa. He was an Italian nobleman who, though well known as an intellectual, wrote nothing of great note until his late sixties when he was told that he was incurably ill. Spurred on by this news he set about writing a novel which had been planned for many years. *The Leopard* was published after his death, and was immediately recognised as a modern classic.

FURTHER READING

1 Anthony, S. (1971), *The Discovery of Death in Childhood and After.* Just as its title describes; interesting even enjoyable reading.
2 Bromley, D. B. (1966), *The Psychology of Human Ageing.* A summary of research findings about the ageing process from mid-life onwards.
3 Caplan, G. (1964), *Principles of Preventive Psychiatry.* Probably the original work which expounded the concept of crisis, in mid-life and in other phases.
4 Jaques, E. (1970), *Work Creativity and Social Justice.* Of particular note for his essay 'Death and the mid-life crisis'. Its language is psychoanalytic, but easy reading and a classic of its kind.
5 Malleson, J. (1948), *Change of Life.* Perhaps a bit old-fashioned but still a straightforward introduction to problems of the menopause.
6 Neugarten, B. C. (1968), *Middle Age and Ageing.* A technical, psychodynamically oriented study on the subject, but of general interest.

Chapter 15

OLD AGE

Respect for the Old

In a static society we might expect the old to be respected. Having lived longest, they can act as the most assured carriers of techniques and beliefs which may be passed on virtually unchanged from one generation to the next. This reverence for the old certainly occurs in many societies, especially if they have both tight family organisations needing an old person's authority, and a plentiful food supply for those who are too old to be producers themselves. However, where food is scarce and living conditions are hard as, for instance, with the Eskimo, the old become a burden upon the young and may expect to be discarded.

The conditions of our society seem to bear some resemblance to both these forms. With a prolonged expectation of life and a highly developed economy, a large proportion of the population is aged and apparently unproductive, yet can be supported. At the same time, old people are not seen as essential carriers of culture. Their contributions are indeterminate, so that very many of them have the appearance of being useless and unwanted.

The ageing person is presented with threats to his well-being from two directions, firstly from the deterioration of his bodily functions and secondly from social expectations that he will become useless on account of his age, irrespective of his real capacities. Many people are compulsorily retired at a fixed age, not just for their own benefit but more so that the younger generations can step into their shoes. There are also vague but widely influential attitudes which match this compulsory retirement; for instance, an old person's ideas tend to be dismissed as old-fashioned simply because they come from an aged mind. He may be physically cared for, but is not reverenced and frequently not even respected.

The Crisis of Retirement

Just as middle age was perhaps epitomised by withdrawal from intimate parenthood, so, for many people, old age is marked by retirement from money-earning work. This is another crisis of life. New integrations of functions must develop for life to continue fruitfully and in contentment. Retirement from work is only one facet of ageing, but it is clear-cut and easy to recognise. Similar, smaller retirements and withdrawals are occurring throughout old age, and likewise call for internal development and reorganisation. I shall stress retirement from work here simply because it epitomises much about this time of life.

A wage-earning man or woman's identity or sense of self will have been largely oriented around working capacity. He may or may not have invested much of himself and his imagination in it, but will inevitably know himself by the work he does. With retirement this identity is taken away from him. So also is a good part of his income. Here are a few examples of how this crisis is managed.

Mr H said he had mixed feelings when retirement was approached. He looked forward to not having to work, but wondered what he was going to do with himself. His wife said she did not want him hanging around the house all the time. On the actual day, he went to work as usual and wished his friends good-bye at the end of it. They settled down to being pensioners. The greatest readjustment was living on a reduced income, but the first ten years proved to be happy. They were both healthy. Mr H took an allotment, so they never had to buy vegetables. They lived close to their children and helped to look after the grandchildren. In the summer Mr H returned to work part-time, but in the winter they could relax with their friends and social activities.

Mr I says he enjoyed every minute of his life as a mechanic. But he looked forward to retirement and, although offered a number of part-time jobs, turned them all down because he felt he needed a complete break. During the first months Mr and Mrs I had a series of holidays visiting children and grandchildren and two weeks away on their own.

After this Mr I turned into a Jack of all trades. He moved around on a bicycle doing gardening, decorating and small repair jobs. His evenings were taken up with committee work. His health was good, but he noticed that there was not so much spring in his legs, and now needed a rest after two or three hours' work. His memory was also not so good, and it took a little longer to think things out. He might not do as much as he used to, but the quality of his work remained satisfyingly high. He also had a freedom which was denied him when in employment.

In contrast here are two other people who did not develop new patterns of living and despair set in.

Mrs F went on working in a pub until she was over 70, when she slipped and bruised herself one day. She lost her job through being off sick. She recovered quite quickly, but never went back to work. Her husband remained lively and full of jokes, but she slowly became quiet and apathetic. She complained of aches and pains, but managed the house-work and cooking. Then she began to lose weight and looked drawn, gave up doing her hair or using make-up. She usually shuffled about the house in boots and several layers of clothing.

Mr G had been a pig farmer for most of his life. He never gave a thought to retiring. By the time he was over 70 there was a noticeable deteriora-tion in the farm. Roofs were leaking and fences broken. Mrs G realised her husband could no longer keep up, and suggested he employ a farm-hand. But he was too stubborn to admit his declining abilities and would not listen to his wife. Finally he became acutely ill and was taken to hospital, where he was overcome by despair as he lay in bed. For many years he had dreamt of his family buying up the land around and continuing in his traditions of farming. But he had no sons, and his daughters had all married townsmen.

When he dies he will be the last of a long line of farmers.

What functions come into play in this crisis? We have already noted the losses from physical deterioration and attendant depressive feelings. As with any loss, this usually sets in train a process of *mourning*. Here fear, rage and regret may be followed by finding substitute satisfactions and then peaceful sadness at the change.

On the positive side, the crisis involves finding new investments. One particular psychological quality seems to be important here. We saw how children approach new activities with awe and enthusiastic roman-ticism. If a person has kept this childlike quality as part of his function-ing identity, he is likely to be able to use it even late in life to discover and develop new investments.

However, such internal changes as these at the crisis of old age can only take place when the external social situation presents opportunities for new investment. For instance, Mr I the mechanic lived in a fairly built-up area, so that his leaning towards becoming a general handyman met a local need. Mr G the pig farmer, on the other hand, could not have turned to this even if he had wanted to, because there were few houses in his rural neighbourhood.

The enjoyment of old age seems to rest, as it does throughout life, upon fusing the satisfaction of personal, selfish urges with contributions to others. The environment delimits both of those aspects as much as does an individual's psychological character.

A great pleasure of old age is that few responsibilities are now expected of a person, and self-centred pursuits can be enjoyed without recrimina-tion. This absolution from guilt must lie at the heart of many old people's enjoyment of their lives, which seem sparse in other ways. Perhaps the most common handicaps to this carefreeness are lack of money and health, or fear of this lack in the future. Anyone acquainted with old people will have encountered real poverty as well as ill health.

Just as vital to many individuals, especially in early old age, is the desire to continue contributing to others. Our present social situation is such that although people are tending to lead longer lives, they still have single careers, so that the last quarter-century of a life may be economically unfertile. This is perhaps slowly being recognised, and agencies for employment in part-time work are being set up. Perhaps in the future a life of several different careers, each attuned to age, will become a normal part of our social order. I am personally sceptical that this will come easily as so many vested interests conspire to have the old out of the way.

The break up of extended families living in close proximity to relations has lessened the opportunity for old people to help in child rearing. But this does not mean that the need for such help has disappeared. It is a great strain for a mother to bring up children without assistance either from grandparents or other help. A mother who has no grandparents or aunts to fall back on when needed is often chronically worried about exhaustion or illness. The illustrations given earlier in this chapter show how both old men and women may turn to being auxiliary parents. It is often noticeable that particularly affectionate bonds grow up between children and their grandparents. Grandparents are not burdened with the parents' anxiety and responsibility, so that they can be both more patient and have more time to relax and play in a childlike way with children. Communication and a sense of equality often grows between the old and young which makes them very fond of each other.

Many other activities readily spring to mind to which old people may contribute. I have already mentioned paid work, odd jobs and committee organisation. The more subtle functions arising from ordinary informal conversations seem none the less important. For instance, old people are the living *historians* of a society. By personal reminiscence they tell younger people how things were in the past, both in their own lives and those of their parents and grandparents. Thus their span of personal memory may bridge a century or more. The young individual may not be called upon to copy their ways as in a traditional society, but historical conversations help to impress the reality of his place in time. He is made aware that he has grown out of people before him, and that others will come and take over from him in turn.

More generally, an old person, having experienced many things and being close to death, can often express himself about living with a cool, dispassionate clarity devoid of the grandiose illusions and denials to which younger people are prone. With this natural wisdom they can broaden our minds and make us humble.

Depression and Ageing

The common feature of ageing is, of course, shrinkage of body functions. Cell tissue is not replaced as in youth, so that hair thins, skin and muscles lose their vibrance, blood circulation malfunctions and brain cells die. In the last chapter we discussed how, from childhood onwards, there is an impact upon awareness when body parts become diseased. With ageing 'small deaths' become widespread, and moods of depression arise; this happens at any time of life whenever there is a loss of enjoyable functioning. With old age there is less opportunity than before to hope for the future, so that a valuable defence against depression is no longer effective. Coupled with physical deterioration comes the loss of friends and loved ones who will also be ageing and dying, and this also brings depression.

Many individuals accept the shrinkage of their lives with resigned equanimity. Perhaps one factor in this is that loss of vitality can act as a release from guilt. The inner commands of 'ought, must and should' may lose their grip now that it is no longer physically possible to carry them out. The old person is in the position to relax into unambitious contentment. Perhaps those people who have been forced on many previous occasions to accept their fate in a passive way find this contentment of old age most easily. On the other hand, those who have characteristically dealt with uncertainty by self-assertive activity may feel the losses of age more acutely. But no matter how it is received, ageing seems to be inevitably attended by deep and widespread depressive feelings. These can vary from utter misery to quiet peacefulness. It may sound strange to refer to depressive feelings as peaceful. However it is well recognised that, after the first depressed pain of the experience of a loss, acceptance can lead to a dignified sense of peace.

Persecutory and Paranoid Feelings in Old Age

Physical deterioration means that there is a concomitant depletion in ego-functioning and shrinkage of the sense of self. The individual feels smaller and more helpless, so that the outside world is consequently larger and less controllable. Events in the external world tend to be experienced passively, and hence may become more persecutory and threatening. This is manifest in an old person's natural fears of roads, trains, and whirl and bustle generally.

As ego-functioning and the sense of self tend to shrink, so we would expect primitive, less integrated patterns of thought and feeling to emerge. This regression is manifest not only in an old person's generalised fearfulness, but also in his tendencies to use projective mechanisms. In the prime of life, these are often held in check or elaborately covered by rationalizations. With ageing, these defences often fall away so that projections emerge more nakedly. This is most evident in senility.

But even a person in full command of his faculties can slowly subside into paranoid cantankerousness. For instance:

A widow had had a very active life. She reared a large family, and was also respected throughout her town for being generally interested in people and helpful. As her body slowed up, so she began to become bitter and suspicious. The first sign was an argument with neighbours over a dilapidated fence. This grew into bitter resentment, which spread to anger at all the people she had helped in the past and who now seemed callous towards her. She would, however, let no one near her to help, because she was convinced that they would make matters worse. Perhaps when young this woman had overcome her passive feelings of being helpless and uncared for by developing a very active and helping character. When this activity was no longer possible, her sense of persecution and helplessness emerged and consumed her whole attitude to life.

Another instance of projection is commonly seen with regard to awareness of physical deterioration. Thus the sense of body malfunctioning, 'little deaths' as I have called it, is often projected on to the external world, so that dreadful things are felt to be happening outside rather than inside the individual. For instance:

An old countryman was looking at the thatched roof of a cottage and said, 'That thatch is good for another ten years. I'm 80 and never had a day of illness in my life, but the thatch will outlive me, no doubt.' He then lapsed into projection and said, 'But then such terrible things are happening in the world now that it will all be over for everyone on this earth before then, that's for sure.'

Such collapses into awareness of persecution are common but not universal. They are most marked when physical functions have deteriorated and little activity is possible. There is much more to old age than this, but we have discussed deterioration, depression and persecutory anxiety because these are underlying background feelings in ageing. They have to be dealt with by every individual as he grows older, however fit and active he may be.

Dependency upon Others

We have so far been considering the position of old people who still retain their vigour. So long as a person can think and move, he maintains his independence of judgement and hence his individuality. But the progress of shrinkage is inevitable, and the old person has to sink into dependence upon others. This must be painful for all concerned and is often bitterly resisted.

Dependence provides the ground for neurotic satisfactions for both old and young. This is often evident between old parents and their children. For instance, an old person losing his independence of action can gain malicious pleasure in being a ruthless baby who will never be satisfied. The impulse to behave in infantile ways may have been grudgingly held in check for many decades from the days of the old person's own childhood, and only now given vent. The younger person, on the other hand, may take pleasure in holding a parent helplessly at his mercy. Perhaps, having felt subservient all his life so far, he can only now both wreak revenge and also appear virtuous in taking up a succouring stance. There are many other ruthless games played between old and young. No doubt fantasies like these play through the minds of everyone. However, they only become ruthless or neurotic when fantasy invades and blots out each person's recognition of the other's individuality. It may also be noted that such games are not confined to parent–child relationships. They are readily detectable in some professionals working with the aged.

Where mutual recognition of each other's dignity is maintained, underlying fantasies will inevitably still be active. But they will be held in check and used as a spur to activity rather than being a dominating force. When this occurs, care of the aged may still be painful and sad but also deeply rewarding, for both old and young are together close to the elements of life and death.

Senility

The progression into muscular incapacity is deeply depressing, but deterioration of brain function is perhaps worse because communication then becomes transient and difficult. With brain deterioration the usual modes of conversation disappear, so that helpers are left embarrassed and confused. With the lapse of highly integrated thought process, more primitive mental functions emerge unfettered. In particular, the paranoid projective mechanisms mentioned earlier in the chapter often dominate a senile person's thoughts and speech. These are often directed at helpers who can be made to feel hurt and confused.

Bitter paranoia does not occur with every senile person, but all seem to revert to primitive modes of symbolic thought and communication. This regression is disturbing to helpers who are naturally attuned to ordinary objective speech. The primitive symbolism of a senile person can often, however, be deciphered by a listener. When this is achieved, the contact between him and the old person can be very moving for both.

The code of this primitive symbolism is like that of dreaming, and can be roughly described as one where generalised abstract ideas are expressed in terms of specific body functions, and conversely body functions are expressed in terms of generalised or external events. If a listener knows the old person well he can often carry out the necessary translation, so that he understands what is being said.

Here is an example of an abstract idea being expressed in terms of body functions.

An old man was clouded and wandering in his mind. His son came to ask for his signature for a power of attorney to manage affairs, and was worried whether his father would understand and comply. The old man seemed to wander off to another subject when he said, 'I must now climb up on to your shoulders. I hope I won't be too heavy.' The son, realising what he meant, said, 'Oh no, everything is in order and we shall be able to manage things quite well', and then handed him the pen and paper. The father signed it and with a sigh said, 'That's much more comfortable now, but then you always were a broad-shouldered boy'.

Here is an example of a body function being expressed in terms of an external event.

An old woman was found crawling in the corridor whimpering, 'There has been an earthquake'. The nurse looked and found that she had soiled herself.

We can see here how external and internal reality have become confused, as may happen to all of us when waking up from a dream, or like a person in psychosis. A young baby has also probably not yet made the differentiation between self and external reality. Such differentiation is one great task of early childhood. In adult life we use our inner fantasy to feed our creative imagination in relation to the outside world. Then with senility the differentiation breaks down, and we can communicate only through concrete symbolic language. Perhaps as people become more sensitive to primitive symbolic communications, the loneliness of old and senile people will be somewhat alleviated.

FURTHER READING

1 Bromley, D. B. (1966), *The Psychology of Human Ageing*. A summary of research findings.
2 Chown, S. W. (ed.) (1972), *Human Ageing*. A series of research articles on ageing.
3 Neugarten, B. C. (1968), *Middle Age and Ageing*. A psychodynamic approach; technical but readable.
4 Townsend, P. (1963), *The Family Life of Old People*. Perhaps a classic text, this is a warm and sensitive description of old peoples' lives by a sociologist, but deserves being read by people of any discipline.
5 Zinberg, N. (ed.) (1963), *The Normal Psychology of the Ageing Process*. A series of technical articles exploring this subject; not difficult reading.

Chapter 16

DYING, GRIEF AND MOURNING

Industrial society has may be enhanced the possibilities of individuality, but a price has been paid in loneliness, particularly for the mother of young children and in old age. Dying, too, tends to be hidden and often solitary. Gorer (1965), among others, has amply demonstrated this.

In close-knit communities we would expect a dying person to be surrounded by people who know him; death would then be a public, shared event in living. In some rural areas of Britain, this is still not uncommon. Many local people may help in nursing, and it is often assumed that after death any acquaintance old or young can pay their last respects to the body laid out in a bedroom or the parlour. In areas of mobility such public intimacy is most unlikely; it is unthinkable for the inhabitants of a suburban road to crowd in to see a body, for most would be strangers. What is more, modern medicine means that many people die in hospital, often alone except for the staff. Sudnow (1967) has shown that within a hospital the staff themselves develop social ways of coping with death, which often continues the isolation of the dying person.

Death is frightening from childhood onwards and taboos grow to keep the anxiety at bay. In Britain, these taboos, in the recent past at least, seem to have been directed at hiding death away to allow the living to deny its omnipresence. Younger people then have little direct experience of real death and the personal humility it can bring. The old and dying for their part tend to be left isolated and alone. Thanks largely to the work of such writers as Hinton (1967), Gorer (1965), Kubler-Ross (1970) and Saunders (1959) perhaps this taboo is beginning to melt, how far I cannot say.

Terminal Illness
Here is a description of the last weeks of an old man. He was very much of an individual, so his way of growing old and dying was his own, but many of the features are common to others' experiences. (He was not known to me, and I am indebted to Barry Palmer for the description.)

For four years Mr J had been partially paralysed and was unable to move outside his home except in a wheelchair. Even so, although 87 years old, he was very alert and able to converse on many subjects through his daily reading. His favourite topic of conversation was, nevertheless, his past career as a soldier. He was very proud of being an active man.

He had steadily deteriorated in physical health, and on many occasions it was thought that he might die. But he was never willing to admit that his health was declining and, when asked how he was, would say that he was better, and even demonstrate this by getting out of his chair and walking across the room. Each step might take upwards of ten seconds, but it would satisfy him that he had convinced the onlookers that he was not dead yet. His will to live was extraordinarily great. Mr J was afraid of being forcibly admitted to hospital. On many occasions it was advisable for the sake of his wife's health that he should leave home for a couple of weeks. He refused on every occasion, and one felt that this was because he had the fear that entry to hospital would be the end of him. On one occasion his wife had to go into hospital, and in spite of the fact that he was most uncomfortable and not properly cared for, he would not leave the house. Mr J was always conscious of death. He was very fond of his children, but if they called without warning he would get very heated and suggest that they had been sent for. I do not know whether he was afraid of death, but he was of losing command of his life situation. It was always clear that he wished to be the boss of the house and in command of every aspect of his life. The thought of losing his independence, which he had largely done but would not admit, was very apparent.

Three weeks before he died Mr J was walking to the toilet when he began to slip, and eventually sat helplessly on the floor. Normally he would claim that he was all right, though someone would have to help him to his feet. On this occasion he said, 'Joan, I'm going'. He did not say much more, except that he wanted to see his children. From this point on he was no longer the man who wished to appear in command, but allowed himself to be cared for. A few days later, having seen his children, he became unconscious much of the time. The one thing which differed from his former collapse was that, though it appeared much the same to the onlookers, he knew that this time he was going to die.

This was one man's way of dying. Although there have been countless millions of deaths in human history most of us really know very little of what it is like. Only recently has it been carefully studied and systematic understanding begun. This is not surprising because, apart from our fears that make us shy away, it is very private, mostly silent and alone, for dying people are not much given to talk. It is perhaps only nurses, even more than doctors, who have a wide experience of the last weeks of life.

There is even physiological doubt about when an organism can be said to be dead. Some argue that absence of cerebral activity is decisive, others that absence of pulse and heartbeat is, but for our practical purposes this is an academic question. What happens just before death and after it does concern us. In traumatic instances death, of course, may be instantaneous. But in other cases a terminal phase can usually be recognised. It may last only a few hours in, say, a coronary thrombosis or be drawn out over weeks and months in slow-working diseases like cancer.

The terminal phase has begun when a disease or deterioration of tissue has such a hold that it is irreversible. Those around may not be aware of this, but there is some evidence that the grip of the lethal process is signalled to the mind of the dying person. For instance, it has been noted that the quality of dream imagery changes. We know little about this as yet, however Hinton is convincing when he suggests that dying people are usually fundamentally aware of their dying, even though it may be dim and often denied.

Pain is frequently a person's greatest dread. Many dying people do experience chronic pain and as a direct result comes exhaustion and often deep depression. Pain is often made more acute by anxiety. Perhaps because of this the old tend to feel less pain than younger people. A younger person is less prepared for death, has more to lose and often is distraught about dependents left behind and life-work uncompleted. Nurses often say that the most harrowing experiences are caring for young children and parents of young children who are dying.

Almost as dreadful as pain is chronic discomfort and immobility, this, too, is terribly depressing. So also is guilt and shame at being a nuisance and incontinent in front of others.

These are probably all at their worst in the earlier stages of terminal illness when a person is still very aware of other people and attached to them. During this time there often seem to be many memories to be relived and settled in the mind. So also are there bonds of affection to things and people to bid good-bye to. This is rarely done explicitly in an orderly manner, but it can be often seen and heard happening none the less. Then, perhaps a day or so before the end, maybe longer, a person seems often to release his interest in those around him. He withdraws into himself; he may talk a bit to those around, but they do not matter to him much any more and he seems to be waiting to let death take him. He may become unconscious, but even if this does not happen a subtle change takes place so that those around usually recognise that death is very close.

The above description gives the impression of a natural sequence: the loosening of bonds, mourning, getting things in order both externally and internally. Then come farewells, if only indirect ones, and finally giving in to death. Only rarely is it clear-cut like this; denials can hide the smoothness and so can pain, depression, anxiety and dementia. But this sequence is commonly enough noticed for it to be thought of as a natural development phase.

This may appear to be stretching the theoretical framework of this book to obsessive limits. But I do not think so, for if looked at in this way, those around can recognise that the dying person still has work to do. In some aspects of this especially the earlier stages of farewell and mourning, they can help him actively. In other aspects he needs to be quiet, alone perhaps, or with another person in the room. It is helping a natural process, which dying is.

Many people around will often be more frightened and frantic than the dying person himself. With their flurry and tricks of mind they can often make dying confusing and more painful and lonely than it need be. People quite often say to a considerate attendant, 'I know I'm dying, but don't tell my relatives they'd be too upset'. I cannot help feeling that this is the fruit of the taboo of death, so common in our own culture, yet hardly known in many others.

Awareness of death and its recognition by those around can mean that a person ends with dignity and peace, and will be remembered for it with gratitude by those remaining. Here are three instances:

An old man in considerable pain said to his son, 'When this nonsense is over you will find the will in the desk downstairs'. He then proceeded to give instructions about his affairs.

An old man said to his niece, 'I think I shall be gone by the time you visit me again next week-end, so think we had better say good-bye now'.

An old woman in Nigeria was nearly 90 when she fell ill. However, she said to her children, 'Don't waste your money preparing for a funeral now, because I am not going to die yet'. She did not die, but one day some months later she got up and began to make her preparations by walking round to all her friends saying good-bye. The next morning her daughter was due to go to market and the old lady said, 'I think we had better say good-bye now before you go'. A few hours later she died.

After this the living person changes into inert, shrunken remains. What is left alive of him on this earth now lies in the minds of other people. His relatives, children, friends and acquaintances, all those who have experienced him in some measure, probably have learnt from him and have something of him inside themselves. I shall now turn to these survivors, for they have the task of transforming their experience of the dead person, from someone outside themselves into an internal, living and usable memory.

Grief and Mourning
Here is a description by a woman of her experiences of death.

When I was 13 my grandmother died. She was a much-loved, very elegant lady, with long, black skirts and button boots. I thought as a very young child that she must be a close friend of the Queen. One Saturday she decorated my bedroom, putting on wallpaper that I had been allowed to choose myself for the first time. She sat eating her tea with my new puppy trying to bite the buttons off her boots. She was laughing and happy. I slept in my newly-decorated bedroom which smelt of the new wallpaper. That night I was very conscious of how much my grandmother loved me. On Monday morning an aunt came round to our house, just as I was leaving for school. It was the day I was due to take an English examination. My mother and aunt tried to make me go to school, but something in their faces terrified me and I refused to go. Eventually they told me that my grandmother was dead. She had died very suddenly the previous night. I then went to school, sat the examination and did not think about my grandmother. I did not think about her again until the funeral, when I sat in the carriage with the hearse and the coffin covered in flowers, surrounded by relatives, dressed in black, and I had a black coat too. I did not think about my grandmother herself, because I was too busy trying not to laugh and laugh, and I knew that if I did nobody would understand why, and my mother would be ashamed. When the results of the examinations came out I was top of my class. It seemed as though this was the most shameful thing I had ever done.

A year later my school-friend died. She had pneumonia. I had seen her and she was getting better. The next day my mother told me when I came home from school that she was dead. I did not believe her. I went to see her mother, who told me that my friend died because the doctor would not wake her up to give her medicine. I was very afraid. I dare not go to sleep that night in case I should see my friend. I had loved her, but her death had turned into a terrifying horror.

When I was 15 my grandfather died. He was ill for a long time, and we knew for a week that he was going to die any day. Perhaps he wanted to die because my grandmother was dead. We had an end-of-term school dance on the Friday, and all I could think of was that I hoped he wouldn't die until that was over, or I should not be able to go. He died on Friday night whilst I was enjoying myself at the dance. I hated him for dying then, and became even more afraid of death.

My next experience was years later, when my own daughter was 15. Normally she returned home from school with three friends, two boys and a girl. This particular day she was delayed at school and they left without her. A thunderstorm broke as they came across the common. They sheltered under a tree with their bicycles, lightning struck them and all were killed. I could not find words to console my daughter. I could only be thankful that she was alive.

A little later my father died, driving his car home from a football match. My mother did not ring me up to tell me until two hours after his death, because she 'wanted me to have my tea first'. I was kept very busy looking after her during the next two weeks, and hardly thought about him.

When I was 44 my mother died. She insisted on living alone. She was very independent and had enough money to do so comfortably. I was always afraid she would have an accident and lie unable to get help. She had a minor stroke and lay unconscious for a whole day before she was found. Nobody told me she was ill; she died before I could get there. I did not say good-bye to her. My aunt said she didn't tell me that she was ill. She thought I might be upset and I 'couldn't do anything anyway'.

A few months later my dearly loved father-in-law died. He died of cancer and we knew that the end was near. We received a telephone call to go to the hospital. Our car was caught in a traffic jam and we arrived at the hospital five minutes after he died. We never talked of any of these people and their deaths.

The last one was my husband and he died after three months of torture. He had cancer and refused an operation, which would have been useless anyway. I used to pray that he would hurry up and die, and was glad when he did.

After they had taken him away his dog ripped up his bed and his pillows and scattered the feathers all over the stairs. I changed all the furniture around the day he died, and then I carried on doing all the same things that I had done before. I used to pretend he was at work.

I couldn't stop buying the foods he liked from the grocers. I didn't know when to go to bed or when to get up. My son drove his father's car, and the dog nearly went mad every day when the car came down the drive. We sold the car. Eventually we had to find a new home for the dog, who would have died of misery if we hadn't. My friends were all very kind. They kept me very busy with empty business. I was lonelier with people than without them. Nobody could talk about my husband. Christmas was hell. We always wound up our special clock on Christmas Day. I let it stop. My birthday, our wedding anniversary, his birthday and his children's birthdays were hell, but we never spoke about him. After a few months people started to say how brave I'd been, and what a wonderful new life I'd made. There was relief in their voices. They could look me in the eye again and didn't need to be embarrassed. I remember the relief that he was dead and couldn't suffer any more, or was it that I didn't have to watch him suffer? I never talked about him.

More recently I have thought about the cruelties of our culture, that demands a 'stiff upper lip' and no embarrassing show of emotion. I think I may have learnt how to say good-bye, and that through sorrow and

conscious weeping the horror of pain and disease-riddled bodies can be
allowed to sink into the background and mourning to become more joyful.
When this happens, memories can be of the happiness known of a loving
mother, warm and alive, of a husband walking in the sunshine across the
paddock, his pipe in his mouth, his dog by his side, coming in to tea.

This is not only a report, it is also a plea for greater openness about
death. Fortunately, a great deal of careful work on bereavement has been
done recently so that much is known about it, although this knowledge
might not yet be widely disseminated. It has been recognised intuitively
for a long time, but it is only recently that its internal processes have
begun to be systematically understood. It is only with this coherent
knowledge that ways of consistent and thoughtful care can be learnt by
any ordinary intelligent person. This has certainly now begun. Parkes
(1972) is, I think, a classic work, moving and straight-forward, it is essential reading for which this brief summary is no substitute.

Parkes summarises the evidence which makes it plain that bereavement is a state of acute stress with all the features which were outlined
early in this book. Cerebral disrhythmia, cardiovascular changes, hyperactivity, panic and flight–fight reactions all occur. Being a state of distress
means that it is a *normal illness*, and should be seen as such. For, not only
do mental disturbances arise very commonly indeed, but individuals are
prone to physical disease as well. This to the extent that the death rate
among certain groups of bereaved people is very significantly higher than
that of similar non-bereaved people. After the death of a close loved one,
a person is at risk.

Following on from this, it is fairly clear that a sequence can be detected
in the months after a death. From the storm of painfulness that goes with
mourning, Parkes suggests that the following movements can be seen as
the essence of it. Acute grief in the few days after a death is when distress
is at its height and is best epitomised by the term *alarm*. The whole
organism is in a biological state of alarm, the person is not likely to be
noisy, on the contrary he is usually very quiet. But the signs of alarm
are omnipresent, sleep is disturbed, there is often subdued hyperactivity
and hallucination in otherwise normal people. At this time it is still
difficult for a grieving person to believe that the loved one has gone; he
is automatically spoken to, heard around the corner, his place even
automatically laid at table. As the loss begins to sink home a phase of
searching, usually quite unconsciously and automatically driven, sets in.
Then this is felt as hopeless and waves of weeping and despair at loss
well up. Somehow, arising out of these tears, periods of calmness begin
to emerge which come in *mitigation* of the loss. A person begins to warm
again inside and become interested in the world around, sad at the loss
but feeling glad to be alive.

This is laid out very neatly here, but it does not happen in this way, for moods come and go. Past life together is relived and re-sorted. Waves of guilt assail the bereaved person and so does rage at being let down. Old recriminations gnaw and further guilt wells up.

It is not only a state of distress, it is an acute depressive crisis (as mid-life was a more chronic depressive crisis). It is a crisis striking a person from the outside rather than arising from within. And, like any crisis, it entails breaking of old patterns, regression, withdrawal and then the slow discovery and testing out of a partially *new identity*.

It is his shattered distress that makes it important for a mourner to have the opportunity for conversation with another understanding person. Probably at heart this allows a person to continue, unconsciously, connecting those primitive patterns of the earliest conversations he had in life which we saw as part of our innate propensity, and which sooth even an infant's distress. Sometimes it hardly matters what is actually talked about, the tone of the conversation itself is enough: without this company the 'going to bits' of distress and its possible hallucinations can be terrifying. The frantic defensive manoeuvres that arise often become wild and even self-destructive. Open destructiveness of others is not much reported upon but it does happen. For instance, an observer at the time reported that Shaka Zulu's grief caused the massacre of about 7,000 people on the day after his mother's death. Vendettas and vengeance are not openly practised in our society but are present in hidden forms. Relatives can become particularly unpleasant with each other, not usually at the time of the funeral but in the months after.

So not only is another person a soothing presence, he can also act as a check to the mourner's ideas and more violent impulses. He can be a continuing reminder that there is enjoyable benevolence in reality which often seems empty. As well as this, being regressed, a person often needs a vigilant helper to carry out essential tasks that the mourner cannot or forgets to do.

However, most bereaved people are adults and have their own dignity. They need to be alone frequently and also to prove their own competence to themselves. Fussing is particularly seductive at this time but fundamentally choking and usually extremely irritating.

In the later phases, working out what to do next, and finding a new integrity or identity is mostly done alone. But people nearly always need to voice their ideas to check them with another person.

With our greater awareness of mourning, it is not only specialists who are alerted to its dangers and its pathology which can continue for years. The clergy, particularly aware of grief for centuries, now are tending to take special care, and other organisations like Cruze Clubs and the Samaritans are perhaps forging a new aspect of our culture.

Grief in Childhood

A young child's inner representations of his world and loved people are less stable than an adult's. He cannot explicitly recognise or manifest his sense of loss. He rarely weeps at a loved person's death. His mental organisation is not sufficiently coherent for him to do so. This raises the question as to whether children who have lost a parent should be told about it or not and, if so, how. Very many people avoid the issue by saying they are too young to understand. And the young child, usually thunderstruck by his loss and by the depression of others in the family, rarely asks questions about it spontaneously. He has not developed the integrative capacity to put his ideas into words. From his silence, adults then often make the assumption that grief means nothing to him.

Some people will go to remarkable lengths to prevent a child knowing about a parent's death. For example:

The mother of three young children died after a long illness. Their father decided it was best to pretend that their mother was still in hospital and would be home again one day. He asked the children's teacher to keep the news from them. The teacher, trying to be considerate and helpful, asked all the others in the children's classes and their parents not to talk about the death. However, the school was large and many children in other classes knew what had happened and naturally talked about it. Throughout the neighbourhood, children were baffled and ill at ease, some having been told not to talk about it, but not knowing why, while others felt guilty for talking quite freely, having no instructions to the contrary. Eventually matters were sorted out by someone mentioning the problem to the teacher, who got someone to talk things over with the father.

The father cannot really be condemned; he was distraught after the death of his wife with three young children to look after. The teacher, too, was trying to help him. But a lie arose which caused more trouble to his children than it was worth, for not only were they surrounded by grief at home but also by embarrassment, secretiveness and confusion among their school friends.

We can see from this that not to tell a child about the death of a parent is to withhold the truth about an important reality. Naturally enough, this does not matter if the child is too young to attach meaning to the spoken word. It would, for instance, be absurd to talk to a young baby of his parent's death. So the question arises first as to how much children understand about what has happened and secondly how much of verbal explanation is helpful. Anthony's (1971) work helps us to work out guidelines.

It seems that children dimly realise at a very early age that something terrible has happened. What is more, even if they do not feel much at the time, the death of a parent soon becomes evident, for they never see him again. This is the main meaning of a death to a young child. A parent has disappeared and never returns. As we saw in earlier chapters, loss and separation can have far-reaching effects upon the child's capacity to feel and think.

The situation is made more complex by the fact that a young child cannot yet communicate his grief coherently. He may *act* in a disturbed way, but he has not yet organised his ideas in order to speak or openly weep about it as an older mourner does. A helping adult cannot wait until the child is openly ready to talk, because he may never be able to verbalise his grief coherently. It seems that it is best for adults to give an explanation which is within the comprehension of the child, and then to leave it to the child to ask what questions he can as time goes by. Answers can then be simple and truthful, confined to what is understandable to the child. Over and above this, the adult must expect anxiety and disturbed behaviour from a little child about ideas and feelings which he cannot yet put into words. Sensitive people find their own ways intuitively about how to respond in these circumstances. Specific rules and procedures are out of place. Without understanding, the child is left with his own grief in an alien, uncommunicative world. This aberration must remain if his adults do not recognise and feel his anxiety and loss, however kind they may be in other ways.

Completion of Mourning

The stage of acute distress may last for only a few weeks, but critical changes inside the individual go on less dramatically for many months and more quietly for years.

Slowly the grieving person finds a new distribution for his energies, and new objects to love and hate. And yet, if mourning is successful, awareness of the dead person is not lost. The immediate experience of the person as dead loses force and gives way to living memory of the person as he was when alive. The mourner in doing this has not necessarily 'become' the dead person, though this sometimes happens, but rather he has internalised him, and has his experience of him from the past ready to use in present and future situations.

This is the natural end product of mourning. The mourners slowly come alive again. The dead person has gained a certain immortality in the memory of his loved ones. They themselves are then perhaps ready to carry on living, and are a little more prepared to die themselves one day, for other generations to carry them on also into the future.

FURTHER READING

1 Gorer, G. (1965), *Death, Grief and Mourning in Contemporary Britain*. A survey of attitudes to death, exposing the means by which it is hidden and denied.

2 Hinton, J. (1967), *Dying*. Its title describes what it is about. A classic text and essential reading.
3 Parkes, M. (1972), *Bereavement*. Also a classic text and essential reading.
4 Schoenberg, B. (ed.) (1970), *Loss and Grief*. A series of technical articles on the subject, but readable.
5 Sudnow, D. (1967), *Passing On*. A sociological study showing how dying is dealt with in hospitals.

REFERENCES

The starred references in this list are specialised technical texts of use only for detailed further study.

Anthony, E. J. and B‹ nedek, T. (eds) (1970), *Parenthood. Its Psychology and Psychopathology* (Boston: Little Brown).

Anthony, S. (1971), *The Discovery of Death in Childhood and After* (Harmondsworth: Penguin).

Arendt, H. (1969), *The Human Condition* (Chicago: University of Chicago Press).

Becker, E. (1971), *The Birth and Death of Meaning* (Harmondsworth: Penguin).

Bell, E. W. and Vogel, N. (1968), *A Modern Introduction to the Family* (London: Macmillan).

Bernard, J. (1972), *The Future of Marriage* (Harmondsworth: Penguin).

Berne, E. (1964), *Games People Play* (Harmondsworth: Penguin).

*Bibring, G. (1961), 'A Study of the Psychological Processes in Pregnancy', *Psychoanalytic Study of the Child*, vol. xiv (London: Hogarth).

Blood, R. O. and Wolfe, D. M. (1960), *Husbands and Wives* (Glencoe: The Free Press).

Blos, P. (1962), *On Adolescence* (London: Macmillan).

Bowlby, J. (1953), *Child Care and the Growth of Love* (Harmondsworth: Penguin).

Bowlby, J. (1969), *Attachment* (Harmondsworth: Penguin).

Bowlby, J. (1973), *Separation, Anxiety and Anger* (London: Hogarth).

Boyle, D. G. (1969), *A Student's Guide to Piaget* (Oxford: Pergamon).

Brecher, R. and E. (eds) (1967), *An Analysis of the Human Sexual Response* (London: Panther).

Britton, J. (1970), *Language and Learning* (Harmondsworth: Penguin).

Bromley, D. B. (1966), *The Psychology of Human Ageing* (Harmondsworth: Penguin).

Bruner, J. (ed.) (1976), *Play, its Role in Development and Evolution* (Harmondsworth: Penguin).

Butcher, H. J. (1968), *Human Intelligence, Its Nature and Assessment* (London: Methuen).

*Cameron, N. (1963), *Personality Development and Psychopathology* (Boston: Houghton Mifflin).

Cannon, W. B. (1929), *Bodily Changes in Pain, Hunger and Fear* (London and New York: Appleton).

Caplan, G. (1964), *Principles of Preventive Psychiatry* (London: Tavistock).

Caplan, G. (ed.) (1969), *Adolescence* (London: Basic Books).

Carter, M. (1966), *Into Work* (Harmondsworth: Penguin).

Chamberlain, G. (1969), *The Safety of the Unborn Child* (Harmondsworth: Penguin).

Chertok, L. (1969), *Motherhood and Personality, Psychosomatic Aspects of Childbirth* (London: Tavistock).

*Chown, S. W. (ed.) (1972), *Human Ageing* (Harmondsworth: Penguin).

Clarke, A. M. and A. D. (1975), *Early Experience, Myth and Evidence* (London: Open Books).

Cromer, D. (1975), in Lewin, R. (ed.), *Child Alive* (London: Temple Smith).

Danziger, K. (1970), *Readings in Child Socialisation* (Oxford: Pergamon).

Davie, R., Butler, N. and Goldstein, H. (1972), *From Birth to Seven* (London: Longman).

Davies, D. R. and Shackleton, V. J. (1975), *Psychology and Work* (London: Methuen).

de Mause, L. (ed.) (1974), *The History of Childhood* (London: Souvenir Press).

*Deutsch, H. (1944), *The Psychology of Women*, vol. II: *Motherhood* (London: Research Books).

Dicks, H. V. (1967), *Marital Tensions* (London: Routledge & Kegan Paul).

Dominian, J. (1969), *Marital Breakdown* (Harmondsworth: Penguin).

*Dunbar, F. (1946), *Emotions and Bodily Change* (New York: Columbia University Press).

Erikson, E. H. (1963), *Childhood and Society* (Harmondsworth: Penguin).

Erikson, E. H. (1964), *Insight and Responsibility* (New York: Norton).

Erikson, E. H. (1968), *Identity, Youth and Crisis* (London: Faber & Faber).

*Escalona, S. (1969), *The Roots of Individuality. Normal Patterns of Development in Infancy* (London: Tavistock).

Eysenck, H. (1953), *Uses and Abuses of Psychology* (Harmondsworth: Penguin).

*Fenichel, O. (1946), *The Psychoanalytic Theory of Neuroses* (London: Routledge & Kegan Paul.)

Fisher, S. (1973), *Understanding the Female Orgasm* (Harmondsworth: Penguin).

Fleming, C. M. (1967), *Adolescence, Its Social Psychology* (London: Routledge & Kegan Paul).

Fordham, F. (1966), *An Introduction to Jung's Psychology* (Harmondsworth: Penguin).

Fraiberg, S. H. (1959), *The Magic Years* (London: Methuen).

Freud, A. (1928), *Introduction to the Technique of Child Analysis* (New York: NMD Publishing Co.).

Freud, A. (1937), *The Ego and the Mechanisms of Defence* (London: Hogarth).

*Freud, S. (1900), *The Interpretation of Dreams*, Standard Edition, vol. IV (London: Hogarth).

Freud, S. (1913), *Totem and Taboo*, Standard Edition, vol. XII (London: Hogarth).

*Freud, S. (1915a), *Instincts and Their Vicissitudes*, Standard Edition, vol. XIV (London: Hogarth).

Freud, S. (1915b), *Introductory Lectures on Psychoanalysis* (Harmondsworth: Penguin).

*Freud, S. (1917), *Mourning and Melancholia*, Standard Edition, vol. XIV (London: Hogarth).

*Freud, S. (1923), *The Ego and the Id*, Standard Edition, vol. XXIII (London: Hogarth).

Friedmann, G. (1961), *The Anatomy of Work* (New York: The Free Press).

Fromm, E. (1957), *The Art of Loving* (London: Allen & Unwin).

Gavron, H. (1966), *The Captive Wife* (Harmondsworth: Penguin).

Goffman, I. (1959), *The Presentation of Self in Everyday Life* (Harmondsworth: Penguin).

Gorer, G. (1965), *Death, Grief and Mourning in Contemporary Britain* (London: Cresset).

Gorer, G. (1971), *Sex and Marriage in England Today* (London: Nelson).

Green, J. H. (1968), *Basic Clinical Physiology* (Oxford: OUP).

Green, L. (1968), *Parents and Teachers, Partners or Rivals* (London: George Allen & Unwin).

*Guntrip, H. (1961), *Personality Structure and Human Interaction* (London: Hogarth).

*Harlow, H. (1961), 'The Development of Affectional Patterns in Infant Monkeys,' in Foss, B. (ed.), *Determinants of Infant Behaviour*, vol. I (London: Methuen).

Hayley, J. (1968), 'The Family of the Schizophrenic' in Handel, G. (ed.), *The Psychosocial Interior of the Family* (London: George Allen & Unwin).

Herzberg, B. (1966), *Work and the Nature of Man* (Cleveland: World Publishing Co.).

Hinton, J. (1967), *Dying* (Harmondsworth: Penguin).

Holt, J. (1964), *How Children Fail* (Harmondsworth: Penguin).

Hunt, S. and Hilton, J. (1975), *Individual Development and Social Experience* (London: George Allen & Unwin).

Hutt, C. (1975), *Sex Differences in Behaviour* (London: Crosby Lockwood).

Isaacs, S. (1930), *Intellectual Growth in Young Children* (London: Routledge & Kegan Paul).

Isaacs, S. (1933), *Social Development in Young Children* (London: Routledge & Kegan Paul).

*Jacobson, E. (1964), *The Self and the Object World* (London: Hogarth).

Jaques, E. (1970), *Work Creativity and Social Justice* (New York: IUP).

Jehu, D. (1967), *Learning Theory and Social Work* (London: Routledge & Kegan Paul).

Kelly, G. A. (1963), *A Theory of the Personality* (New York: Norton).

Kelmer-Pringle, M. (1974), *The Needs of Children* (London: Hutchinson).

*Khan, M. M. (1974), *The Privacy of the Self* (London: Hogarth).

Klein, J. (1965), *Samples of English Culture*, vol. II (London: Routledge & Kegan Paul).

*Klein, M. (1932), *The Psychoanalysis of Children* (London: Hogarth).

*Klein, M. (1948), *Contributions to Psychoanalysis* (London: Hogarth).

Klein, M. (1952), *Developments in Psychoanalysis* (London: Hogarth).

Kline, P. (1972), *Fact and Fantasy in Freudian Theory* (London: Methuen).

*Kohlberg, L. (1969), 'State and Sequence', in Goslin, D. A. (ed.), *Handbook of Socialisation Theory and Research* (Chicago: Rand McNally).

*Kohut, H. (1971), *The Analysis of the Self* (London: Hogarth).

Kubler-Ross, E. (1970), *On Death and Dying* (London: Tavistock).

Laing, R. D. (1959), *The Divided Self* (Harmondsworth: Penguin).

Laing, R. D. and Esterson, A. (1964), *Sanity, Madness and the Family* (Harmondsworth: Penguin).

Laing, R. D. (1970), *Knots* (Harmondsworth: Penguin).

Landreth, C. (1967), *Early Childhood* (New York: Alfred Knopf).

Laufer, M. (1974), *Adolescent Disturbance and Breakdown* (Harmondsworth: Penguin).

*Laufer, M. (1976) 'The Central Masturbation Phantasy', in *Psychoanalytic Study of the Child*, vol. XXXI (London: Hogarth).

*Lévi-Strauss, L. (1966), *The Savage Mind* (Chicago: University of Chicago Press).

Lewin, R., ed. (1975), *Child Alive* (London: Temple Smith).

Lidz, T. (1963), *The Family and Human Adaptation* (London: Hogarth).

*Ling, T. (1973), *The Buddha* (Harmondsworth: Penguin).

Lomas, P. (ed.) (1967), *The Predicament of the Family* (London: Hogarth).

Lowe, G. (1972), *The Growth of Personality* (Harmondsworth: Penguin).

Lynd, H. M. (1958), *Shame and the Search for Identity* (London: Routledge & Kegan Paul).

*Maccoby, E. C. and Jacklin, C. N. (1975), *The Psychology of Sex Differences* (Oxford: OUP).

*Mahler, M. S., Pine, F. and Bergman, A. (1975), *The Psychological Birth of the Human Infant* (London: Hutchinson).

*Malinowski, B. (1916), *The Sexual Life of Savages* (London: Routledge & Kegan Paul).

Malleson, J. (1948), *Change of Life* (Harmondsworth: Penguin).

*Matte Blanco, I. (1975), *The Unconscious as Infinite Sets* (London: Duckworth).

May, R. (1967), *Psychology and the Human Dilemma* (Princeton: D. Van Nostrand).

Mayerson, S. (ed.) (1975), *Adolescence and the Crises of Adjustment* (London: George Allen & Unwin).

Mead, M. (1950), *Male and Female* (Harmondsworth: Penguin).
*Meade, G. H. (1932), *Mind, Self and Society* (Chicago: University of Chicago Press).
Mee, S. A. and Mayes, A. R. (eds) (1973), *Dreams and Dreaming* (Harmondsworth: Penguin).
Millar, S. (1968), *The Psychology of Play* (Harmondsworth: Penguin).
Mitscherlich, A. (1969), *Society without the Father* (London: Tavistock).
Neugarten, B. C. (1968), *Middle Age and Ageing* (Chicago: University of Chicago Press).
Newson, J. and E. (1963), *Patterns of Infant Care* (Harmondsworth: Penguin).
Parkes, M. (1972), *Bereavement* (Harmondsworth: Penguin).
Persig, R. M. (1974), *Zen and the Art of Motorcycle Maintenance* (London: Corgi).
*Piaget, J. (1929), *The Child's Concept of the World* (London: Paladin).
*Piaget, J. (1935), *The Moral Judgement of the Child* (London: Routledge & Kegan Paul).
*Piaget, J. (1950), *The Psychology of Intelligence* (London: Routledge & Kegan Paul).
*Piaget, J. (1951), *Play, Dreams and Imitation in Childhood* (London: Routledge & Kegan Paul).
*Piaget, J. (1953), *The Origins of Intelligence in the Child* (London: Routledge & Kegan Paul).
*Piaget, J. (1955), *The Child's Construction of Reality* (London: Routledge & Kegan Paul).
Rapoport, R. N. (1970), *Mid-Career Development* (London: Tavistock).
Richmond, P. G. (1970), *An Introduction to Piaget* (London: Routledge & Kegan Paul).
*Rochlin, G. (1973), *Man's Aggression, The Defence of the Self* (New York: IUP).
*Rosen, I. (ed.) (1964), *The Pathology and Treatment of Sexual Deviation* (Oxford: OUP).
Rutter, M. (1972), *Maternal Deprivation Reassessed* (Harmondsworth: Penguin).
Rycroft, C. (1968), *A Critical Dictionary of Psychoanalysis* (London: Nelson).
Rycroft, C. (1971), *Reich* (London: Fontana).
Saunders, C. (1959), *Care of the Dying* (London: Macmillan).
*Schilder, P. (1935), *The Image and Appearance of the Human Body* (London: Kegan Paul, Trench, Trubner).
*Schoenberg, B. (ed.) (1970), *Loss and Grief* (New York: Columbia University Press).
Schofield, M. (1965), *The Sexual Behaviour of Young People* (Harmondsworth: Penguin).
Segal, H. (1973), *An Introduction to the Work of Melanie Klein* (London: Hogarth).
Sheridan, M. (1968), *The Developmental Progress of Infants and Young Children* (London: HMSO).
*Skinner, B. F. (1953), *Science and Human Behaviour* (New York: Macmillan).
Skynner, R. (1976), *One Flesh, Separate Persons* (London: Constable).
Smith, A. (1970), *The Body* (Harmondsworth: Penguin).
Snow, E. (1937), *Red Star over China* (Harmondsworth: Penguin).
Spitz, R. (1965), *The First Year of Life* (New York: IUP).
*Stoller, R. (1968), *Sex and Gender* (London: Hogarth).
Storr, A. (1960), *The Integrity of the Personality* (Harmondsworth: Penguin).
Sudnow, D. (1967), *Passing On* (Englewood Cliffs, N.J.: Prentice-Hall).
*Suzuki, D. T. (1949), *Essays in Zen Buddhism*, First Series (London: Rider).
Tillich, P. (1952), *The Courage to Be* (London: Fontana).
Toffler, A. (1970), *Future Shock* (London: Pan Books).
Townsend, P. (1963), *The Family Life of Old People* (Harmondsworth: Penguin).
West, D. J. (1960), *Homosexuality* (Harmondsworth: Penguin).
Willmott, P. (1966), *Adolescent Boys of East London* (Harmondsworth: Penguin).
*Winnicott, D. W. (1958), *Through Paediatrics to Psychoanalysis* (London: Hogarth).
Winnicott, D. W. (1964), *The Child, the Family and the Outside World* (Harmondsworth: Penguin).

*Winnicott, D. W. (1965), *The Maturational Processes and the Facilitating Environment* (London: Hogarth).

Witkin, H. and Lewis, H. (eds) (1967), *Experimental Studies of Dreaming* (New York: Random House).

Wright, D. (1971), *The Psychology of Moral Behaviour* (Harmondsworth: Penguin).

Zinberg, N. (ed.) (1963), *The Normal Psychology of the Ageing Process* (New York: IUP).

INDEX